Stalin's War

German troops tear down the border post at the Lithuanian front, June 23, 1941. *(Courtesy Lithuanian Photographic and Video Archives)*

Stalin's War

Tragedy and Triumph,

1941-1945

Edwin P. Hoyt

Published by Cooper Square Press
A Member of the Rowman & Littlefield Publishing Group
200 Park Avenue South, Suite 1109
New York, New York 10003-1503
www.coopersquarepress.com

Distributed by National Book Network

Library of Congress Cataloging-in-Publication Data

Hoyt, Edwin Palmer.
    Stalin's war : tragedy and triumph, 1941–1945 / Edwin P. Hoyt.
    p. cm.
    Includes bibliographical references and index.
    ISBN 0-8154-1032-8 (hardcover : alk. paper)
    1. World War, 1939–1945—Soviet Union. 2. World War, 1939–1945—
Campaigns—Eastern Front. 3. Stalin, Joseph, 1879–1953—Military leadership.
I. Title.

    D764 .H697 2002
    940.54'217—dc21   2002013410

Printed in the United States of America

⊗™ The paper used in this publication meets the minimum requirements of American National Standard for Information Sciences—Permanence of Paper for Printed Library Materials, ANSI/NISO Z39.48-1992.
Manufactured in the United States of America.

Contents

Preface

Stalin's Way

ONE MAN, ABOVE ALL OTHERS, DOMINATED RUSSIA for thirty years, murdered millions of his fellow citizens, and made his country into a giant flytrap from which very few managed to escape. His arms were long. He murdered Leon Trotsky in Mexico without ever leaving the Kremlin. He was shrewd rather than intelligent, conspiratorial, secretive, given to secret bouts of fear and trembling. He was a monster in human form and when he died in his sleep in 1953 half the world cheered, and no one cried. He had no friends, only subordinates, whom he bullied unmercifully. He was Josef Vissiaronovich Djugashvili—Stalin—the man of steel who ruled Russia as absolute dictator from the 1920s until his death.

Ernst Topitsch, professor of philosophy at Graz University in Austria, has evolved a unique theory about World War II: Stalin was planning to attack Hitler and was building up his armies to that end; but Hitler got in the first blow.

The Topitsch theory ties in with the influence on Stalin of Marshal G. I. Kulik, the chief of artillery of the Red Army, who was responsible for many errors, and was finally cashiered, but not before he had put the whole war effort in jeopardy. From Kulik, Stalin got the theory "attack, attack, attack," which he followed in the first weeks of the war, uselessly sacrificing millions of men.

This book is the story of Stalin's war against the black forces of Naziism. But more than that, it is the story of his attempts to shape the world in the communist image. Stalin nearly succeeded; had it not been for the stubborn opposition of America and Britain, he could have. But, in the end, it all came to naught, proof once more that a despot cannot control his own succession.

An Unholy Alliance

TO THE RUSSIAN GOVERNMENT WORLD WAR II WAS only an extension of the Bolshevik Revolution that had begun in 1918. Germany and Japan were pawns to be used to destroy the capitalist system of Western Europe and America. After they had been used, they were to be discarded on the scrap heap of history, while the international revolution forged on until it had the world in thrall.

In the 1930s, Josef Stalin was pursuing the twin aims of assuring his continued power by a campaign of terrorism and the continuation of the Bolshevik Revolution that, in his mind, would bring all the world under communist rule. Two factors entered the equation to threaten his plans. First, the stubborn resistance of Finland to Russian territorial demands, which led to the celebrated Winter War, wherein the Soviet armies took a thrashing before overwhelming the Finns with sheer numbers. Russian casualties in that three-month war were 200,000 dead and more than twice that number wounded. Finnish casualties were 24,000 dead or missing and 43,000 wounded.

The second unexpected factor was the attack on Soviet forces on the Mongolian-Manchukuo border. The Japanese Kwantung Army was testing the water for a full-scale invasion of Siberia. In the summer of 1940 the Japanese attacked, expecting an easy victory. Instead, they ran into a buzz saw.

General Georgi Zhukov, commander of the Soviet Siberian armies, at first seemed content to wage defensive warfare. But in July he laid plans for a counteroffensive. To supplement the plans he waged a spectacularly successful disinformation campaign. First, he distributed to his troops a handbook, *What the Soviet Soldier Must Know in Defense*, and he made sure that copies fell into the hands of the Japanese enemy. He transmitted false radio reports about the construction of defense facilities and backed these up with inquiries about the fate of various pieces of nonexistent engineering equipment. He had trucks and tanks drive backwards and forwards along the front, night and day, in an effort to get the Japanese used to the constant revving of engines. Meanwhile, he amassed his armor for the attack.

After a bloody artillery battle in mid-July that lasted two days, the Japanese were pinned down in their trenches while the

---

The Pact Becomes Reality

21 August 1939

To the Chancellor of the German Reich, Herr A. Hitler:

"I thank you for your letter. I hope that the German–Soviet Nonaggression Pact will bring about a decided turn for the better in the political relations between our two countries.

The peoples of our countries need peaceful relations with each other. The assent of the German government to the conclusion of a nonaggression pact provides the foundation for eliminating political tension and for the reestablishment of peace and collaboration between our two countries.

The Soviet government has instructed me to inform you that it agrees to Herr von Ribbentrop's arriving in Moscow on 23 August."

—J. STALIN

Russians, who had air superiority, began moving their force up for their attack. The Russians were assisted by bad flying weather in the week of August 12 to 19, which effectively prevented the Japanese aerial reconnaissance planes from spotting troop concentrations.

The Japanese were planning an attack of their own—for August 24—a fact known to Zhukov from reconnaissance and the Sorge spy ring. But by August 19, Zhukov had moved thirty-five infantry battalions and twenty cavalry squadrons, supported by an armored force of 346 armored cars and 498 tanks. In the air, Zhukov had 500 planes. Against him, the Japanese had twenty-five infantry battalions and seventeen cavalry squadrons. The Russian force was far superior.

The Japanese were overconfident, one of the characteristics born of the new Bushido, which declared that the Japanese soldier was superior to any in the world. So confident were the Japanese that a number of senior officers had left the lines to seek recreation in the *geisha* houses of the nearby towns and villages. The Russians were aware of this, and timed their offensive accordingly.

Sunday, August 20, dawned warm and quiet, with the promise of a sunny, hot day. At 5:45 AM the Soviet artillery opened its barrage and 250 Soviet aircraft bombed and strafed Japanese positions. At 8:15 AM the second wave came, and a half-hour later red rockets signaled the movement of the armor and infantry.

The battle was joined by the Japanese and lasted day after day. By August 23, the Russians had encircled the Japanese, but still the Japanese continued to attack at every opportunity. General Zhukov's ruthless determination was now proved: at one point the commander of a division reported for fresh orders after having beaten off a savage counterattack.

"Attack again!" Zhukov ordered.

A short time later, he called the division to find out what was happening.

"When will you start the attack?" he demanded.

"Well, er, uh . . ."

"Let me speak to your chief of staff," the general said.

"Can you get the division moving?" Zhukov asked.

"I think so," said the chief of staff.

"Then, as of now, you are in command," Zhukov said.

But the new chief of staff was no more successful than the previous had been, so Zhukov replaced him with an officer from his own staff. The division attacked again and, although it suffered heavy losses, this time overrunning the defenses. The last Japanese position was taken on August 28, and by the morning of August 31 the Russians had regained all the disputed territory.

The Kwantung Army wanted to continue the fight.

"Next time," said the commander, "it will be different."

He announced that he was sending fresh troops to carry on the battle and that the offensive would be resumed in a few weeks. But when the casualties were assessed—55,000 Japanese to 10,000 Russian losses—wiser heads in Tokyo prevailed and Japan turned away from its Siberia adventure, making plans to move south against Malaya and the Dutch East Indies. On April 13, 1941, the day that the Yugoslav army surrendered to Hitler's Wehrmacht, the Russians signed a neutrality pact with Japan.

Deviousness

The Soviets could be just as devious as the Germans when it came to disguising assistance the Soviet Union was giving to Germany. Trade Commissar Mikoyan, for example, told Karl Schnurre in October 1940 that the Soviet government was perfectly agreeable to the transit of raw materials through Black Sea ports, notably Odessa, as well as Murmansk. However, he pointed out, other shipments would need to be camouflaged. The Soviet officials were prepared to buy raw materials on behalf of Germany and ship them to Odessa in neutral vessels, ostensibly for Soviet use. "One way of camouflaging," he said, "would be to mix the contraband goods destined for Germany with other cargoes which would first be unloaded in Bulgarian or Rumanian ports."

✳ ✳ ✳

The Nazi–Soviet Pact of 1939 was the result of the unbridled cupidity of two men bent each on fooling the other. When the pact was signed, Hitler showed his joy, "Now I have the world in my pocket," he said. Stalin was equally satisfied with the secret division of the eastern border states, which gave the USSR rights to Finland, Estonia, Latvia, Bessarabia, and Poland east of the line formed by the rivers Nasrev, Weichsel, and Sann.

Stalin intended to attack Germany but in 1939 was not yet prepared to do so. It would be another three years before he could strike. The Soviet army was in a state of flux, slowly recovering from Stalin's disastrous purge of 1937, in which the cream of the officer corps had been wasted. The Soviet war plan called for 170 divisions and two brigades; as of June 1941, those were deployed.

The Soviet forces had 21,000 tanks, 17,775 aircraft, and 67,000 major artillery pieces. Many of these weapons were obsolete. However, two new tank types were superior to anything the Germans had: the Soviet T-34 tank (28 tons), which outweighed, outgunned, and outperformed the German Panzer IV; and the KV (named for Kliment Voroshilov), which was heavier and slower than the T-34 but carried the same 76-mm gun. The best Soviet fighter planes matched the German ME 109. But the major weakness of the Soviet army was in transport, still relying on the horse-drawn vehicles of World War I. Soviet Chief of Staff Meretskov carried out war games in January 1941, with Zhukov leading the Blue Force (Germans) against the Red Force (Soviets). The Blues followed a plan envisioning the actual attack of June 22, and won. Stalin reviewed the results of the war games on January 13. When Chief of Staff Meretskov could not explain this, Stalin sacked him and replaced him with Zhukov.

The alliance of 1939 served the purposes of both dictators. It gave Stalin time to build up the army he had wrecked with the purges

---

First Strike

Immediately after the signing of the Non-aggression Pact, Stalin began planning the first strike in the coming war with Hitler. Work began to deploy the Red Army. Man concentration was to be on the Western Front. War production, recruiting, and training of airborne troops were all increased. By 1941 Stalin had a million parachute troops.

Hitler also knew why Stalin had stationed a powerful striking force on the Rumanian border. Rumania hid Hitlers life's blood—oil. That action was the reason for Operation Barbarossa.

In February 1941, Stalin relocated his command posts, and on May 5 he told a graduating class at the Red Army Academy, "There will be war and the enemy will be Germany." He said that the army had been reorganized and strengthened to 300 divisions, one-third of them mechanized. He projected a change in defense philosophy, Russia would go on the offensive.

In May a proposal for establishment of a Supreme Military Headquarters was offered. The nation was to be put on a war footing with the direction of the General Staff.

Stalin proceeded with his plan to strike the first blow.

---

of 1937. It gave Hitler a promise that he would not be attacked by Russia while assaulting Poland.

❋ ❋ ❋

In 1939, the Germans needed raw materials. Even after exercising rigid economies on the civil population and conversion of all available used materials, they still had a shortage of 25 percent in zinc, 50 percent in lead, 70 percent in copper, 90 percent in tin, 95 percent in nickel, 98 percent in bauxite, 66 percent in mineral oils, and 80 percent in rubber.

Stalin was punctilious in honoring the agreement, sending raw materials to Germany on schedule and, after Poland was defeated, in splitting the remains with Germany. In return Stalin demanded armament and industrial equipment. Germany was not nearly so punctilious in delivering, but by 1941 Russia's rearmament program was well underway and the Red Army had weapons superior to those of Germany. Stalin's obduracy, however, nearly threw the advantage away.

As one example, the T-34 tank equipped with the ZIS 376-mm gun was superior to the Germans' best tank. But in 1937, G. I. Kulik was appointed head of the artillery directorate and, single-handedly, he nearly managed to scuttle it by wrong-headed, arbitrary decisions backed by Stalin. The combination of Kulik's effusiveness and Stalin's intractability caused the introduction of a 107-mm gun, which proved to be disaster in the Finnish campaign, and the imprisonment of Col. Gen. V. L. Vannikov, one of the artillery geniuses, for obstructionism because he opposed the 107-mm gun.

Only after the German attack had been underway for a month was Vannikov released from jail and rehabilitated.

One of the major problems with the Soviet defense in the early days of the war was the Kulik doctrine, backed by Stalin, that the Soviet armies must attack, attack, attack, even when they were enormously inferior in weaponry.

✳ ✳ ✳

Hitler was fortunate that France collapsed in 1940, leaving Britain as the sole enemy in the west and making it possible for Germany to concentrate on the buildup for the attack on Russia. On December 18, 1940, Hitler signed the directive for Operation Barbarossa. "The German Wehrmacht must be prepared to crush Soviet Russia in a quick campaign," he said. Preparations were to be complete by May 15, 1941.

Stalin had plenty of warning that the attack was coming—from Britain and his own intelligence agents—but he was trapped by his own conspiratorial nature, scornfully rejecting all the signs of German military buildup as "provocations" engendered by the capitalist powers. He even ignored a June 15 warning from Richard Sorge, head of the Russian spy ring in Tokyo, that war would begin within a week. Thus the war was upon him before he knew it.

Beginning in 1940 more than half the troops of the Special Western Military Region were concentrated around Bialystok and west in an area that projected into enemy territory. From that disposition, historian Ernst Topitsch concludes, the Russians clearly were planning a preemptive attack on Hitler.

On April 10, Marshal Timoshenko called a council of war and declared a state of emergency for the Soviet fighting forces. Topitsch concluded that this was done to encourage the Greeks and Yugoslavs to resist the German incursion into the Balkans and also to test the operational readiness of the Russian troops. It is a far-out conclusion, for the alert came at a time when Stalin was beginning to protest that anything indicating German readiness to attack was "provocation."

War Games

On New Year's Eve, 1940, Stalin called his marshals together and inquired about war games scheduled for the following day. He wanted to be in on the critique he said. Next day the war games began under supervision of Marshal Timoshenko. General Zhukov commanded the blues, the attackers, and General Pavlov, commander of the Western Military District, commanded the Red Army defense. Zhukov mounted three powerful concentric attacks, wiped out most of the concentrations of the Reds, and smashed his way deep into Russia. In the critique that followed, Stalin lost his temper and fired General Meretskov, the chief of the Red Army General Staff and appointed Zhukov in his place.

It was not until about a month before the attack that Stalin finally accepted the truth that there would be war with Germany. But, even then, he was wrong; he said it might come in a year, not in a month. He called up 800,000 reservists to strengthen the 21 divisions in the frontier military districts, thus bringing the total military force to 5 million men, but this was only about two weeks before the attack. He also ordered the camouflaging of military installations along the frontier and the dispersal of aircraft on the fields—reluctantly, ever mindful of not upsetting the Germans. The German General Staff saw this timidity in his actions, and concluded that the Russians were going to be a pushover. But General Halder, chief of the German army General Staff, wrote in his diary on April 7, 1941, that he was concerned lest the Soviets stage a preventive strike.

The Germans were building their assault forces in the east slowly, so as not to alarm the Russians. The reason for Halder's concern was that as of April 6, the Wehrmacht had only forty-seven divisions on the frontier, including three tank divisions opposing the Red Army, a force declared to be far too weak for an offensive. The German plan for Operation Barbarossa was threatened by the necessity of dealing with threats from Yugoslavia and Greece, which in April and May tied up units expected and needed for the Russian invasion. Operation Barbarossa called for 3 million men, or 75 percent of the German forces. Besides this, there were 67,000 German troops in Northern Finland, 500,000 men of the Finnish army, and 150,000 Rumanians. The Germans would have 3,350 tanks, 7,184 artillery pieces, 600,000 motor vehicles, and 625,000 horses. The *Luftwaffe* would furnish 2,770 aircraft, 65 percent of its total front line force.

Dmitri Volkogonov, head of the Russian Institute of Military History and the first biographer to publish after glasnost, concluded that Stalin's miscalculations and his wrong assessments stemmed from his absolute control of Soviet society. Everyone was afraid of him—as he had shown so ruthlessly and so recently, he had the power of life and death over them.

So, to please Stalin, everyone talked about the Invincible Red Army, knowing they were parroting lies, and the day that the internal stresses of capitalism would bring explosion from within. There were a few sober minds at work. A group at the Lenin Military Political Academy prepared a thirty-five-page study of the causes of the debacle of the Russo-Finnish War. "Talk of invincibility leads to arrogance, superficiality and neglect of military science," they said. Stalin was shown the paper.

Finnish War, 1940

The Russians considered the Soviet-Finnish frontier, twenty miles north-west of Leningrad, to be a potential threat to Russia's second largest city and asked that it be pushed back a few dozen kilometers in exchange for which they would grant Finland a much larger piece of territory elsewhere. The negotiations went on for several months but collapsed when the Finns shelled the frontier, killing several Soviet soldiers. Russia declared war on Finland and troops began to march. The Red Army advanced, capturing Petsumo and tried moving up the Karelian Peninsula. The Finns resisted manfully and soon the hospitals of Leningrad were full of Russian wounded.

The first month of the war was an unmitigated disaster for Stalin. After very heavy fighting the Soviet troops reached the Mannerheim defense line, about forty miles away, but there they came to a halt after encountering heavy snow. The few roads were defended by the Finns and the Russians had no ski troops. The Finns were armed with tommy guns and automatic rifles and the Russians were not. The temperatures were -30° F and most of the Soviet troops did not know how to use skis, and they had no experience in breaking into pillboxes and other permanent fortifications.

At the beginning of January, the offensive stopped. Timoshenko was appointed commander in chief and he planned an assault on the Mannerheim line. Three infantry divisions were assigned—as were engineers, tanks, planes, and guns—for an all-out effort against the Finnish fortifications. A diversionary attack was to be launched against Viborg across the ice in the Gulf of Finland. The storming of the Mannerheim line began on February 11, preceded by a bombardment. The advance was slow. The Russians captured many pillboxes, but the Finns resisted desperately. The reinforced concrete defenses were almost—but not quite—impregnable. After almost a week following the breakthrough along an eight-mile front, the Russians struggled but finally overran the western portion of the line, but suffered heavy casualties.

Their losses were so great that the units had to regroup and heavy reinforcement brought up before the advance could be resumed. Full-scale operations were restarted on February 28 . When the troops approached Viborg,
they encountered another obstacle—the Finns had flooded large areas—but
they finally reached the Viborg-Helsinki highway. There the Finnish resistance
slowed. On March 4, Mannerheim informed the Finnish government that the
army could no longer resist successfully. The Soviet-Finnish Peace Treaty was
signed in Moscow on March 12, 1940.

"File it," he snorted.

In biographer Volkogonov's opinion, Stalin's biggest prewar error
was to sign the Treaty of Friendship and Borders on September 28,
1939, thus reversing the longstanding Soviet policy that held the Nazi
dictatorship of Germany to be "terrorist, militarist, and the phalanx
of world imperialism." Overnight, the Russian people were told to
change their opinions—not only to change but to reverse their view.
Overnight, the Germans ceased to be Russia's worst enemy and,
according to official Soviet doctrine, became a best friend.

The Coming Storm

THE GERMAN CAMPAIGN IN YUGOSLAVIA ENDED WHEN
Belgrade surrendered on April 13, 1941, and the Yugoslav army
gave up four days later. Greece surrendered on April 23, and Hitler
then sent airborne troops to capture Crete, which was accomplished
against an incompetent British defense at the end of May. Actually,
the Balkan campaigns had not slowed the German preparations
appreciably. The worst problem was weather: the winter and spring
of 1941 were unusually wet, and much of Poland was flooded. Even
in early June the Bug River was over its banks.

When the Balkan campaign concluded the Germans wasted no time
in rushing the troops to the Soviet border. Three army groups were
established for the attack on Russia—Army Group South, under Field
Marshal Gerd von Rundstedt, Army Group Center, under Field
Marshal Fedor von Bock, and Army Group North, under Field Marshal
Ritter von Leeb. Army Group South would operate south of the Pripet
Marshes; Army Group Center would work between the Pripet Marshes
and the Suvalki Peak; and Army Group North would begin in East
Prussia and drive toward Leningrad. All together 145 divisions were

available for operations against Russia—nearly 3.2 million men of a total German field force of 3.8 million.

The Germans were confident of quick and easy victory. In September 1940, the German General Staff predicted victory in eight to ten weeks. On June 18, 1941, Heinrich Himmler predicted victory in six weeks. Hitler and his generals even postulated a postvictory plan, one that called for the conquest of Afghanistan and India.

The Soviet forces included the Northwest Front, of twenty-four divisions under General V. I. Kuznetsov; the Western Front, thirty-eight divisions under General Dmitri Pavlov; the Southwest Front, fifty-six divisions under General Mikhail Kirponos; and the South Front, sixteen divisions under General Armii Tyulenev.

> **And with the Fleet...**
>
> On June 13, Admiral Kuznetsov had given Stalin the latest naval intelligence about German ship movements. Soviet fleet commanders, he said were convinced that the Germans were planning a major offensive against the Soviet Union from the Barents Sea to the Bosphorus.
>
> The Germans had also stopped work on the cruiser they had sold to the Soviet navy and was being fitted out in the Leningrad Shipyard with the aid of German technicians.
>
> When he had finished, Stalin looked up from his papers, "Is that all?" he demanded.
>
> Yes, that was all.

But the fact was that Russia was not prepared for the attack, morally or physically. Russian industry had barely begun to produce modern war materials. The Russian air force planes were mostly obsolete, the Yak-1 and Mig-3 fighters and the Pe-2 bombers had gone into production in 1940 but in a very small way, for example: only twenty Mig-3s were produced in 1940.

The same was true of tanks. In 1940, only 243 KV tanks and 115 T-34 tanks were produced. On June 21, there were only 508 KVs and 967 T-34 tanks in all five of the military districts. Similarly, the production of guns, mortars, and automatic weapons proceeded at a pace that was "intolerably slow," as Alexander Werth noted in his *Russia at War*. The responsibility was with the Russian bureaucracy, which dragged its heels.

The ammunition situation was even worse. Russia also suffered from the lack of an auto industry: there were only 800,000 motor vehicles, which was not enough to draw the artillery. The Russian army had to depend on farm tractors or horses for transport.

On the eve of the German invasion, most of the troops along the frontier were scattered; in the western district they were scattered over a depth of 60 to 190 miles from the frontier.

The situation of the air force was even worse. A vast construction program had been ordered with the People's Commissariat of Internal Affairs (NKVD) responsible for rebuilding airfields; therefore, simultaneous to the attack, dozens of fields were torn up. As a result, Soviet fighter aircraft were concentrated on a handful of airfields—thus vulnerable—while the Germans had built or modernized 250 airfields and fifty landing strips in Poland to handle their Heinkels, Dorniers, and Messerschmitts.

Almost everything else was wrong, too. Russian railroads had only a third of the capacity of the German roads on the other side of the New Frontier. The building of fortifications had just begun. Every Russian plan was predicated on a German attack that would threaten in 1942 or 1943, not 1941.

In spring 1941, Germans began to violate the new Soviet borders with air incursions, and sometimes land raids, as they built their offensive line. Stalin was furious when his frontier commanders proposed to attack the intruding planes and flatly ordered that these "provocations" must be ignored.

Even a week before the German invasion, the TASS News Agency issued a communiqué that could only have originated with Stalin:

> According to the information of the USSR, Germany is observing the terms of the Soviet–German Nonaggression Pact just as strictly as is the Soviet Union. In view of this, in the opinion of Soviet cir-

cles, rumors about Germany's intention to break the pact and attack the USSR are devoid of all foundation, and the recent dispatch of German troops released from operations in the Balkans to the eastern and northeastern areas of Germany is connected, it must be presumed, with other motives which have nothing to do with Soviet–German relations.

From this it must be inferred that Stalin was well aware of the German concentration on the frontiers. The motives, not the concentration, are brought under question. Any commander bent on increasing combat readiness ran the risk of obloquy from his fellows, superiors, and the OGPU. His loyalty would be brought into question and he would be labeled a provocateur and panic monger. General R. I. Malinovski, a corps commander on the Southwest Front, asked: "Could we open fire if the enemy invaded our territory?"

The response from Moscow was, "Do not succumb to provocation and do not open fire."

Such directives were sent to the troops in the field, the last of them only three hours before the German assault began.

At the end of May, Marshal Timoshenko and General Zhukov were summoned urgently to the Kremlin.

"Aha," they said. "At last we will be permitted to put the border districts on high alert."

But no. All Stalin wanted to tell them was that the German ambassador had asked permission to search for the graves of German officers and men killed in World War I.

✳ ✳ ✳

General M. I. Kazakov was assigned to training exercises in the Near Eastern theater and was there on June 11, when he was summoned from Moscow. A plane took him from the training exercise to Tashkent, and the next day he flew to Moscow. They flew over a railroad line and he noted many trains passing, all of them headed northwest. The trains were from the Trans Baikal, heading toward the Western Front. In Moscow, Kazakov sought out General A. M. Vasilievsky, asking him what was going on.

"Finland's armed forces are mobilizing and German forces are already concentrated on our frontiers," was the response.

"When will war begin?"

"We'll be lucky if it doesn't begin in the next fifteen to twenty days."

When Kazakov's work was finished, he reported to Marshal S. K. Timoshenko, the People's Commissar of Defense, and was invited to see a film of the German invasion of the Balkans. He was annoyed to see that the film showed Slavic girls serving wine to German soldiers. After the film, Timoshenko had a dinner engagement with Chief of Staff Zhukov, so the lesser lights had to spend a few hours waiting in the Operations Office. They did not see Timoshenko again that day. He returned about 1:00 AM and immediately went home and to bed. Zhukov left shortly afterwards. The next morning, June 20, Kazakov waited on Chief of Staff Zhukov, who arrived at the office at 11:00 AM and saw him immediately. Kazokov never did get to meet with Timoshenko but went back to Tashkent on June 21.

> **Provocations**
>
> There was no shortage of warnings to the Russians that Hitler was about to attack. The historical analysts have documented eighty-four such warnings. But Stalin's answer was always the same: "Provocations! Provocations! Always Provocations!"
>
> Richard Sorge, head of the Soviet spy ring in Tokyo, gave several warnings, complete with dates. Stalin refused to believe as he refused to believe any other warnings.

✳ ✳ ✳

Admiral N. G. Kuznetsov, chief of naval operations, was stationed at naval headquarters in Moscow. In February he complained to Stalin that the Germans were delaying deliveries for the cruiser *Luetzow*, which was under construction. Stalin expressed concern and told the admiral to keep him informed. Later he heard that Zhdanov, a member of the Supreme Naval Council, said that war seemed improbable and that violations of Soviet airspace were simply precautionary measures on Hitler's part.

The last time he saw Stalin before the war began, he reported on the readiness of the fleet but then was abruptly dismissed because Stalin obviously had other things on his mind. He wanted to report also that German ships were leaving Russian ports, which seemed ominous, but had no chance.

The next day he saw Foreign Commissar Molotov. When he remarked that the German ships were leaving and that this indicated a coming attack, Molotov said, "Only a fool would attack us."

On Saturday, June 21, the air of Moscow seemed unusually quiet. That evening the telephone at Kuznetsov's office did not ring at all until 11:00 PM when he had a call from Marshal Timoshenko.

"Come to my office at once. There is very important news."

When the admiral and an aide arrived at the office of the marshal they found him pacing the floor and dictating. Marshal Zhukov was sitting at a desk, writing. Both officers had their tunics unbuttoned (it was a very hot night) and had apparently been working for long time.

"The fleets must be ordered to combat readiness," Timoshenko said.

"In the event of attack are they allowed to open fire?" the admiral asked.

"They are."

Admiral Kuznetsov sent his aide running to naval headquarters to send a telegram to the fleets. It was already after midnight; June 22 had begun. He did not know that the first clash of the navy with the Germans was less than three hours away.

At 3:15 the commander of the Black Sea Fleet reported that an air raid was in progress against Sevastopol.

The war had begun!

The admiral attempted to reach Stalin and failed, but G. M. Malenkov returned the call, and when Admiral Kuznetsov reported on the Sevastopol attack, Malenkov did not believe him and telephoned Sevastopol.

✳ ✳ ✳

General of the Army I. V. Tiulenev was at Moscow District Headquarters on June 21.

At 2:00 PM he had a call from Stalin, ordering him to bring Moscow's air defense command to 75 percent of readiness. But that was the only indication of tension.

Darkness fell, he left the office, and his car took him home to Rzhevskii Street. As the car moved along he read the papers: hostilities in Syria, situation on the Libyan–Egyptian Front, a Reuters report of a few German planes over Britain.

The Germans Move

Eight hundred thousand copies of Hitler's proclamation to the troops starting the invasion of Russia were issued secretly to the armed forces on the evening of June 20.

"At this moment, soldiers of the Eastern Front, an assembly of strength on a size and scale such as the world has never seen is now complete.

"German soldiers! You are about to join battle, a hard and crucial battle. The destiny of Europe, the future of the German Reich, the existence of our nation, now lie in your hands alone."

"May the Lord God help us all in this struggle."

News of Russia, the all-union agricultural exhibit in Moscow, the departure of the Young Pioneers for camp, a brief report of the forthcoming opening of a water sports stadium in Khimki. These were the news items of the day.

The general's family had gone to their country dacha for the weekend, and later, after checking with air force headquarters, he drove out to join them. At 3:00 AM the general was awakened by a call, summoning him to the Kremlin at once. On the way he stopped at General Staff Headquarters and found Marshal Zhukov on the telephone.

"The Germans have bombed Kovno, Rovno, Sevastopol, and Odessa," Zhukov said. "We have reported it to Stalin but he continues to believe it is merely provocation by German generals."

General Tiulenev hurried on to the Kremlin where he learned that he had just been appointed commander of the Southern Army Group and was ordered to leave that very day.

Violations of the frontiers by German aircraft were becoming more frequent. In the Baltic, a flight of German aircraft was forced to land. Still, the air force was not allowed to fire at the Germans.

The German Attack

O N THE EVENING OF JUNE 19, 1941, COL. I. T. STARINOV, the leading Soviet expert on land mines, left Moscow for Brest-Litovsk and troop exercises of the Western Military District. He thought about the coming exercises and was eager to see old friends, General Nikolai Aleksandrovich Klich and General of the Army D. G. Pavlov, with whom he had fought in Spain.

When he arrived at Minsk, Starinov was put off a bit when he saw Pavlov's chief of staff, who was totally concerned with telephone reports he kept getting of German incursions into Soviet territory.

"They're stirring up panic with constant reports like that."

He was taken to General Pavlov's office.

When he entered, Pavlov was on the phone.

"Never mind," the general snapped. "More self-control. I know. It has already been reported. More self-control."

Finally, Pavlov put down the receiver and turned to his guest. But they had hardly shaken hands, when the telephone rang again.

"I know. It has already been reported." He said. "Those at the top know better than we. That's all." And he slammed down the receiver.

The chief of staff came in. General Pavlov excused himself. He was very busy, he said. He would have time to discuss old times with Starinov at the coming exercises, he said.

Starinov then called on General Klich, and asked him what was going on.

"Something bad is happening," Klich said.

"What specifically?"

"Specifically the Germans are moving tanks, troops, and artillery up to the border. Their airplanes are constantly flying over our territory."

"And what are we doing?"

"We are reforming and rearming the troops. It is strictly forbidden to shoot down enemy planes. Then there is also the TASS statement of June 14. It calmed us but it also lowered our level of combat readiness."

May Day

Marshal Timoshenko was one of the few military leaders who had Stalin's confidence. He had led the May Day parade to Red Square, riding a handsome chestnut stallion (because Stalin could not ride a horse). He had also made the May Day oration. Standing next to Stalin, he said, "The government of the Soviet Union firmly and consistently carries forward the wise foreign policy of Stalin, the policy of peace among the peoples and the guarantee for the security of our Fatherland. In this it meets with the sympathies of the countries waging war. The Soviet Union stands outside the war and fights against its extension. That is the purpose of the neutrality pact with our eastern neighbor, Japan, as well as all other international acts of the Soviet government. We are for peace and for the consolidation of friendly and good neighborly relations with all countries which are seeking to establish the same relations with the Soviet Union. The Bolshevik Party and the Soviet government take account of the fact that the international situation is very heated and harbors all sorts of surprises. That is why the entire Soviet people, the Red Army, and the navy must be prepared to fight."

"Understand what is bothering me. I have many guns, but the artillery men are mainly youngsters, and they are not adequately trained. On top of that, the trucks of many artillery regiments have been taken for the construction of fortified areas. They have even sent the tractors there. The result is guns without traction power. Do you understand? No traction power."

"Naturally you have reported this to Pavlov?"

"And Pavlov reported it and called Moscow. Everywhere we get the same answer—'the boss knows all about it. Don't panic! Keep calm!'"

A telephone call ended the meeting. Klich was summoned urgently by the district commander.

On Saturday, June 1, Colonel Starinov left for Brest-Litovsk, traveling with another colonel. They stopped at Kobrin, headquarters of the Fourth Army. Here the chief of engineers, Colonel A. I. Proshliakov, invited them to spend the night, saying he would send a car for them the next morning to drive to the maneuvers area.

The usual Saturday bustle prevailed at Fourth Army Headquarters, which was responsible for the Brest-Litovsk sector. Later that day they were informed that the maneuvers had been canceled and they spent the evening in the picturesque town. After dinner they returned to the office of the chief of engineers, and settled down for the night on sofas.

Colonel Starinov woke up suddenly, aroused by an explosion. He looked at his watch. It was 4:20 AM. Only the monotonous sound of airplane engines broke the quiet.

Not far away a thud was heard, and then an explosion.

Demolition works, the colonel thought.

But it quickly became apparent that this noise was bombing. They raced to the windows; the sky over Kobrin was growing light. Then the sound of boots was heard on the other side of the wall; the radio in the hallway began to blast.

"Everyone is to leave the building immediately."

Colonel Starinov pulled on his boots, put on his tunic on the run, and dashed into the street.

Operation Barbarossa

When Hitler knew he had been defeated in his attempt to invade England he turned to the attack on Russia. The code name was selected at random: Operation Barbarossa. The timing was established during one of Molotov's visits to Berlin. Molotov came to meet German Foreign Minister von Ribbentrop. They met during a British air raid, in a shelter. As they sat there talking von Ribbentrop said, "England is finished."

"So why are we sitting in this place?" asked Molotov.

It was December 1940, six months before the German attack.

For six months, Stalin had warnings from everyone from Winston Churchill to Soviet spy Richard Sorge. He believed none of them. Winston Churchill failed because Stalin said he was trying to drag Russia into the war, Sorge because he refused to return to the USSR. Who could believe a defector?

When Hitler began his Balkan campaign in spring 1941 this seemed to be proof that he was aiming for Suez. Also, if the Germans were aiming to attack so late in the year, they would need winter clothing. Sheepskins. But the market for fleece was not going up, further proof that the warnings were all faked. So, the conventional wisdom has it, Stalin was completely surprised by the attack on June 21.

Just in time!

A squadron of planes was heading for the headquarters building. "Air attack," someone shouted.

He ran across the square, jumped a ditch, and flung himself down in an orchard. On the run he saw thin small bombs detach themselves from the planes. The bombs began to fall, the headquarters building was quickly concealed by smoke and dust.

Another flight of planes—Stuka dive bombers—appeared and bombed the headquarters. When the raid ended, much of Fourth Army Headquarters had been destroyed, smoke was rising from the ruins, and a fallen tree lay across the street. Somewhere a feminine voice was crying hysterically, a desperate, inconsolable "aaaah."

Colonel Starinov decided to make his way to Brest-Litovsk, and caught a ride with the first passing vehicle. He saw officers running along the side of the road, hastening to their posts. A long line of refugees, women, and children was moving, carrying bundles and baskets, leaving the military settlement. The streets of Kobrin, so hospitable the day before, were full of fires. The rasp of a loudspeaker stopped the car in the square. The driver opened the door and leaned out. The familiar Moscow call signal invaded the confusion and turmoil. Everyone in the square looked up hopefully, the round black loudspeaker mounted on a telephone pole.

"It is 6:00 AM Moscow time. We begin our broadcast of the latest news."

The announcers cheerfully reported on the labor achievements of the Soviet people, the rich harvest, the fulfillment of a factory ahead of schedule. Celebrations in the Mari Autonomous Republic. . . .

Finally they heard, "The German Information Agency reports—"

A girl standing next to Colonel Starinov rose on tiptoes. . . .

However, the announcer reported sunken British vessels, German air raids on Scotland, a Reuters communiqué on the downing of twenty-seven German bombers over England, the war in Syria, and that was all. . . .The newscast ended with a weather report. The girl no longer stood on tiptoe. The crowd stared at the loudspeaker.

"Let's wait. There may be a special communiqué," said Starinov's companion.

But the morning calisthenics began as usual.

The driver spat and slammed the door.

"Stretch your arms out, Bend! Livelier! Up, Down, livelier. That's it."

The girl looked around and then ran off through the dispersing crowd.

✳ ✳ ✳

Starinov and his friends decided to go back to Minsk for instructions. They had reached Pinsk by noon, to see the airfield torn to pieces, planes wrecked and burning, and firefighters out in force, trying to salvage what they could. Yet they still believed that the damage was local, that elsewhere the Soviet air force was counterattacking. After all, there had been so much evidence that the front lines were prepared.

✳ ✳ ✳

General of the Army I. V. Boldin at Western Army Headquarters came home late on Saturday. He was extremely tired but could not sleep. Horrid thoughts kept running through his mind. On Friday, intelligence had reported that six German planes had crossed the border and penetrated Soviet territory for several kilometers. Soviet fighters went up and escorted the Germans back to the border. They did not shoot them down because the air force was under categorical orders not to open fire on German planes, no matter what they did.

That Saturday evening Lt. Gen. V. I. Kutznesov, commander of the Third Army, reported that the Germans had removed the barbed wire barriers along the border at then Avgustov-Seini Road. The roar of many engines had been heard from the forest in that area. In the area of Suvalki and Aris, troops were coming up from the rear, and German artillery had taken up firing positions. A large number of tanks were concentrated south of Suvalki. Trainloads of pontoon equipment, sectional bridges, and ammunition were arriving at the Biala–Podliaska Station.

The German troops concentrated opposite the Western Special Military District had taken up an attack position.

General Boldin called the operations duty officer at headquarters and asked for news. There was nothing.

Boldin, deputy commander of the Western District, had often visited the border garrisons. All the signs now indicated a coming German attack and Boldin had so informed General Pavlov. More than once he had been rebuked.

"Ivan Vasil'evich, believe me, in Moscow they know the military and political situation and our relations with the Germans better than you and I do."

Quite recently, Major General Klimovskikh, chief of staff, had tried in his presence to report a plan for measures to increase combat readiness. Pavlov had blown up, swept away the map with his hand, and said sharply, "War is possible, but not within the near future. Now we must prepare for autumn maneuvers and take steps to see that no alarmist answers German provocation by opening fire."

"He was probably right," Klimovskikh said. "He spoke with Moscow every day. He must be more fully briefed."

But Boldin was still worried, and was worrying when a call came for him to appear at headquarters at once.

Fifteen minutes later he was in the commander's office and found Corps Commissar Fominykh and General Klimovskikh there.

"What has happened?" Boldin asked Pavlov.

"I can't make it out myself. A few minutes ago I had a call from Kuznetsov. He says the Germans have crossed the border in the sector from Sopotskin to Avgustov and are bombing Grodno. Wire communications with units have broken off. Two radio stations have been demolished. The reports are incredible. The Germans are bombing."

The conversation was interrupted by a phone call from Moscow. Marshal Timoshenko, the Commissar of Defense, was calling Pavlov.

Pavlov reported. A few minutes later there was another call from Kuznetsov. The situation was worse. At daybreak on June 22, more than thirty German infantry, five tanks, and two motorized divisions had attacked the Western Army Group.

Calls kept coming in. Finally Pavlov said, "Golubev called once and then there were no more reports. I'll fly there now, and you stay here in my place."

"In the present situation the commander of the military district should not leave headquarters," Boldin said.

"You, Comrade Boldin," Pavlov said, adopting an official tone, "are first deputy commander. I request that you take over for me at headquarters. I see no other solution to the situation that has arisen."

Very shortly afterwards Pavlov left the office.

The General Staff

On the eve of the German attack the highest agitation ruled in the Soviet General Staff. On June 21, they received information pinpointing the night of June 22 as the beginning of the attack. A German deserter informed the Soviet frontier commander that his unit had been ordered to go into action at dawn. War Commissar Timoshenko and Chief of Staff Zhukov waited on Stalin with that news at 5:00 PM, as well as an order that would put all Russian units on a war alert. Stalin's first reaction was to dub the business an obvious provocation. The term seemed to have lost all concrete meaning and become simply an expression of despair.

At 12:30 Stalin had been persuaded to approve the order and it was ready to be sent out, "There has arisen a possibility of a sudden German attack on June 21–22. The German attack may begin with provocations. It is ordered in the course of the night of June 21 to occupy secretly the strong points on the frontier. To disperse and camouflage planes at special airfields, to have all units battle ready. No other measures are to be employed without special orders."

It was already June 22. How could the Russians move hundreds of thousands of troops and thousands of planes on the shortest night of the year, before dawn? This was Stalin's Russia, where everything had to be in writing so Stalin would know his orders were being obeyed explicitly. Out went the telegrams to commanders. By the time the operational units got theirs it was 2:25 AM. The Germans struck at 3:14 AM, while the officers were deciphering the words "no other measures are to be taken without special orders."

The man bearing the responsibility for this negligence was asleep in his dacha at Kuntsevo.

Marshal Timoshenko called again. Boldin reported, since Pavlov was out of the office. He said that German planes were continuing to strafe Soviet troops and the civil population. The enemy had crossed the border in many sectors and was advancing.

Marshal Timoshenko said, "Bear in mind Comrade Boldin, that no actions are to be started against the Germans without our consent."

"What?" Boldin shouted. "Our troops are forced to retreat, cities are burning, people are dying!"

"Stalin thinks that these may possibly be provocations on the part of some German generals. I am issuing an order that aerial reconnaissance be conducted no deeper than sixty kilometers."

"Comrade Marshal, we must act. Every minute is precious. This is no provocation. The Germans have started a war."

Boldin finally got permission to fly to Belostok, Tenth Army Headquarters, with which there were no communications, to clarify the situation.

Pavlov came back into the office and Boldin reported to him. At about 3:00 PM on June 22, he finally left for Belostok. Flying over Baranovichi, he saw the station was on fire. Trains and warehouses were burning. German planes were streaking through the sky. Boldin's pilot dropped down to the deck and turned away from the railroad, but they were chased by German fighters. The situation was impossible. Up ahead they saw a small airfield with several planes burning on the ground. Boldin signaled the pilot to land. As they approached the field they were attacked by a Messerschmitt, which luckily broke off without doing any damage. They landed; immediately after that the field was bombed again by a flight of German planes. Their aircraft was destroyed.

There was no car at the airfield so they rode in a light truck to General Golubin's headquarters. Gasoline and grain warehouses were burning on the outskirts of Belostok. When they reached Tenth Army Headquarters they found that General Golubin had gone to the field command post, so they set out to follow. They found it twelve kilometers southwest of Belostok, in a small wood—two tents with wooden tables in each. On one table was a telephone. Some distance away stood a truck with a radio. This was the Tenth Army Command Post at 7:00 PM on June 22.

Speaking to General Golubev, Boldin learned that losses were heavy: the Fifth Corps had been overwhelmed by three enemy corps. General Boldin discovered how grave the situation was. The Thirteenth

---

The Attack

The Politburo was in session all day on June 21. After the meeting the black limousines carried Stalin and his drinking buddies to his dacha. He needed distraction.

They were with him until midnight, but the forced cheerfulness was a failure. Stalin instructed Molotov to send a coded telegram to Berlin to the Soviet ambassador instructing him to demand answers from the German foreign minister to the questions Ambassador Schulenberg had dodged. Molotov drove to the Commissariat for foreign affairs and sent the telegram to Berlin at 12:40. At 3:30 AM, German planes bombed Belorussia; at 4:00 they were bombing Kiev and Sevastopol. Meanwhile, Stalin was snoring in his dacha.

Zhukov telephoned him there and got the night man.

"Who's calling?"

"Zhukov—chief of staff. Please connect me with Comrade Stalin. It's urgent."

Three minutes later, Stalin came to the phone. Zhukov reported.

Silence.

"Did you understand what I said?"

Silence.

Then finally, "Where's the commissar?"

"Bring him down to the Kremlin. Tell Poskrebyshev to summon the whole Politburo."

That was how the war began.

Mechanized Corps, with a handful of tanks, had been sent to the Nurets River to stop a German flanking maneuver. But General Golubin had no hope that the Thirteenth Corps could carry out its mission. They were short of fuel and ammunition.

Why were they short of fuel?

In the first hours of the attack, enemy planes had set fire to many fuel dumps. They knew where they were. The Germans used incendiary bullets to destroy railroad cars filled with fuel. They knew where they were. Not for nothing had the *Luftwaffe* been overflying the Soviet positions for all these weeks.

Minsk was calling, and soon Boldin was talking to Pavlov.

"Here is the order," Pavlov said.

"You are to organize an attack force made up of the Sixth and Eleventh Mechanized Corps, and the Thirty-Sixth Cavalry Division."

"Destroy the enemy on the left bank of the Neman River, with a counterthrust, making sure that the Germans do not break through in the area of Vokovysk. After that the whole force will be transferred to the command of General Kuznetsov."

"Tell Golubev that his assignment is to occupy Osovets, Vizna, Bel'sk, and Kleshchele"—all to be done that very night.

Boldin tried to tell Pavlov that this was impossible.

Pavlov was silent for a moment, and then said, "That is all I have to say. Get started."

With that, the conversation ended. Boldin thought, "How far from reality Pavlov is."

The Tenth Army was heavily engaged in fierce fighting with the advancing enemy, yielding one position after another. Effective counterattack was out of the question.

But if Pavlov was far from reality, it was because he had been led down the garden path by Stalin.

Here is what Marshal Zhukov had to say later about Stalin's military leadership, "It appeared to us before the war that Stalin knew no less and even more than we did about matters of war and defense and had a deeper understanding and foresight. When we had to encounter difficulties in the war, however, we understood that our views about Stalin had been erroneous."

—⚬⚬—

4

The First Days of War

EARLY HISTORIES OF THE WAR PORTRAY STALIN AS going into deep shock at the attack and retreating to remain incommunicado in his dacha for a week. But recently new documents have come to light that tell quite a different story.

The streetlights were still on when his car drove into the Kremlin that morning. He waited for news of casualties, alone, because he was first to arrive at the Kremlin. The other members of the Politburo, aroused by Poskrebyshev, soon began filing in—Molotov, Beria, Timoshenko, Mekhlis, Zhukov, Malenkov, Mikoyan, Kaganovich. Timoshenko gave his report; the German attack must be considered to be an accomplished fact. The enemy had bombed the airfields, ports, and major arterial junctions.

Then Stalin began to speak. He spoke slowly and sometimes his voice broke. When he was finished, everyone was silent for some time. He then spoke to Molotov, "We must get in touch with Berlin again and ring the embassy." Molotov rang the commissariat for foreign affairs and spoke to someone who asked him to come. Count von der Schulenberg, the German ambassador in Russia, was asking to see him.

"Go," said Stalin.

Vatutin, first deputy chief of the general staff, left the room for a few minutes and returned to report that German troops were moving rapidly into Soviet territory without meeting notable resistance.

Molotov went to his own office in the Kremlin, looking out on the church of Ivan the Terrible, and Schulenberg was shown in. After talking to Schulenberg, Molotov came back to Stalin's office and stated, "The Germans have declared war on us."

This announcement threw the Politburo into confusion, for they had believed and hoped that it was just a provocation.

"The enemy will be beaten, all along the line," said Stalin calmly.

He turned to the military leaders, "What do you recommend?"

Zukov spoke first. "Order the troops to attack all along the whole front and halt the enemy. He has gone too far, too fast."

"Destroy, not halt," answered Timoshenko.

On this first day of the war everyone believed the German attack was a short-lived venture that would fail. Orders were given to fall on the enemy with all the forces and means at their disposal and destroy them in areas where they had crossed the frontier. Pending further orders, they were not to cross the frontier. Russian planes would bomb the enemy, including the forces on occupied territory.

On this first day, everyone appeared to be optimistic.

But, in reality, everyone was feigning that optimism.

Timoshenko and the Politburo were feigning it because they knew that Stalin would never forgive them if they did not. He would harbor a grudge, and he would make them pay for it later. Here was the proof of Stalin's absolute authority as dictator. Everyone feared him.

Stalin was also feigning optimism. He knew that what had happened was a disaster. Hitler had all the advantages of the aggressor. But what was the extent of the disaster?

Chadayev, chief administrative assistant to the Council of Peoples Commissars, was given the responsibility of taking notes at these meetings. "I caught a glimpse of Stalin in the corridor. He looked tired, worn out. His pockmarked face was haggard. During the first half of the day the Politburo approved an appeal to the Soviet people and Molotov read it over the radio at noon."

Stalin had put Molotov on display deliberately. Molotov had signed the pact with Germany; let him take the consequences. Molotov said Stalin did not want to come forward first. He wanted time to get the picture, to have some room to decide what the tone should be and what approach to use.

The nation heard the appeal at noon on this first day. Tuned to their radios, some citizens listened as bombs were crashing around them. Molotov spoke haltingly and ended with words written by Stalin: "Our cause is just; the enemy will be smashed; victory will be ours."

This was to become Stalin's mantra throughout the war.

At 2:00 PM, Chadayev was called into Molotov's office and Stalin came along.

"Well, you sounded a bit flustered but the speech went well."

Molotov was happy. He knew Stalin would start looking for people to blame. But it seemed now that Molotov would not be one of them.

The nation was waiting for Stalin to speak, but he was silent, waiting to see what would happen at the front and choosing his first culprits. That evening, Stalin was in a somber mood. "Pavlov isn't even in communication with the headquarters of his army group. He says the order reached him too late. Why was it late? And what if we hadn't managed to give an order? With or without orders the army ought to be completely ready for action. Surely I shouldn't have to give my watch orders to keep working?"

Pavlov was the commander on the Western Front, which had taken the first blow from the Germans.

Stalin had found his first scapegoat. "We must order them to evacuate the population and the enterprises eastward. Nothing must

Bombast

After the German attack sent Stalin into shock, he was confused and panicky. He refused to go on the air to tell the Russian people that they were at war and dispatched Molotov to do it. When that had been decided, he recovered a little and prepared, with Marshal Timoshenko's help, Order No. 2 of the Supreme War Council:

On 22 June 1941, at 0400 the German air force carried out totally unprovoked bombing raids on aerodromes and towns along our western frontiers. In view of the brazenness of the German attack, I order that:

1. The forces use all their strength and means to destroy the enemy where he has crossed the border. Until further orders, our troops are not to cross the border.
2. Reconnaissance and combat aircraft are to pinpoint the sites where the enemy has concentrated his aircraft and his ground forces. Bombers and dive-bombers must utterly destroy the enemy's aircraft on the ground and his main groupings of ground forces. Bombing attacks are to be carried out up to a depth of 100–150 kilometers into German territory. Koenigsberg and Memel are to be bombed. Finnish and Rumanian territory is not to be bombed until further orders.
22.6.41 07 15

—TIMOSHENKO, ZHUKOV, MALENKOV

The problem with this order is that there was no earthly way it could be carried out.

The initial German bombings had ravaged the front line Soviet airfields and destroyed almost all of the front line aircraft. The Luftwaffe had been very efficient. Bombers had wiped out most of the fuel dumps in the front areas, and ammunition dumps and railway stations were blazing.

Stalin did not know any of this and he was in no condition to be instructed. The situation on the Western Front was total chaos, and it threatened to grow worse as Stalin fumbled with orders to bring in more untrained troops to fight an efficient, disciplined German Wehrmacht.

fall into the hand of the enemy." This was the progenitor of the scorched earth policy, which became a reality a little bit later.

* * *

Desperate news arrived from the front. Timoshenko reported that in the first hours of the war the enemy planes had made mass attacks on airfields and troops.

Stalin said many planes must have been destroyed on the ground but surely the Germans had not managed to reach every airfield?

Unfortunately, they had.

"How many planes were destroyed?"

"About seven hundred."

The Western Front suffered heaviest losses. "This is a monstrous crime," Stalin said. "Those responsible must lose their heads." He instructed Beria to investigate.

The workday ended at 5:00 PM. Beria was the last to leave Stalin's office, after hearing the usual parting instructions to shoot those responsible.

Work began again in the middle of the night. There was an uninterrupted stream of visitors until the middle of the following night. During the day, Stalin created the Stavka, General Headquarters (GHQ) of the high command, the highest administrative unit of the armed forces. This was an exact copy from the days of Nicholas II. He also brought back the officers' epaulets. Internationalism and revolution went to the bottom of the agenda. The emphasis was on the Fatherland.

Stalin appointed Timoshenko as the chief of the Stavka, ad interim.

It was now June 24 and Stalin's last visitors, Timoshenko and Molotov, did not leave the office until 6:00 AM. The mask of impassivity was dropped. There was no sign of exhaustion or helplessness. His constant state now was one of rage. He hated everyone and everything, all for the error he alone had committed.

Timoshenko reported that the Soviet troops were bravely trying to carry out the orders to counterattack, they had not yet succeeded.

Stalin listened and at the end flew into a rage. He blamed the western command for everything. Then he heaped reproaches on Vatutin and Timoshenko. Timoshenko turned pale, but hid his resentment and asked to be sent to the front.

"The front can wait a bit longer," Stalin said. "But who's going to clear up the mess we have here at GHQ; who's going to correct the present state of affairs?" The request had only fueled his indignation. The People's Commissar for Tank Production, Malyshev, was summoned. Stalin interrupted as Malyshev read his report: "You're a long time getting a move on."

He then began making suggestions—on how to expand arms production, how to best organize production of armor plating, and the like. It was decided to create new bases for tank production in the Urals and Siberia. If worse came to worst, and the Germans occupied all of European Russia, then the limitless expanses of Siberia and the mineral wealth of the Urals would be left. The war could be carried on from there.

Stalin telephoned General Vasilievsky, deputy chief of staff, and instructed him to tell the front commanders that Stalin was very displeased with their failure to attack.

G. M. Popov, the secretary of the Moscow City Committee of the Party, and the city district secretaries had been sitting in the waiting room. They were called in. Stalin stroked his mustache with the telephone receiver.

"The Central Committee is receiving a large number of requests from the Soviet people for the creation of a Soviet peoples' militia . . . to meet the wishes of the citizens of Moscow, we shall set up a number of volunteer divisions of citizen soldiers."

A murderous scheme was evolving in his mind. He would hold back and keep fresh the new divisions then assembling in Siberia, a land of hunters, full of young men skilled in the use of arms. He would plug the front with cannon fodder, the peoples' militia, the four-eyed intelligentsia, the boys fresh from universities and technical colleges, together with the hemorrhaging remnants of the retreating armies.

The call to arms was sounded. Joining up was supposedly voluntary but those who refused to join were showered with contempt and threats of retribution.

✳ ✳ ✳

The search for scapegoats continued. He came down heavily on Marshal Kulik, an incompetent, who he had substituted during the purge of the army. "That good for nothing Kulik needs a kick in the ass." Day after day was filled with fits of rage. By this I mean there was no disguising the real dimensions of the tragedy. Timoshenko reported that the Russian troops were regrouping to check the enemy's advance.

Stalin said, "You mean you are no longer getting ready as you promised to smash the enemy?"

"No that's not possible but after we have concentrated we will smash him."

He began to lose his temper more frequently. He would stand before a map, arms folded, and give orders. Before his generals had time to do one thing he told them to do another.

He decided to start speaking the truth although no one else dared. "We were hoping against hope that the enemy could be halted, and smashed, but he continues to move forward."

At 3:00 AM on June 24, an air raid alarm sounded. The commander of antiaircraft artillery reported that enemy planes were flying toward Moscow. Sirens roared, the people took refuge in air raid shelters, antiaircraft guns opened fire. Damaged planes left fiery trails as they crashed to the ground. But clarification soon followed. The district commander of aircraft telephoned Stalin to say that it was a mistake.

"Our people have made a bit of a mess of things. They have been firing on our own planes coming back from a bombing raid." He omitted adding that they had largely succeeded in shooting them down.

From the first days of war, panic and fear reigned in Moscow. Windows were blacked out. Street lamps went unlit. It was a paradise for lovers who could kiss out on the streets.

As always, Stalin tried his hand at everything. He concerned himself with the design choice of a sniper's rifle and rifle bayonet, either knife blade or three sided.

He could usually be found in his office with Molotov, Beria, and Malenkov. They never asked questions but sat and listened. He was now beginning to pay for the universal fear he had inspired. Reports from the front usually understated Russian losses and exaggerated enemy losses. All this helped convince him that the enemy could not take such losses for long and would soon suffer defeat.

But the Germans were advancing rapidly. Minsk was about to fall, which meant that Smolensk would also fall, leaving the way to Moscow open.

On the morning of June 27, the members of the Politburo assembled as usual in Stalin's office. When the meeting ended, Stalin, Molotov, and Beria got into a car. It was clear from their actions that the Germans had taken Minsk. Shortly afterward the telephone rang. It was from Stalin's chief body guard, saying that the party had arrived at the Commissariat for Defense. Their arrival had caused great surprise. Stalin went into Timoshenko's office and said abruptly that they had to acquaint themselves with affairs. Stalin stood by the operations map without saying anything, obviously trying to control his fury. At a sign from Timoshenko, Zhukov and Vatutin remained in the office.

"What's happening at Minsk?" Stalin asked. "Isn't the position yet stabilized?"

Timoshenko said, "I am not yet able to report on that."

Stalin said, "It is your duty to have the facts clearly before you at all times. And to keep us up to date. You are simply afraid to tell us the truth."

Zhukov, who had been on edge before Stalin's arrival, flared, "Comrade Stalin, have we your permission to get on with our work?"

Beria butted in, "Perhaps we are in your way?"

Zhukov said, "You know that the situation on all fronts is critical. The front commanders are waiting for instructions from the commissariat, and its better that the commissariat and the general staff do it ourselves."

Beria said, "We, too, are capable of giving orders. If you think you can do it."

"If the party tells us to, we will."

Zhukov remained angry, "So wait 'til it tells you to. As things are, we've been told to do a job."

There was a pause then Zhukov went up to Stalin. "Excuse my outspokenness, Comrade Stalin, we shall get it all worked out and then come to the Kremlin and report."

Stalin looked at Timoshenko.

"Comrade Stalin, our first priority must be to think how we can help the armies at the front. After that, we can give you the information you want. You are making a crass mistake in trying to draw a line between yourselves and us. We all must join in thinking how to help the fronts."

Then Stalin looked gloomily at each of the Politburo members in turn and said, "There we are then; let them get it sorted out first. Let's go, comrades."

And he was the first out of the office.

✳ ✳ ✳

He had seen it with his own eyes. The most dreadful thing imaginable had happened. They were no longer afraid of him. And if they were no longer afraid of him it could be the end.

Lenin founded our state and we've fucked it up!

And that's when Stalin disappeared from view. No one knew where he was. Or when he would return. People tried to get him day and night without success.

Poskrebyshev began to accumulate papers that must be signed. Since Voznesensky was chairman of the Council of People's Commissars, he was asked to sign. Voznesensky telephoned Molotov, listened, and put down the receiver saying, "Molotov asks you to wait one more day. And wants members of the Politburo to meet in his office in two hours."

Voznesensky picked up the hotline, waited a minute, and then said there was no reply from the dacha.

✳ ✳ ✳

Stalin usually got to the Kremlin about 2:00 PM. For half an hour one car would drive up after another, with Stalin in one of them, no one knew which. His workday went until 3:00 or 4:00 AM. Everyone had to observe this routine.

And suddenly Stalin had failed to turn up. No one was summoned; the telephones were silent.

Everyone knew he was at the dacha; the staff said he was there and was well. But no one had the nerve to go and see him. The members of the Politburo met every day in Molotov's office, trying to decide what to do.

Finally, the members of the Politburo decided to visit him as a body.

✳ ✳ ✳

What had happened?

Stalin's great hero was Ivan the Terrible. One work in his personal library that was much thumbed was Tolstoy's play, "Ivan the Terrible."

No, Stalin was not behaving like a neurotic. He was adopting Ivan's methods to be his own. In the Commissariat for Defense that day he had seen a change in attitude and had drawn his own conclusions. He knew that Minsk would fall and then the juggernaut would roll toward Moscow. If so, his pathetic slaves might rebel. So Stalin emulated his teacher, Ivan the Terrible.

Ivan the Terrible's trick was to pretend that he was dying, watch how people behaved, then rise from his sickbed and punish them to discourage rebellion. Ivan also made a habit of disappearing to show everyone how helpless they were without him. Stalin was behaving as Ivan the Terrible had.

The experienced courtier Molotov saw through the game immediately and was wary of signing important papers. Not signing was proof of loyalty. By leaving his blind kittens to themselves Stalin was making them feel their insignificance and reminding them that without him the military would sweep them away. Molotov organized the trip to the dacha. And there the great actor performed his role in the play "The Retirement Game."

They found their leader thin and haggard. He looked gloomy. "The great Lenin is no more," he said. "If only he could see us now, those he entrusted with the fate of his country. I am inundated with letters from the Soviet people rebuking us, saying 'you surely can't halt the enemy.' Maybe some of you wouldn't mind putting all the blame on me."

Molotov responded, "Thank you for your frankness, but I tell you that if some idiot tried to turn me against you I'd see him damned. We are asking you to come back to work and we will do all we can to help you."

"Yes, but how can I live up to the people's hopes anymore, can I lead the country to victory? There may be more deserving candidates."

Voroshilov said, "I believe I am voicing the unanimous opinion there is no one more worthy."

This was followed by the chorus. Right!!!

They pleaded earnestly with him, knowing that to do less would be fatal.

The game was over; they had begged him yet again to be their leader, as if they had reinvested him with power.

Writing of this moment, biographer Edvard Radzinsky consulted the calendar for June 1941. Stalin had indeed disappeared on June 27 and had not turned up again until July 1.

He had won his little game.

The *Blitzkrieg*

G ENERAL HEINZ GUDERIAN COMMANDED PANZER
Group 2, one of the striking forces of Army Group Center. His
assignment on the first day of Operation Barbarossa was to cross the
Bug River on both sides of Brest-Litovsk, break through the Russian
positions, and advance to the area Roslavl-Elnya-Smolensk.

On the morning of June 22, Guderian went to his command
post, in an observation tower, south of Bohukaly, nine miles northwest of Brest-Litovsk. He arrived at 3:10 AM. It was still dark. At
3:15 the German artillery opened its barrage. At 3:40 the first Stuka
dive bomber attacked. At 4:15 advance units of the Seventeenth and
Eighteenth Panzer Divisions began to cross the Bug. At 4:45 the leading tanks of the Eighteenth Panzer Division forded the river, protected from immersion by waterproofing, which had been developed
for Operation *Sea-Lion* and never used.

At 6:50 AM General Guderian crossed the Bug in an assault boat
in the neighborhood of Kolodno. His command staff consisted of
two armored wireless trucks, several cross-country vehicles, and
some motorcyclists. They began by following the tank tracks of the

General Boldin

General Boldin had gone to the Minsk Army Officer's Club to see a play. He was sitting in a box with General Pavlov when suddenly Colonel Blokhin, the intelligence officer of the Western Military District, appeared and carried on a whispered conversation with General Pavlov.

"It can't be true," Pavlov said. "Seems nonsense to me. Our reconnaissance says that things are very ominous at the frontier. The German troops are supposed to be ready for action and to have shelled some of our positions."

That was the end of the conversation. But later in the night, Boldin had an agitated call from Pavlov asking him to come to headquarters. He arrived there ten minutes later.

"What's happened?" Boldin said.

"Can't quite make it out," Pavlov replied. "Some kind of deviltry going on, General Kuznetsov phoned. Germans have crossed the border on a wide front and bombing Grodny. Telephone communications have been smashed and we have had to switch over to radio. Two wireless stations are out of action. Must have been destroyed. Calls from Golubev and Colonel Sandalow say the Germans are bombing everywhere."

The conversation was interrupted by a call from Marshal Timoshenko in Moscow, who wanted to know what was going on. In the next half-hour, more and more news came in, all of it bad. They were bombing Grodno, Lida, Brest, Volkovysk, Slonim, and other towns. Many Russian planes had been destroyed on the ground.

Timoshenko called again, "Comrade Boldin remember that no action is to be taken against the Germans without our knowledge. Please tell Pavlov that Stalin has forbidden to open artillery fire against the Germans."

"But how is that possible?" Boldin yelled into the telephone. "Our troops are in full retreat. Whole towns are burning, people are being killed."

"No artillery," Timoshenko repeated.

"There is to be no air reconnaissance more than thirty-five miles beyond the frontier!"

Boldin tried to argue but Timoshenko shut him up.

Eighteenth Panzer Division and soon reached the bridge at Lesna. There they found no one except a few Russian pickets who took to their heels when they saw the German vehicles. Two of Guderian's orderly officers set off after them, and never came back. It was an abrupt lesson in the dangers of pursuing Russians behind the lines.

At 10:25 AM the leading tank company reached Lesna Bridge and crossed. And General Guderian accompanied the Eighteenth Panzer Division on their advance until midafternoon, when he returned to his command post.

The Germans had taken the Russians by surprise along the entire Panzer Group Front, to the southwest capturing all the bridges, and to the north building bridges.

The average penetration that first day was fifty kilometers.

But the fortress of Brest-Litovsk was a tough nut, which held out for several days, depriving the Germans of the road and rail communications across the Bug and Muchaviec Rivers. By the end of the first week Guderian's troops had reached Bobruisk on the Beresina River. General Hoth's Panzers had captured Minsk. All along the three sectors, the Germans were advancing at top speed.

✳ ✳ ✳

On the day that war broke out, Stalin's eldest son, Lieutenant Yakov Djugashvili, telephoned his father before leaving for the front. Stalin was laconic on the telephone.

"Go and fight," he said.

A month later, Lieutenant Djugashvili was taken prisoner by German Panzer troops. The Russian POWs were lined up and an SS officer barked, "All commissars, communists, and Jews step forward. [Hitler had ordered that all commissars and communists be shot on capture. His policy regarding Jews was well known.] A few men stepped forward. The SS officer stepped up to one man and stuck a pistol in his belly. "Why don't you step out? You're obviously a Jew."

"I'm not," was the response. Then some other men stepped up and shouted, "That's Stalin's son. He's a Georgian, not a Jew."

Lavrenti Beria—Agent Provocateur

Security Chief Beria's history with Stalin went back to their mutual Georgian beginnings. In October 1936, when Stalin's mother died in Tbilisi, Beria was the one who informed him of the fact, and when Stalin and his family came to the funeral the children stayed with Beria in his luxurious apartment. Beria got to know all of them well, and soon realized that Stalin hated his eldest son Yakov and would have nothing to do with him. When the family returned to Moscow, Stalin took with him his daughter Svetlana and second son Vasily and Beria came along as a guest. Yakov was not invited.

When the war began for Russia, Yakov was called up as a reserve officer. In the early fighting he was wounded and captured. Stalin and Beria had adopted a harsh policy against those who were captured willy-nilly. They were treated as traitors and their families were arrested. This policy apparently applied to all, so when Yakov was captured Beria informed Yakov's wife, Yulia. Without trial, he condemned her to three years in prison, despite the fact that she was the sole support of Stalin's four-year-old granddaughter, Gulya. Beria checked before he acted so precipitously and discovered that Stalin hated Yulia so much because she was a Jew. As Beria's biographer Taddeus Wittlin wrote, "The imprisonment of the woman was a secret sweet triumph for Beria, who always experienced a peculiar joy when he could make someone miserable. And this time it was not only Yulia but Stalin's son to whom Lavrenti delivered a blow. If Beria could cut the throat of Josef Stalin, whom he so glorified in his books and speeches, he would do it more eagerly. But it was not yet the right moment. For that chance, the commissar of internal affairs and state security decided to wait."

Yakov's story came out in interrogation by a German Major Walter Holters on July 18, 1941.

"Did you surrender of your own accord or were you taken by force?"

"I was taken by force."

"In what way?"

"On July 12, our unit was surrounded. There was heavy bombing. I tried to reach my men but was stunned by a bomb blast. I would have shot myself if I could."

"Do you believe your troops still have a chance of reversing the war?"

"The war is still far from ended."

Marshal Kulik

General Boldin was sent to buck up the Tenth Army, which had been nearly wiped out in the initial stages of the German attack. General Pavlov had ordered them to attack that night, which was patently impossible, given their casualties and shortage of fuel and ammunition. In this desperate situation, Marshal Kulik suddenly appeared out of thin air from Moscow. Kulik was a Stalinist, and he owed his promotion to high rank to toadyism and the wiping out of most of the officer corps in the purge of 1937. He was hopelessly incompetent, and later army historians blamed him for the failure of the military suppliers to supply the infantry with modern machine guns and other automatic weapons.

"He listened to my explanations," Boldin later wrote, "then made a vague gesture, and mumbled 'Yes, I see. . . .'" It was quite obvious that when leaving Moscow he had no idea the situation was as serious as this. Soon after the marshal left our command post. When saying good-bye he said he would see what he could do.

A few minutes later, General Hatskilevich arrived in a great state of agitation.

"We are firing our last shell. Once we've done that, we shall have to destroy the tanks."

"Yes," I said. "I don't see what else we can do."

Within a few hours, General Hatskilevich died a hero's death on the battlefield.

As for Marshal Kulik, he disappeared from the scene almost immediately after the shooting started and was never heard from again.

"And what if we shortly get hold of Moscow?"

"You will never take Moscow."

"Why are there commissars in the Red Army?"

"To raise the fighting spirit and give political guidance."

"Do you believe the new government in Russia is better suited to the needs of workers and peasants than the Czar's government?"

"I have no doubts about that."

"When did you last speak to your father?"

"I rang him up on June 22. Upon hearing that I was leaving for the front he said to me 'Go and fight.'"

Yakov rejected a suggestion that he write to his family and also refused to send a message. The Germans took a picture of him in conversation with two German officers, which they used as propaganda. They forged a letter that read, "Dear Father. I am in a prison camp. I am well. I will soon be transferred to an officers' camp in Germany. I'm treated well. Wishing you good health."

✳ ✳ ✳

A second interrogation was conducted by intelligence officer Wilfred Strick. He said that all attempts to win Yakov over to the Germans had failed.

Strick described Yakov in the following way, "He has a fine intelligent face, with sharp Georgian features. He is self-possessed and carries himself well. He flatly rejected any compromise between capitalism and socialism. He refused to believe in Germany's final victory."

The Germans took Yakov to Berlin and handed him over to Dr. Goebbels' propagandists. But they found that attempts to turn him were useless and in December 1941 he was sent to an ordinary POW camp.

POW Alexander Uzinsky recalled seeing Yakov, "He had lost weight, his face was black, and a heavy dismal look came from his sunken eyes. He was wearing a much-worn greatcoat and a torn army shirt."

As a prisoner, Yakov's position was unique. His father was on record with Order No. 270. "Those who surrender to the enemy shall be considered traitors who have violated the oath of duty and betrayed the Motherland." Yakov took this very seriously. He believed that he could never go home again even if the Germans released him.

Uzinsky recalled that one of the guards came up with a bucket of red paint and began painting the letters SU on Yakov's chest.

Yakov said, "Let him paint. The Soviet Union is my Motherland."

The other POWs were startled.

Such words were punishable by death.

Yakov Stalin did not seem to care.

—ᴟ—

6

Moscow

O N THE EVENING OF JUNE 22, 1941, GENERAL KIRPONOS, commander of the Kiev District, reported several cases of German deserters coming over. They reported that the German attack would begin that night. Kirponos telephoned Marshal Timoshenko, who called Stalin. There was a pause, and then Stalin ordered Timoshenko to come to the Kremlin with General Zhukov and Major General Vatutin. When they arrived, the entire Politburo was assembled. Stalin was pacing up and down. On seeing them he turned.

"Well, what now?" he said.

Silence.

"We must immediately order all troops of the frontier districts on to full battle alert," said Marshal Timoshenko.

"Here, read this," said Stalin, thrusting a paper into the marshal's hands.

It was the draft of a general order that stressed the need for decisive action.

Stalin broke in, "It would be premature to issue that order now. It might still be possible to settle the situation by peaceful means. We should issue a brief order saying that an attack might begin if provoked by German action. The border units must not allow themselves to be provoked into anything that might cause difficulties."

As the military men were leaving to issue their orders, Stalin muttered, "I think Hitler is trying to provoke us. He surely hasn't decided to make war?"

✳ ✳ ✳

The Politburo dispersed at 3:00 AM. It was the shortest night of the year. Stalin gazed through the windows of his limousine at the empty streets of Moscow, unaware that German planes were already on their way to attack Soviet towns and air-dromes. He reached his dacha and went to bed. He had scarcely lain down when there was a knock on his door.

> ### The Near Surrender
>
> The fact was that Stalin had come near to surrendering to Hitler. How near did not become clear until after the war. As early as 1941 Stalin, Beria, and Molotov had discussed the advisability of trying to placate by handing over to Hitler the Soviet Baltic republics, Moldavia, a large part of the Ukraine, and Belorussia. They tried then to make contact with Hitler through the Bulgarian ambassador. When they approached him, he brushed them off. Hitler would never beat the Russians, he said, and Stalin should stop worrying about it. He declined to act as mediator. "Even if you retreat to the Urals," he said, "you'll still win in the end."

"General Zhukov is asking to speak to you on the phone on a matter that can't wait."

Stalin picked up the phone and listened.

Zhukov outlined the enemy attacks on Kiev, Minsk, Sevastopol, Vilna, and other places.

Silence.

"Do you understand what I said, Comrade Stalin?"

Silence.

Again Zhukov said, "Comrade Stalin, do you understand?"

Stalin said he understood. It was 4:00 AM on the morning of June 22.

"Come to the Kremlin with Timoshenko," Stalin said. "Tell Poskrebyshev (his secretary) to summon all the members of the Politburo." He returned to the Kremlin.

As he went up to his office by the entrance reserved for him alone he snapped at Poskrebyshev, "Get the others here, now!"

Silently, the members of the Politburo filed in, followed by Timoshenko and Zhukov.

"Get the German consul on the phone."

Molotov left the room. The others sat around the table in tense silence: Andreyev, Voroshilov, Kaganovich, Mikoyan, Kalinin, Shvernik, Beria, Malenkov, Voznesensky, and Scherbakov.

Molotov returned, all eyes on him. "The ambassador reported that the German government has declared war on us," he stammered. "The formal reason is the standard one: Nationalist Germany has decided to forestall an attack by the Russians."

The silence was severe. Stalin sat down and looked at Molotov angrily, recalling in his mind the foreign commissar's confident prediction six months earlier that Hitler would never wage war on two fronts. The USSR had plenty of time to strengthen its defenses, Molotov had indicated, "Plenty of time."

The blame was Molotov's, of course. It could not be Stalin's. Never.

✳ ✳ ✳

Timoshenko finally broke the silence, "Comrade Stalin, may I get a report of the military situation?"

"Yes."

The First Deputy Chief of Staff, Vatutin, entered the room. His report contained little new information. After air attacks in the northwest and western sectors, large German forces had invaded Soviet territory. The border units had sustained serious losses but had not deserted their posts. The General Staff had no further news.

Stalin had just suffered the greatest shock of his life. He was angry with everyone, for he laid the blame with a trowel for the surprise, quite forgetting the many attempts to warn him, which he had ignored as "provocation."

The Politburo remained in session all day, awaiting news from the war fronts. One by one, members went to the bathroom, stretched their legs, made phone calls, and returned.

On the morning of June 22, the members of the Politburo realized that they must tell the Russian people something about the war. All eyes turned to Stalin.

He refused.

Traditional wisdom has it that Stalin was depressed because he had not believed Hitler would attack.

Biographer Volkogonov said that early on the morning of June 22 it was agreed that Molotov would address the people. Stalin demanded that the military "destroy the enemy with crushing blows," showing how far out of reality he had drifted. All that first day he waited for good news, lifting his head expectantly every time someone entered the room. He was so nervous he drank only one cup of tea all day. The disaster was complete but he did not seem to sense it, and he bullied the others, demanding action. He could not concentrate, suddenly breaking off a discussion with Molotov, Zhdanov, and Malenkov of a proposal from Timoshenko to create a headquarters chief of command. He began barking orders, sending his associates to the fronts. That very day Shaposhnikov and Kulik were sent to join Pavlov on the Western Front "immediately."

For the next few days Stalin functioned irregularly, issuing orders that demanded immediate attack with forces that did not exist. On June 23, he ordered establishment of a new superdefense committee, an order that went out to the military districts but died a sudden death without ever functioning. On the sixth day he lost control completely. On June 29, when leaving the defense commissariat with Molotov, Voroshilov, Zhdanov, and Beria, he burst out, "Lenin left us a great inheritance, and we, his heirs, have fucked it all up."

There was no good news. At the end of the first week, the German tanks were approaching Minsk. The Western Front had virtually collapsed. The other fronts were in chaos. Orders were sent for troops to attack, after retreating for 300 kilometers under orders that often could not be obeyed because of lack of fuel or ammunition. If a commander lacked the resources to carry out an order, his superior was likely to threaten him with execution. In the first two days the Soviet air force front line was virtually destroyed and the Germans had complete mastery of the air.

Vatutin showed Stalin the map that told the story: the Eighth and Eleventh Armies were retreating in divergent directions and the gap between them had reached 130 kilometers. The main forces of the Western Front were either destroyed or encircled.

Why hadn't Stalin listened to his generals when they asked him to build up the Western Front? In the Western European campaigns, Hitler had headed straight for the national capital in order to force the most rapid capitulation of the country. Why hadn't Stalin's advisors pointed this out?

The answer was that they had, but Stalin, the absolute master, refused to listen to advice.

Stalin's state of mind was so negative and confused that he was powerless to act sensibly. He divided his time between the Kremlin and his dacha. On the night of the twenty-eighth he went to his dacha and lay down on his usual couch without undressing. He could not sleep so he got up and wandered around in the darkened rooms, pausing in the dining room before Lenin's picture, which was lighted as always. He waited for telephone calls to bring more terrible news, but they did not come.

Molotov, Voznesensky, and General Volkogonov decided to go and see him at the dacha. Molotov would lead the way; the others would follow.

When they got to the dacha they found Stalin in an armchair in the small dining room. He looked up and said, "What have you come for?"

The Kulik Mystery

The mystery of Marshal Kulik's sudden appearance on the Western Front was solved on that second day. He had been sent by Stalin's personal order. On the first day, after issuing the famous Order No. 2, Stalin and his associates had staggered around in shock, with Stalin obviously the most affected victim. One half-baked plan followed another, with Stalin growing angrier with his associates every moment. It was as if he blamed them for the success of the Germans in breaking through the Soviet lines. That conjecture was not far from the fact. The truth was that the Russians had planned to attack the Germans, and the creation of the military districts along the Western Front had been preliminary buildup to such an attack. But Russian readiness was still months away, and they had believed the Germans would stand still and allow themselves to be sucked into a vortex and destroyed. The sudden realization that the plan had been undone was a major cause of Stalin's shock. When he began barking orders and sending marshals this way and that he was truly out of his mind. Kulik had fumbled his words in conversation with General Boldin because he did not really know why he was there on the front except that Stalin had sent him.

"Comrade Josef Vissiaronovich, power has to be concentrated in order to ensure rapid decision making and get the country back on its feet," Molotov said.

Stalin looked surprised and said nothing but, "Fine."

Headquarters staff now began to establish a new line of defense to replace the Western Front. Stalin turned up twice on June 29 at the defense commissariat and subjected everyone there to abuse. His face was gray and he had huge bags under his eyes. At last he had recognized the danger that hung like a shroud over the country. If something were not done swiftly the Germans would be in Moscow. His first step to regain control of the situation and himself was to begin sacking military leaders.

Marshal Timoshenko had already begun that process.

On June 22, General A. I. Yeremenko received a call from the chief of staff of the Far Eastern Army Group telling him of the German attack on the Western Front. Yeremenko was ordered to Moscow to report to Timoshenko. He set out that day by train, but was stopped at Novossibirsk and ordered to fly to Moscow. He arrived on June 28 and went directly from the airfield to the People's Commissariat of Defense. Timoshenko said, "We have been waiting for you," and immediately got down to business. He showed Yeremenko on the map the territory that had been lost. Yeremenko was astounded.

"The reason," Timoshenko said, "is that our commanders in the border districts were not up to the mark." Particularly he criticized General Pavlov, commander of the Western Army Group.

"Well, Comrade Yeremenko," he said, "now the picture is clear to you."

"Yes. It's a sad picture."

"General Pavlov and his chief of staff have been relieved of command. By decision of the government you are appointed commander of the Western Army Group and Lt. Gen. G. K. Malandin has been named chief of staff. Both of you are to depart for the front immediately."

"What is the army group's mission?"

"To stop the enemy advance," Timoshenko said, and he handed Eremenko his orders to take command. Yeremenko and Malandin left immediately for the Western Army Group Headquarters, which had been moved from Minsk to a point in the forest near Mogilev.

They arrived at the command post early in the morning and found that General Pavlov was having breakfast in a small tent. Malandin went off in search of the chief of staff. Yeremenko entered the tent to be greeted noisily by Pavlov.

"How long it has been since we met? What fate brings you here? Are you staying long?"

Rather than reply, Yeremenko handed Pavlov the copy of his orders to take command. Pavlov read the document and then asked, "And just where am I going?"

"The People's Commissar has ordered you to Moscow."

"Sit down. Have you eaten? Do you want breakfast?"
Yeremenko declined to eat.

"We have to analyze the Army Group's situation as soon as possible. We must discover the state of our troops and the enemy's intentions."

Pavlov started to talk, "The stupefying strikes of the enemy caught our troops unaware. We were not prepared for battle. We were living peacefully, training. Therefore we sustained heavy losses in aircraft, artillery, tanks, and personnel. The enemy has penetrated our territory. Bobruisk and Minsk have fallen."

Pavlov also referred to the tardy receipt of the order to put the troops on combat alert. The delay was due to the fact that Stalin, as head of the government, put his trust in the pact with Germany. He did not pay attention to the reports that the Germans were preparing to attack and considered those reports to be provocations. He did not execute urgent defense measures, fearing that this would give the Germans a pretext for attacking. As head of the government, Stalin bore the principal responsibility for the Russian defeats.

Pavlov laid this out, and Yeremenko knew it was true. But also Marshal Timoshenko had to carry part of the burden for there were actions he could have taken that would have made the response of the armies much quicker.

At the end of the talk with Pavlov, he and Yeremenko decided to call together the leadership of the Army Group, but before the officers arrived, Yeremenko called on Marshal Voroshilov and Marshal Shaposhnikov, who had arrived from Moscow to survey the situation.

They blamed Pavlov. "Things are very bad," Voroshilov said. "Pavlov's command is very poor. Reserves and second echelons must be brought up immediately, in order to close up the gaps and halt the enemy advance."

Shaposhnikov was equally critical of Pavlov.

After this talk, Yeremenko had a talk with the secretary of the Communist Party of Belorussia, who joined in the criticism of Pavlov. It was obvious that Pavlov had been chosen to be the major scapegoat of the early days of the war.

The First Fall Guys

B Y JUNE 30, STALIN HAD RECOVERED HIS APLOMB
enough to function again. On that day the State Defense
Committee was created, with Stalin as its head. His first step was to get
rid of General Pavlov as commander of the Western Front. General
Yeremenko was appointed to his place, and Pavlov and his senior
commanders were all arrested.

That same day, General Kuznetsov, commander of the Northwest
Frontier, ordered retreat from the Dvina River and the fortified districts of Ostrov, Pskov, and Sebezh. He was immediately dismissed
and replaced by Major General Sobennikov, but he escaped Pavlov's
fate. Pavlov was so naive as to believe he would be reassigned,
but when he reached Moscow he was put on trial with General
Klimovskikh, General Grigoryev, and General Korobkov, convicted
of treason, stripped of his rank, and shot.

This exhibition of terror frightened everyone involved. Colonel
Starinov came to headquarters seeking someone to whom he could report
on his efforts to lay mines. He was shunted here and there, finally received
by General Malandin, but sent off to another commander for action.

Accompanied by the two NKVD officers who had been escorting him ever since he reached the front, Starinov sought audience with this commander, who was at the moment talking to a major.

"May I enter?" Starinov asked.

Seeing the green hats of the NKVD officers, the commander and the major froze. The major snapped to attention. The commander gulped, turned pale, and began to babble, "I was with the troops, I did everything—I am not guilty."

Starinov looked with pity on the man. He understood the reaction all too well.

* * *

Stalin then began issuing orders to try to stop the Germans. He threw whole armies into the field without regard to their equipment or readiness, only to see them ground up like hamburger by the Wehrmacht. On July 3, Stalin addressed the nation by radio. He began by exculpating himself from all blame, called on the people to wage a patriotic war, and lied about German victories and strengths. From now until the battle of Stalingrad, Stalin was to cut a wide swathe, sacrificing one army after another to gain time.

On July 10, the Staff Headquarters was transformed into Headquarters High Command (later called Headquarters of the Supreme High Command). Stalin was in charge from that day until the end of the war, and he meddled shamelessly with his military commanders. His orders were often erratic, superficial, and incompetent, turning victory into defeat.

The Germans captured Smolensk on July 16 but the Soviet Front remained intact. Army Group Center needed reinforcements to continue the drive on Moscow. If the drive continued without reinforcement, Army Group Center would be vulnerable to attack from the Russian Central Front.

On July 17, General Rokossovsky was ordered to the Western Front to take command of miscellaneous troops who had escaped the German encirclement and several reserve divisions that eventually

---

General Boldin Observes

After the German attack began and General Boldin had been summoned by General Pavlov to Western District Headquarters, with Marshal Timoshenko's permission, General Boldin flew to Belostok. There he found chaos. And it was not until evening that he reached the headquarters of the Tenth Army, which had moved to the little wood outside the city. There he met with General Nikitin, commander of the Sixth Cavalry Corps, whose unit had been almost entirely wiped out.

General Pavlov gave Boldin preemptory orders to mount an attack with the Tenth Army, which had been virtually wiped out. Boldin could see that the orders were being given for effect, in fact to cover Pavlov's behind—orders issued for the record to show Moscow that something was being done.

The ploy did not work. Pavlov was the first to go.

The German advance continued without a hitch, trapping large Russian forces in the Belostok pocket, and eleven divisions in the Minsk area. Soon the Germans reached Minsk and pushed deep into the Baltic Republics and were approaching Pskov, on a line straight in for Leningrad.

---

became the Seventh Mechanized Corps. Rokossovsky had no great opinion of Pavlov, whom he regarded as unfit for his position.

As head of the Western Front, Rokossovsky had fallen victim to the Stalin purge of the army and had served three years in prison, accused as a Polish spy. He had been released in 1940, on the assurances of Timoshenko to Zhukov that he was loyal and given the rank of major general and command of the Fifth Cavalry Corps. He rose to command of the Ninth Mechanized Corps, which he was leading in the Southwest Front when the war began.

On July 29, Chief of Staff Zhukov briefed Stalin on the situation, telling him that the Germans would use part of their strength to defeat the Central Front and the Southwest Front, thereby securing their right flank before continuing to Moscow. To counter his move,

Zhukov recommended that the Southwestern Front move all its forces to the left bank of the Dnieper and prepare for a blow from the north. He also recommended reinforcing the Central Front, even at the expense of withdrawing some of the troops before Moscow.

When Stalin asked about Kiev, which is on the right bank of the Dnieper, Zhukov said it was indefensible and should be abandoned. He also recommended that the El'nia salient be eliminated by a counterstrike.

"You are talking nonsense," Stalin said. "Soviet troops do not know how to attack. And who could come up with the idea that Kiev should be abandoned?"

Zhukov lost his temper, "If you think that I talk nonsense you should send me to the front and get another chief of staff."

That afternoon Zhukov was placed in command of the Reserve Front. Shaposhnikov replaced him as chief of staff. Zhukov had lasted as chief of staff for just six months. Before they parted company, Stalin again asked Zhukov's advice about the future plans of the enemy. Once more Zhukov said that the Germans were planning to envelop Kiev. Stalin said he would discuss the matter with Shaposhnikov but when Shaposhnikov offered the same advice that Zhukov had given, Stalin ignored it.

Stalin continued to work in his masterly way, and brought about the loss of Kiev under tragic circumstances. The city was surrounded by General Guderian's tanks on September 15. The staff of the Southwestern Front tried to escape through the ring, and General Kirponos was killed. Altogether more than 600,000 troops were lost in the debacle. It could easily have been avoided had Stalin listened to advice.

Rokossovsky became commander of the Sixteenth Army and in September was promoted to Lieutenant General. Meanwhile, Zhukov went to the Reserve Front and August 30 found him directing the attack of the Soviet Twenty-Fourth Army against the Germans at El'nia. After the battle began, Zhukov had a telephone call from Stalin's Secretary Poskrebyshev, asking him to come to Moscow to see Stalin.

Zhukov begged off. His presence with the troops was necessary, he said.

On September 6, the battle was won and the next day Zhukov appeared at Stalin's office. The conversation was about Leningrad.

"When will the Germans resume their effort against Moscow?" Stalin asked.

General Fedyuninsky Reacts

General Fedyuninsky was commander of the Fifteenth Infantry Corps of the special Kiev Military District. On June 18, he questioned a German deserter and was convinced that the Nazis were soon going to attack. He telephoned the local army commander, General Potapov, but was told that this was merely a provocation. He went on the alert anyhow and when the attack came on June 22, Fedyuninsky's troops withstood the first German rush, but by the end of the day they were in retreat. Two of his regiments were surrounded by the Germans but broke out after eight days of heavy fighting. Fedyuninsky listened to Stalin's July 3 broadcast.

"It is hard to describe the enormous enthusiasm and patriotic uplift with which this appeal was met. We suddenly seemed to feel much stronger. When circumstances permitted, short meetings would be held by the army units. Political instructors would explain the position at the front, and tell them how in response to the party's appeal, the whole Soviet people were rising like one man to fight the holy Fatherland War. They stressed that the war would be very hard and that many ordeals, privations, and sacrifices were yet ahead, but that the Nazis would never defeat our powerful and hardworking people."

The retreat continued; by July 8 Fedyuninsky's troops had withdrawn to the Korosten fortified line in the Ukraine, already well inside the old borders of the Soviet Union. On August 12, after a further retreat towards Kiev, Fedyuninsky was summoned to Moscow. There, Stalin ordered him to fly to Leningrad where the situation was becoming desperate.

"Not until they have captured Leningrad," Zhukov replied.

"How was the behavior of the Twenty-Fourth Army?" Stalin asked.

"Unexceptionable."

Without another word Stalin handed Zhukov a handwritten letter to Marshal Voroshilov, instructing him to turn over command of the Leningrad Front and the Baltic Fleet to Zhukov and return to Moscow.

That was as close to apology as Stalin ever came

(What had brought about this change of heart?)

Stalin knew that he had made a blunder at Kiev when a member of the State Defense Committee had returned from the Leningrad Front to report that Voroshilov was totally incapable of managing troops there. Seeing a vision of another blunder, Stalin had turned to a man he had begun finally to trust.

✳ ✳ ✳

From the maps prepared by the General Staff, Stalin could see clearly the three directions in which Hitler was thrusting: the northwest, toward Leningrad; west toward Moscow; and southwest toward Kiev. He created three commands: the northwest command under Marshal Voroshilov, the western command under Marshal Timoshenko, and southwestern command under Marshal Budenny. But having taken so wise a step he kept interfering and made it impossible for the commands to function independently and efficiently.

He spent much of his time on petty detail, because it was his habit, refined over the years, to decide and do everything himself. Besides military affairs, he spent several hours a day on economic matters. He took the war to mean confirmation of his absolute dictatorship. One of the first results of this was to be seen in the picture given him of comparative losses of the German and Soviet commands in the first two weeks of the war.

Aircraft loss:	enemy	1,664
	Soviet	889
Tanks lost:	enemy	2,625
	Soviet	901
Enemy casualties, killed		1,312,000
Prisoners		30,004
Soviet missing and prisoners		15,000

Actually, Soviet losses were colossal. Thirty divisions had been wiped out and seventy had lost more than half their men. Nearly 3,500 Soviet aircraft had been lost, and more than half the fuel and ammunition dumps. The Germans had lost 150,000 men, 950 aircraft, and several hundred tanks. But the doctoring of the figures made it impossible for Stalin or anyone else to know the truth. The statistics had been distorted by people accustomed by the Stalin cult to lie to him. So Stalin lived in a dream world, believing all these lies. And his concept of warfare was nineteenth century.

"Our army somewhat underestimates the importance of cavalry. In the present situation at the front, when the enemy's rear is extended over several hundred kilometers in wooded terrain and is totally unable to protect itself against major diversionary action by us, raids by Red Cavalry units could play a decisive part in disorganizing the administration and supply of enemy forces."

In these first few weeks Stalin went his bumbling way, sacrificing millions of men and officers to his ignorance and willfulness. General Pavlov and his subordinates, were all loyal men but they were killed to supply goats for Stalin's stupidity. The story of two other officers is also revealing: General V. Ya. Kachalov and General P. G. Ponedelin.

General Kachalov was commander of the Twenty-Eighth Army. General Ponedelin was commander of the Twelfth Army. The NKVD

Stalin Speaks

On July 3, Stalin at last recovered enough to address the Russian people: "Comrades, citizens, brothers, and sisters, fighters of our army and navy! I am speaking to you, my friends!"

This was something new to the Russian people; he had never spoken to the people so intimately before. He began by saying the Nazi invasion continued "although the best German divisions and air force units had already been smashed." He did, however, admit that the Germans had captured Lithuania, a large part of Latvia, western Belorussia, and part of the western Ukraine. German planes had bombed several important cities. "A serious threat hangs over our country," he said. The reason for the German success was that the war had begun under conditions favorable to the Nazis and unfavorable to the Red Army. He then justified the Nazi–Soviet Pact. It had given the Soviet Union time to prepare against German aggression.

"This war has been inflicted on us, and our country has entered into a life-and-death struggle against its wicked and perfidious enemy, German fascism. Our troops are fighting heroically against heavy odds, against an enemy heavily armed with thousands of tanks and aircraft. The main forces of the Red Army, armed with thousands of tanks and planes, are now entering the battle. Together with the Red Army the whole of our people are rising to defend their country.

"The enemy is cruel and merciless. He aims at grabbing our land, our wheat, and oil. He wants to restore the power of the landowners, reestablish Tsarism, and destroy the national culture of the peoples of the Soviet Union and turn them into the slaves of German princes and barons.

"There should be no room in our ranks for whimperers and cowards, for deserters and panic mongers. Our people should be fearless in their struggle and should selflessly fight our patriotic war of liberation against the Fascist enslavers."

"We must immediately put our whole production on a war footing, and place everything at the service of the front and the organization of the enemy's rout."

Then came the famous scorched earth instructions, "Whenever units of the Red Army are forced to retreat, all railway rolling stock must be driven away. The enemy must not be left a single engine, or a single railway truck, and not a pound of bread nor a pint of oil. The *kolkhozniki* must drive away all their livestock, hand in their grain reserves to the state organizations for evacuation to the rear, and valuable property, whether grain, fuel, or nonferrous metals, which cannot be evacuated, must be destroyed."

Then followed instructions about partisan warfare. Stalin had outlawed partisan activity a few years earlier, afraid that it would threaten his power, but now there was a greater threat.

"In the occupied areas partisan units must be formed. There must be diversionist groups for fighting enemy units, for spreading the partisan warfare everywhere, for blowing up and destroying roads, and bridges, and telephone and telegraph wires, for setting fire to forests, enemy stores, and road convoys. In the occupied areas intolerable conditions must be created for the enemy, and his accomplices, who must be persecuted and destroyed at every step."

He spoke of the alliance of the Western powers that was already bringing help to the Soviet Union. Then he concluded, "Comrades, our forces are immeasurably large. The insolent enemy must soon become aware of this. Together with the Red Army, many thousands of workers, *kolkhozniki* and *intellectuals,* are going to war. Millions more will rise. The workers of Moscow and Leningrad have already begun to form a home guard of many thousands in support of the Red Army. Such *opolcheniye* forces must be constituted in every town threatened with invasion."

Stalin's speech was very effective. It raised the morale of the nervous and frightened people. As historian Alexander Werth put it, "Now they felt they had a leader to look to."

had reports that these two officers had surrendered voluntarily and were working for the Germans. They were tried in absentia and ordered to be shot.

Kachalov had been killed in battle on August 4. Ponedelin's army had been encircled, and he was taken prisoner while unconscious. He spent four years in Hitler's prison camps and never weakened. When he was repatriated in 1945 he was arrested and sentenced to five years in Soviet camps. He made a personal appeal to Stalin and on August 25, 1950, he was again sentenced to death. This time the sentence was carried out.

Such perversity on the part of the leader could have lost the Russians the war and nearly did. Only the loyalty and the devotion of the common people saved the day, for from the very first, the Germans learned that in the Soviet people they faced something new. In Western Europe, when the armies were defeated the society collapsed. But in Russia from the first day, the people fought back, tooth and nail. Partisan units sprouted like cabbages, although Stalin had earlier outlawed partisan activity. The partisans represented a second front, and soon they would be accorded official recognition by the Soviet regime.

✳ ✳ ✳

Even Stalin began to learn about war. At the beginning of August, Marshal Shaposhnikov was summoned to Stalin's dacha at midnight to give Stalin an account of the situation on all fronts. What Stalin got was a lecture in failure, as bitter was wormwood in the dictator's mouth.

First Shaposhnikov spread a map out on the desk before Stalin.

"We can say that we have utterly lost the first phase of the war," the Marshal began.

"Battles are already taking place on the distant approaches to Leningrad, the Smolensk district, and the defensive area central to Kiev. Our resistance is still not strong. We have to deploy the troops along the front, more or less without knowing where the enemy might strike with concentrated force tomorrow. The enemy has all the strategic initiative. The problem is exacerbated by the absence of second line troops and powerful reserves in many sectors. In the air the enemy has complete supremacy. Though he has lost many aircraft. Of the 212 divisions of the active army, only ninety have 80 percent or more of their full complement.

"The defense of approaches to Leningrad acquiring some elasticity and the dynamism of the German advance may come to nothing. It looks as though we should move the Baltic Fleet to Kronstadt. Heavy losses are inevitable."

"The engagement at Smolensk enabled us to stop the enemy on the most dangerous (i.e., western) thrust. According to our calculations about sixty German divisions took part, amounting to something like half a million men. As you know, Comrade Stalin, in order to consolidate the front the Nineteenth, Twentieth, Twenty-First, and Twenty-Second Armies were moved there as early as the beginning of July."

The attempt to make counterattack was only partly successful, Shaposhnikov continued. It enabled the Sixteenth and Twentieth armies to escape encirclement. But now there was a single line front, consisting of twenty-four incomplete divisions, and this was cause for concern.

From this, Stalin concluded that the Red Army was capable of stopping the enemy, even where he concentrated his forces. It would be a long war, Stalin decided. It would also be a vengeful war to the death, with no quarter given by either side. From the beginning, Hitler promised terror: all communist officials were to be executed on capture. On the first day of the war, a column of General von Manstein's troops came across a German patrol that had been captured by the Russians. Every man was dead, and each of them had been tortured before he died.

Following is the story of the defense of Kiev.

The first order of business would be the Dnieper and Kiev. That very day Stalin and Shaposhnikov called Kirponos and Khrushchev and demanded that they hold the line, even using cavalry as infantry. Khrushchev and Kirponos replied that they were doing their best to stop the Germans from crossing the river and taking Kiev and asked for reinforcements. Some of their divisions, they said, had been reduced to a couple of thousand men.

The defense of Kiev failed. By early August German Army Group Center and German Army Group South had wrapped their lines halfway around the Russian forces at Kiev and along the Dnieper, creating a trap for almost all the Southwest Front. Chief of Staff Zhukov suggested that Kiev be abandoned and an angry Stalin removed him from his job. Zhukov was appointed to command the Reserve Front a hundred miles east of Smolensk in the Rzhev-Vyazma area. He had six armies under his control and early in August he went into action near Yelnya. The battle lasted twenty-six days and stopped the German drive on the Central Front. Stalin ordered the front onto the defense, summoned Zhukov to the Kremlin, and sent him to Leningrad to pick up the pieces of the military disaster that was looming under the command of Marshal Voroshilov.

On August 4, Stalin ordered the Southwest and South Fronts to hold.

The Sixth and Twelfth Armies were encircled, but fought on until August 7, when they were overrun. Budenny asked permission to move the troops across the Ingul River. Stalin furiously refused. He ordered transfer of nineteen and five cavalry divisions, but these were half-trained troops and they were badly armed. In the fighting, many of them panicked and ran. Whenever Stalin heard of a position being abandoned, he either flew into a rage or he sank into apathy. He jumped to conclusions and he made snap judgments, many of them erroneous. His actions only made a bad situation worse. Here is one of his orders:

> Anyone who removes his insignia during battle and surrenders should be regarded as a malicious deserter, whose family is to be

arrested as the family of a breaker of the oath and betrayer of the Motherland. Such deserters are to be shot on the spot.

Those falling into encirclement are to fight to the last, and try to reach their own lines. And those who prefer to surrender are to be destroyed by any available means, while the families are to be deprived of all state allowances and assistance.

Bold and brave people are to be promoted more actively.

This order is to be read to all companies, squadrons, batteries.

—Stalin

✳ ✳ ✳

Meanwhile tragedy was approaching. On September 15, the Germans closed the circle in the district of Lokhvitsa, surrounding the main force of the Southwestern Front, trapping the Fifth, Twenty-Sixth, Thirty-Seventh, and part of the Twenty-First and Twenty-Eighth Armies.

Stalin and Kirponos then had another conversation. It ended up with Stalin ordering the reorganization of the Kiev defenses with a ridge on the River Pysol. "Kiev must not be abandoned or its bridges blown up without permission of Staff HQ. That is all. Goodbye."

"Kirponos. Your orders are clear. That is all. Goodbye."

It was Kirponos' last goodbye.

✳ ✳ ✳

Stalin expected to be given precise information, yet when his commanders gave him unpleasant facts his reaction was often to accuse them of alarmism. At Kiev, Tupikov reported that the catastrophe was imminent—only the matter of a couple of days. Stalin cabled back that Tupikov's message showed "panic." Stalin's commanders then became cautious about telling Stalin the truth if it was unpleasant. On September 15, General Zhukov upbraided General Rakutin for making false reports about the successes of his Twenty-Fourth Army. Rakutin said he would investigate. Zhukov said, "The main thing is to stop the lying that is coming out of your headquarters."

Rakutin had been let down by subordinates, who had reported nonexistent successes. This often happened because of the fear of Stalin's wrath. Rakutin tried to straighten out this matter, but before he could do so was killed in battle.

On September 17 at 5:00 AM, the War Council again requested permission to break out of the trap, but Stalin refused, allowing only the withdrawal of the Thirty-Seventh Army to the east bank of the Dnieper. By nightfall the situation had become critical and the War Council decided to extract the armies. But too much time had been lost and contact had been lost between front headquarters and the armies. Individual units fought fiercely for the next ten days but the result was disaster: 452,720 men encircled, including 60,000 officers. Kirponos, his chief of staff, Tupikov, and War Council member Burmistenko all died in the fighting. Stalin was mainly responsible. The defeat at Kiev tipped the balance in the enemy's favor all along the war front.

At Kiev alone more than 600,000 men had gone missing.

Stalin said nothing, except to tell Shaposhnikov to "plug the hole." He agreed with Shaposhnikov's suggestion that Timoshenko be appointed to take over the southwest defense and that Khrushchev should be appointed to the Supreme War Council. Little by little, the dictator was beginning to learn how war should be conducted.

CHAPTER

8

The German Advance

A T THE END OF THE FIRST WEEK OF WAR, GENERAL
Guderian's panzers had reached Minsk, 200 miles east of the
Bug River, and linked up with General Hoth's Third Panzer Group.

A quarrel among the generals ensued. The Panzer men wanted to
move fast against the center and capture Moscow. But the infantry
generals of the broad front school wanted to move more slowly,
cleaning up as they went and not letting the tanks outrun the infantry
by too far. Hitler came down on the side of the broad front generals.

On July 7, 1941, Guderian's troops reached the Dnieper River.
He decided to disobey orders and cross. On July 10 and 11, he
crossed, losing only eight men. By July 29, he was only 300 miles
from Moscow.

But on August 4, Hitler assembled all his generals and told them
that Leningrad was the primary objective, then the Ukraine, and
finally Moscow.

General Halder summed up the feeling of the generals in his
diary, "Thus the aim of defeating decisively the Russian armies in
front of Moscow was subordinated to the desire to obtain a valuable

industrial area, and to advance in the direction of Russian oil. Hitler now became obsessed with the idea of capturing Leningrad and Stalingrad, for he persuaded himself that if these two 'holy cities of Communism' fell, Russia would collapse."

By September the Germans were claiming victory. The armies of Marshal Timoshenko were surrounded in front of Moscow. The armies of Marshal Budenny in the south were virtually destroyed. The army of Marshal Voroshilov in the north at Leningrad was also surrounded. General Halder knew that Guderian had influence with Hitler and so he sent him to persuade Der Fuehrer to put Moscow first. Guderian failed. Hitler then made his fatal error that caused his ultimate defeat. He moved forces from the Central Army Group to the south to help von Rundstedt. Guderian's Panzer Group was one of them. In the fall of Kiev in September, the Germans captured 665,000 prisoners. Hitler called it the greatest victory in history. But while that battle was being fought, the Central Army Group was stalled on the Desna River because its armor was in the south. Finally, in late September, Hitler was persuaded to move against Moscow.

"Move in ten days," Hitler said.

It was impossible. First the armor had to be brought back from the south. It was not until October 2 that Operation Typhoon was actually launched. Hitler announced the "final" drive on Moscow in a speech in Berlin. Then the drive on Moscow began. It took the people of Moscow several days to realize what was happening. All attention had focused on the big German offensive in the Ukraine, their breakthrough in the Crimea, and the visit of Lord Beaverbrook of London, which began on September 29.

The Germans struck on the Bryansk Front against armies commanded by General Yeremenko. The front widened to include the Western Front, and the Reserve Front, now commanded by Marshal Budenny. The Germans made a breakthrough in the Orel sector. German armor headed for Tula, sixty-five miles south of Moscow. On the night of October 4–5, Moscow lost contact with the Western Front, at 9:00 AM on the morning of October 5, word was received that the Germans had broken through just south of Yelnya and were moving east on the Warsaw highway toward Moscow. Stalin dismissed this first report as "panic," but at noon a reconnaissance flier reported seeing a fifteen-mile-long German armored column only a hundred miles south of Moscow. The report was questioned and two more planes were sent out. The report was verified and Stalin was notified.

There were no Russian troops in the path of the Panzers. He ordered a scratch force set up to defend the capital. The move was delayed by Secret Police Chief Beria, who did not believe the reports and had threatened to court martial the air reconnaissance men. It was eight hours before any Russian troops moved, and the next day before an air strike was launched against the column.

On October 5, as the German drive on Moscow began, General Rokossovsky was ordered to transfer to the neighboring Twentieth Army and to take his staff to Vyazma where five rifle divisions were concentrating. They were to lead a counterattack in the direction of Iukhnov. Puzzled by this unusual order, Rokossovsky demanded a retransmission with the personal signature of the front commander. He received the order signed by Koniev and Marshal Bulganin. Liaison officers from the Twentieth Army arrived and the Sixteenth Army staff began moving toward Vyazma. En route they encountered

Odessa

Odessa was one of the four "hero cities," along with Moscow, Leningrad, and Stalingrad. Between August 5 and October 16, 1941, it was defended against one German and eighteen Rumanian divisions. The Black Sea Navy and the Marines played crucial roles in the defense. Losses reaching 40 percent overall and with the marines as much as 80 percent.

When Odessa finally fell, 80,000 soldiers and much of the defense equipment were successfully transported to Sevastopol and the Caucasus.

Still, important as Odessa was, the battle for the city was a sideshow on the major actions.

vehicles and personnel from units that had been scattered in an attack of German parachutists and many civilian refugees. The evidence suggested that a large enemy armored column had penetrated deeply north of the Iartsevo-Vyazma highway. The Sixteenth Army staff did not encounter any sign of the promised five divisions and could not establish communication with the front headquarters. No one seemed to know what was going on. When Rokossovsky reached Vyazma, the local commander assured him that there were no troops in the town but Rokossovsky was not in the town long before there was a report that German tanks had been seen.

He confirmed that with his own eyes. The staff of the Sixteenth Army now had to flee because they could not stand up against tanks.

It looked like the German pincers were about to close on Vyazma. On the evening of October 6, the Sixteenth Army staff took shelter in a forest north of the Vyazma-Mozhaisk highway. They established that they were located between the inner and outer rings of the German encirclement. Rokossovsky organized all the stragglers in the vicinity and decided to try to break out. They broke through and reached Russian lines. There, Voroshilov, Molotov, Koniev, and Bulganin were searching for a scapegoat to take the blame for the collapse of the Western Front. Their first question to Rokossovsky was how he managed to be here with the staff of the Sixteenth Army without troops.

Rokossovsky showed them the order signed by Koniev. Stormy conversation then took place between Voroshilov and Koniev. The order seemed to be enough to warrant Koniev's trial for incompetence. Later Zhukov came into the room, and was introduced to Rokossovsky as the new Western Front commander. He had stopped the German drive on Leningrad.

On the night of October 6, Stalin had telephoned Zhukov in Leningrad and ordered him to Moscow to see what he could do to save the city. He arrived on October 7 and went immediately to the Kremlin. Stalin was in his apartment, suffering from the flu, but Beria was also there. Beria by now had direct control of the Russian intelligence and security empire he had inherited from Yezhiv. Beria would soon have a seat on the five-man state defense committee, which then included Stalin, Molotov, Voroshilov, and Malenkov. Beria remained silent as Stalin told Zhukov that the Red Army was not strong enough to resist the German attack on Moscow.

Turning to Beria, Stalin suggested that he find a way of negotiating another Brest Peace—like the one signed by Lenin in March 1918, which took Russia out of the war at the cost of losing the Baltic states,

---

New Objective

By August, Hitler had changed his mind and the new objective was Leningrad, which he planned to obliterate. He called it St. Petersburg, using the old Czarist name. He issued a directive to his generals, "The Fuehrer has decided to have St. Petersburg wiped off the face of the earth. The further existence of this large city is of no interest once Soviet Russia is overthrown. The intention is to close in on the city and raze it to the ground by artillery fire and continual air attack. Requests that the city be taken over will be turned down, for the problem of the survival of the population and supplying it with food is one that cannot and should not be solved by us. In this war for existence we have no interest in keeping even a part of this great city's population."

Hitler now became obsessed by the idea of capturing both Leningrad and Stalingrad. If these two "holy cities of communism" were to fall, Russia would collapse, he told himself. He also wanted to take Moscow and Kharkov before the winter snows set in. But the primary goal was now Leningrad and the second was the Caucasia. General Halder summed it up in his diary, "Thus the aim of defeating decisively the Russian armies in front of Moscow was subordinated to the desire to obtain a valuable industrial area and to advance in the direction of Russian oil."

In September the Germans were claiming that they had already won victory in Russia. They called the fall of Kiev "the greatest victory in the history of the world." When they took Rostov, Dr. Goebbels trumpeted that "the gateway to the Caucasia has now been opened."

Belorussia, Moldavia, and part of the Ukraine. Beria was to ask the Bulgarian ambassador in Moscow to act as intermediary.

The effort failed, because the Germans ignored the Bulgarian ambassador.

Stalin asked Zhukov to go to the front and find out what was happening. He was to telephone Stalin when he found out, no matter the time, day or night. Zhukov checked with Chief of Staff Shaposhnikov, got a map of the Western Front as of October 7 and left for the front. He found Budenny and discovered the extent of the disaster. On October 9, Zhukov was named commander of the Western Front.

✳ ✳ ✳

The Moscow plunge had moved very swiftly. The Germans had encircled two Russian armies and captured 650,000 prisoners, 5,000 field guns, and 1,200 tanks. The German spearhead was forty miles from Moscow, and the Soviet government evacuated to Kuibyshev on the Volga, although Stalin, in a rare display of bravery, refused to leave Moscow. But Stalin was his usual dictatorial self. He proposed to Zhukov that the entire Western Front command be replaced. Zhukov persuaded him to keep General Koniev as deputy commander and to entrust him with the defense of Kalinin. On the morning of October 10, Zhukov reached Western Front Headquarters at Krasnovidovo near Mozhaisk. He found that the situation was indeed serious. The Sixteenth, Nineteenth, Twentieth, Twenty-Fourth, and Thirty-Second Armies had been trapped by the Germans. Stalin asked him to get the Western Front into shape as fast as possible. Zhukov replied that Stalin must begin shifting reserves to meet the German thrust toward Moscow. He moved the Western Front Headquarters to Alabino and set out for Mozhaisk to confer with Colonel Bogdanov, the commander of the Mozhaisk Fortified Area. Then he returned to Alabino and set up the Mozhaisk defense line, along the Lama, Moskva, Kolocha Lucha, and Sukhodrev Rivers, whose steep banks constituted effective antitank defenses.

Zhukov ordered Rokossovsky to defend the Mozhaisk sector, but by October 14 the army was moved to Volokolamsk. Two days later German tanks were attacking the army's left flank. The army's one rifle division was the Eighteenth, made up of Moscow militia. They were soon joined by the Third Cavalry Corps, which entered the Fifteenth Army area through an accident of battle.

From early October until early December, the Western Front stretched in an arc from Volokolamsk to Kalasgva, through Mozhaisk and Maloiaroslavets. Broken armies were reformed. Construction was begun on all likely tank approaches to Moscow. Troops surrounded in the Vyazma and Bryansk pockets continued to fight their way out. When they made it they were collected and debriefed. Some were then arrested on suspicion of desertion and assigned to penal battalions.

As the Germans pressed ever closer to Moscow, Stalin's pressure on Zhukov became intense. The loss of a village became a matter demanding the personal attention of the front commander. The relations between Zhukov and his generals at times became poisonous, a matter that would be remembered and revived.

✳ ✳ ✳

An important element in the defense was the weather. Mid-October brought the wet Russian autumn, with its blinding rains that turned the roads to mush.

"The infantryman slithers in the mud," one junior German officer reported, "while many teams of horses are needed to drag each gun forward. All wheeled vehicles sink up to their axles in the slime. Even tractors can move only with great difficulty. A large portion of our artillery was soon stuck fast."

Moscow was virtually in sight—so near but so far. And with their backs to the wall, the Russian resistance stiffened. In the woods the partisans were now getting organized. *No Mercy, No Quarter*. These were the terms the Germans had laid down, and now, in October 1941, they were being visited on Hitler's troops as well.

Stalin's "Mother Russia" Speech

Ten days before the second German offensive against Moscow began, on the night of November 6, 1941, the Russians celebrated the twenty-fourth anniversary of the Bolshevik Revolution. The Germans were only forty miles away from Moscow and the atmosphere was that of a besieged city; tens of thousands of wounded filled the hospitals and tens of thousands of party workers and soldiers filled the streets. The meeting was held in the ornate hall of the Mayanovsky tube station, a setting humiliating to some, and depressing to others. Stalin spoke, delivering a mixture of black despair and total confidence. First, he said grimly, the war had suspended the building of socialism.

"After four months of war," he said, "we have suffered 350,000 killed, 378,000 missing, and over a million wounded. In the same period, the enemy has lost over four and a half million in dead, wounded, and prisoners. Germany's reserves are running low, while ours have scarcely been tapped."

Probably nobody believed these figures, so far from the truth, but Stalin felt it necessary to overstate the case in order to bring to attention his major point: that the German *blitzkrieg* had failed.

"It failed for three reasons," Stalin continued. "The Germans had hoped that America and England would join them in the war against Russia and that had not happened. The Germans had hoped that the Soviet government would collapse and that had not happened. Instead, the Soviet rear is today more solid than ever. And, finally, the Germans had expected the Soviet forces to collapse in front of them and let them push to the Urals. But we Russians have the advantage of fighting a just war. Moreover, the Germans are now fighting in our territory, far from home with their supply lines constantly harried by our partisans. The defense of Moscow and Leningrad show that in the fire of the great patriotic war new soldiers are being forged, men who will tomorrow become the terror of the German army."

He excoriated the Nazis as imperialists of the worst kind determined to annihilate or enslave the Slav people.

"And it is these people without honor or conscience, these people with the morality of animals who have the effrontery to call for the extermination of the great Russian nation, the nation of Plekhanof and Lenin, of Belinsky and Chernyshevsky, Pushkin and Tolstoy, Gorki and Chekhov, of Glinka and Tchaikovsky. . . . The German invaders want a war of extermination against the peoples of the Soviet Union. Very well, then, if they want a war of extermination they shall have it. Our task now will be to destroy every German to the last man, who has come to occupy our country. No mercy for the German invaders! Death to the German invaders!"

On October 11, the forces of the Mozhaisk Line were combined into the Fifth Army and the defense zone was reinforced with units from the Western and Reserve Fronts and other troops. Everywhere, the Russian people heeded the call for the defense of Moscow. On October 12, a directive from Stalin incorporated all these units into the Western Front. General Lelyushenko, commander of the Fifth Army was wounded and replaced by Major General Govorov. The Fifth, Sixteenth, Forty-Third, and Forty-Ninth Armies had a combined strength of only 90,000 men so they were concentrated in five areas. Headquarters was moved again, to Perkushkovo.

What was needed now was time to build up the Russian defenses and this was given by the armies encircled by the Germans west of Vyazma. They held down units of the German army that would otherwise have been sent to the Moscow attack.

The retreat of the government to Kuibyshev was made on October 15. On October 17, Stalin called a meeting in the Kremlin with Molotov, Malenkov, Mikoyan, Beria, Voznesensky, Scherbakov, Kagaonovich, Vasilievsky, and Artemiev. He laid out details for the evacuation of all important state and party people and the laying of explosives in all important buildings in the event of the capture of Moscow. A plan was made for the evacuation of the government to Kuibyshev and the General Staff to Arzamas. Two days later a state of siege was announced in Moscow. Several antiaircraft batteries were clustered around Stalin's dacha. A few days later, as Stalin returned to the dacha from the Kremlin, he witnessed an air raid on Moscow. A piece of shrapnel fell in his driveway. For the first time he sensed the immediacy of the war and insisted on going to "the front." So, one day a column of cars left Moscow by the Volokolamsk highway and turned onto a country road. Stalin wanted to watch a salvo fired but his security chief would not let him go farther. They waited and watched for a long time, seeing crimson flashes on the horizon and then turned away. As they left the area an armored car sprayed Stalin's limousine with mud. Beria insisted that he transfer to another car.

* * *

A new defense line was established as fallback from Novo-Zavidovsky through Klim and the Istra Reservoir to Aleksin.

The Military Council of the Western Front made an appeal to the troops, "Comrades! In this grave hour of danger for our state, the life of each soldier belongs to the Fatherland. The homeland demands from each one of you the greatest effort, courage, heroism, and steadfastness. The homeland calls on us to stand like an indestructible wall and to bar the fascist hordes from our beloved Moscow. What we require now as never before is vigilance, iron discipline, organization, determined action, unbending will for victory and a readiness for self-sacrifice."

A special train at one of Moscow's railroad stations, and four airplanes were set aside for his evacuation from Moscow. But after long deliberation he decided to stay on in Moscow.

During the month of October, then, these conditions were met by the people of Moscow and the soldiers of the army, the Germans advanced 150 miles from the starting point. But Hitler's plan to seize Moscow was thwarted, the German forces were exhausted, and the panzer units were overextended. The German drive was halted along a line running from Turginovo, Dorokhovo, west to Serpukhov and Aleksin.

By the end of the month, the Kalinin Front had been stabilized and the Twenty-Second, Twenty-Ninth, and Thirtieth Armies had been combined under General Koniev as the Kalinin Front. On October 30, a combined defense force of soldiers and armed workers repulsed an attack by Guderian's panzers in a bloody battle marked by the use of Molotov cocktails and brave attacks by individuals against tanks with bundles of dynamite. They held Tula and tied down the German advance from the south, ultimately causing Guderian to split his force, thus losing cohesion of attack.

The Germans made much of the Russian mud but General Zhukov denied that it was an important factor in the defeat of the effort to take Moscow. The roads were impassable for a relatively short period in October. Then, in November, the Russian winter set in and the terrain and the roads froze. The temperature ranged from 14 to 19° F. The first phase of the battle of Moscow was won by the Russian people.

On November 1, Zhukov was summoned by Stalin to Moscow for advice about the ceremonies to mark the October revolution. Zhukov said the enemy was in no condition to start a new offensive, although one was expected soon. The Germans were reinforcing and regrouping. The traditional parade was held in Red Square on November 7. Around it the Russian armies were regrouping, too. Three days later the whole Tula defense was transferred to the Western Front and the Bryansk Front was disbanded. Now that winter had come, the Russian soldiers got fur coats, felt boots, woolen underwear, padded vests, and fur caps. The Germans were still in summer uniforms. They did their best to keep warm, confiscating the felt boots and furs of the local people, but the freezing time had come. In Berlin, propaganda minister Goebbels opened a *Winterhilfe* drive for fur coats and other warm clothing. The army quartermaster was supposed to have shipped more than a million warm coats and other supplies, but these had not reached the troops of the Eastern Front by the time the Russian winter began.

* * *

In mid-November the Germans in the south captured Rostov at the mouth of the Don River. But five days later an enormous Soviet army appeared to challenge the Panzers, which were well out ahead of the infantry. The Panzers turned around and raced back to the Mius River line. It was the first German retreat of the campaign and Hitler was furious. Marshal von Rundstedt wanted to retreat further, but Hitler ordered him to hold. "Where a German soldier has set his foot," he was to say later, "there will be no retreat."

Von Rundstedt was quick to reply. He demanded permission to retreat. "It is madness to attempt to hold. In the first place the troops cannot do it, and in the second place if they do not retreat they will be destroyed. I repeat that this order must be rescinded or that you find someone else."

That night Hitler replied, "I am acceding to your request. Please give up your command."

* * *

That fall of 1941 the Germans had suffered their first experience with the Russian *rasputitsa*. On October 6, the first snow fell, and for the next three weeks alternate snow and rain and the movement of trucks and tanks pounded the roads into mush. This weather militated in favor of the Russians, whose T-34 tanks had wider treads than the German tanks, and so a few of them could hold up the German advance. And by the end of October, the German advance on Moscow was stalled thirty-five miles away.

The new drive was in preparation, and the Russians prepared to meet it. Zhukov had six armies, but they were extended over a front of 375 miles. He planned to provide protection for the most vulnerable areas on the flanks and to keep some forces in reserve for emergencies, but on November 13 Stalin interfered.

"Shaposhnikov and I feel that we must break up the enemy offensive with a preventive counterattack. One counterattack should bypass Volokolamsk on the north, and the other should be launched from Serpukhov against the flank of the German Fourth Army. Those seem to be the areas where large forces are being massed for the drive against Moscow."

"What forces are we supposed to use for these counterattacks?" Zhukov demanded. "The front has nothing available. We have just enough to hold our present positions."

"In the Volokolamsk area you could use the right flank units of Rokossovsky's army, the Fifty-Eighth Tank Division, a couple of cavalry divisions, and Dovator's cavalry corps. At Serpukhov use Belov's cavalry corps, Getman's tank division, and parts of the Fortieth Army," the dictator said.

"We can't do that," Zhukov said. "We can't throw the last reserves of our front into dubious counterattacks. We won't have any reinforcements when the enemy goes over to the offensive with his shock troops."

"But you've got six armies. Don't tell me that's too little."

Zhukov replied that the defense line of the Western Front was overextended. It measured more than 375 miles, and they had very few reserves in depth, especially in the center."

"Consider the question of counterattacks decided and let me have your plan by tomorrow evening," Stalin ordered. And having had the last word, he hung up on Zhukov.

Fifteen minutes later Bulganin walked into Zhukov's office to say that he, too, had just been dressed down by Stalin.

"You and Zhukov seem to be getting quite a high opinion of yourselves," Stalin had said. "But we'll find a way of dealing with you, too."

And Stalin had ordered Bulganin to get to work immediately on the counterattacks.

Another version of this tale was offered by General Belov. He said that on the day that his cavalry unit was incorporated into the Western Front, Zhukov had told him that Belov's group was to act in collaboration with the Forty-Ninth Army in a counterattack and he was to lay the plans immediately, even without surveying the scene. On November 10,

Moment of Trial

Despite stiff resistance the Germans were closing in on Moscow. During the last days of September and the first days of October, all attention was centered on the big German offensive in the Ukraine and the breakthrough into the Crimea. At a press conference on September 28 Stalin's spokesman assured the press that the Germans were losing many tens of thousands of dead outside Leningrad; that although they had broken through into the Crimea, they had not yet crossed the Perekop Isthmus; and that although Kiev had been lost, the battle was continuing. He dismissed the German claim of having captured 600,000 prisoners at Kiev. Nothing appeared in the Russian papers about Hitler's speech of October 2, announcing his "final drive" against Moscow. It did not become clear until October 4 that the offensive against Moscow had started. But by October 7 the bad news had begun to seep through, with the first Russian official admission of "heavy fighting in the direction of Viazma."

On October 8, *Red Star*, the army's paper, said that "the very existence of the Soviet state is in danger" in Hitler's "last fling," wherein Hitler was throwing in his reserves. "Every man of the Red Army must be prepared to stand firm and fight to the last drop of blood," the paper said. "Hitler has thrown into it everything, even every old and obsolete tank, every midget tank the Germans have collected in Holland, Belgium, and France. The Soviet soldiers must at any price destroy these tanks, old and new, large and small; all the riff-raff armor of ruined Europe is being thrown against the Soviet Union."

On October 12, the rulers decided to evacuate the government and diplomatic offices immediately to the east. Kuibyshev became the goal of many People's Commissariats, and nearly all scientific and cultural institutions. The Stavka and a skeleton administration were to stay on in Moscow, as were the principal newspapers, *Pravda*, *Izvestia*, *Red Star*, *Komsomolskaya Pravda*, and *Trud*. The news of these evacuations was followed by the official communiqué published on the morning of October 16, "During the night of October 14–15 the position on the Western Front became worse. German

Fascist troops hurled against our troops large quantities of tanks and motorized infantry and in one sector broke through our defenses."

In this moment of trial there were three factors:

1. The Red Army, which fought desperately and yielded ground slowly.
2. The Moscow working class, many of whom were putting in long hours and in their free time building defenses and preparing to fight the Germans inside Moscow if they should break through.
3. The mass of Muscovites including high and medium party officials, who participated in "the great skedaddle." Panic, for which many were later bitterly ashamed, set in and people began running this way and that. One journalist who returned to Moscow this day telephoned fifteen of his friends and discovered that all had run away. The stampede engulfed the railroad stations, officials fled in official cars without official permits, the smell of burning paper filled the air, officials burning all documents that might incriminate them as Communist *apparachiki* if the Germans came.

The panic involved the young and the old, men and women, particularly party members, who knew what fate they might expect at the hands of the Germans.

Only Stalin remained. In spite of the panic of others he firmly refused to leave the Kremlin, a fact announced to the Russian people on October 17, which shamed them and persuaded some to return. Two days later a state of siege was announced in Moscow, partly caused by the widespread looting of the official quarters of the city. The NKVD's special troops were put in charge of the city with orders to shoot on sight any provocateurs, thieves, or spies. Emergency tribunals were setup to try the accused and administer justice on the spot.

By the end of October more than 2 million people had been evacuated from Moscow and many more had fled unofficially, some officials did not turn up for three weeks or so. Through all of this Stalin sat, like a rock, in the Kremlin, a symbol of Russian faith and resistance to the Germans.

Zhukov took Belov to Moscow and they met Stalin, whom Belov had not seen since 1933. Belov observed that Stalin had aged twenty years in nine, and seemed to lack confidence. Zhukov addressed Stalin sharply, and Belov had the feeling that Zhukov, not Stalin, was in charge. Zhukov submitted the plans for the operation and Stalin approved them with only one change, a delay of one day in the start.

These versions are not mutually exclusive, Stalin had obviously ordered the offensive, and insisted on it over Zhukov's objections.

In any event, the counterattacks were almost as ineffective as Zhukov had expected. They were carried out mostly by cavalry, and they were not strong enough to materially affect the German buildup. On November 15, the Germans renewed their Moscow offensive, with Guderian moving to bypass Tula. Zhukov had difficulty in pulling Belov's cavalry corps and Getman's tank division out of the line and moving them to the Kashira sector. Stalin's interference had expended men and material without commensurate results, a real waste.

The Germans, having brought in new forces, now faced the Western Front with fifty-one divisions—thirty-one infantry, thirteen tank, and seven motorized divisions all up to full strength. The attack began on November 15 with three thrusts—one against the right flank of the Thirtieth Army on the Kalinin Front, one south of the Shosha River, and one against the Sixteenth Army near Teryayeva Sloboda.

The Thirtieth Army gave way before the assault of 300 tanks against the army's fifty-six light tanks. On November 16, the enemy moved in the direction of Klin, where there were no reserves because Stalin had used them to counterattack in the Volokolamsk sector that was still held down by the Germans.

On November 17, Stalin ordered the Thirtieth Army transferred to the Western Front, which did not solve any problems. He also fired General Khomenko, the commander of the army, and replaced him with General Lelyushenko. In a harsh gesture that had become commonplace with Stalin, Khomenko was arrested.

The Sixteenth Army withdrew from its position to prepared artillery positions and took a stand, inflicting serious losses on the

Germans. But the withdrawal was the cause of a serious quarrel among the Russians.

Rokossovsky wanted to withdraw to the Istra River, but Zhukov refused to permit it. Rokossovsky went over his head to Shaposhnikov who consulted with Stalin and approved it. Zhukov ordered Rokossovsky to stand where he was, but Rokossovsky withdrew anyhow. The incident left a scar that would surface later.

On November 19, Stalin called Zhukov to ask if the Moscow line could be held. Zhukov asked for more troops and this time Stalin agreed to send two reserve armies that were just being formed. They would arrive at the end of the month, but there were no more tanks to be had at the moment.

The Germans began the attack in the Tula area on November 18. On November 21, they occupied Uzlovaya and Stalinogorsk, posing a real threat to Tula. On November 23, there was heavy fighting around Venev, and on November 26, the German Third Tank Division cut the Tula Moscow Road north of Tula. But in the Kashira section the Germans were thrown back by vigorous Russian attacks. The next day the Russians staged a counterattack against the German Seventeenth Tank Division, throwing it back ten miles.

In the fighting of the next three days the Germans suffered heavy losses, and on November 30, General Guderian gave up the assault on the Kashira Tula area and took his Second Tank Army into defensive positions.

Around Istra and Klin the Russian situation was far more perilous. German Panzer broke into Klin on November 23, and the city was abandoned on November 24. The loss of Klin tore a gap between the Sixteenth and Thirtieth Armies. On November 25, the Sixteenth Army was forced to retreat from Solnechnogorsk. The Russians moved up everything they could, including isolated groups of tanks, artillery batteries, and antiaircraft divisions. The enemy had to be contained until the Seventh Rifle Division from Serpukhov and two tank brigades and two antitank artillery regiments could be moved to Solnechnogorsk.

Somehow Stalin got word that Zhukov's troops had abandoned the city of Dedovsk, northwest of Nakhabino, about ten miles from Moscow, and he became very excited. He called Zhukov, "Do you know that they've occupied Dedovsk?" he demanded.

"No, Comrade Stalin," Zhukov said. "I did not know that."

"A commander should know what's going on at the front!" Stalin snapped. He ordered Zhukov to go to Dedovsk immediately and personally organize a counterattack to retake Dedovsk.

Zhukov argued that it was not wise to leave front headquarters at so tense a moment.

"Never mind," Stalin said. "We'll get along somehow. Leave Chief of Staff Sokolovsky in charge."

Zhukov hung up the phone and immediately called General Rokossovsky at Sixteenth Army. "Why does headquarters not have any word that the enemy has occupied Dedovsk?" he demanded.

"Because it's not true," Rokossovsky said. "You must mean the village of Dedovo. The Ninth Guards Rifle Division is fighting a battle down there to prevent the Germans from breaking through along the Volokolamsk highway."

Zhukov then telephoned Stalin again and explained.

But Stalin would not listen. He flew into a fury and insisted that Zhukov go to Rokossovsky and demand that what Zhukov called "this miserable village" be recovered instantly from the enemy. He also insisted that Zhukov take along the Fifth Army commander, General Govorov, because he was an artillery man and could help Rokossovsky organize artillery fire.

When Zhukov telephoned Govorov, the latter objected.

"There is no point in it," he said. "Rokossovsky has his own artillery chief, and besides Rokossovsky can handle this himself."

"The point," Zhukov said, "is that this is a direct order from Stalin."

So he picked up Govorov, then Rokossovsky, and they went to General Beloborodov's Ninth Guards Rifle Division. Beloborodov was not happy to see them. He was up to his neck in problems and now he had to stop everything and explain why the Germans had occupied a few houses of a village on the far side of a deep gully. He made it plain that there was no tactical reason to try to recapture the houses.

Zhukov was reluctant to admit that tactical principles had nothing to do with his presence here on the battle line. Zhukov ordered Beloborodov to send a rifle company and two tanks to drive the Germans out of the village. It was the dawn of December 1.

A communications officer appeared at Beloborodov's headquarters to say that Zhukov should call his command post. He finally managed to get through to Chief of Staff Sokolovsky, who reported that Stalin had called three times asking, "Where is Zhukov?" The enemy had launched a surprise attack on the Thirty-Third Army.

Zhukov and Sokolovsky agreed on what must be done to end this new threat, and then Zhukov got through to headquarters in Moscow. He was told that Stalin had left orders for him to return immediately to his own headquarters.

After he returned to headquarters, Zhukov called Stalin.

"What about Dedovsk?" Stalin asked.

"It wasn't Dedovsk. It was the village of Dedovo. I sent a rifle company and two tanks to oust the Germans."

Stalin had nothing to say to justify his interference that had fouled up two armies, Western Front Headquarters, and a rifle division for half a day to satisfy a royal whim based on misinformation.

✳ ✳ ✳

On the night of November 29, the enemy took advantage of a weak defense of the bridge near Yakhroma across the Moscow-Volga canal and seized the bridge, crossing to the east bank. There the Germans were stopped by the newly formed First Shock Army under Lt. Gen. V. I. Kuznetsov and thrown back across the canal.

On December 1, the Germans made a surprise attack on the center of the line, then advanced along the Minsk-Moscow highway toward Kubinka. They were stopped at the village of Akulovo by the Thirty-Second Rifle Division. Many tanks were destroyed by Russian artillery fire and some were blown up in mine fields. The enemy tanks then turned toward Golitsyno, but by December 4 this break-through was liquidated, with the Germans leaving 10,000 dead, fifty tanks, and many field guns on the battlefield. On December 5, General Guderian ordered his troops into defensive positions.

"The offensive on Moscow has ended," he noted in his journal. "All the sacrifices and efforts of our brilliant troops have failed. We have suffered a serious defeat."

✳ ✳ ✳

In those first days of December, it became apparent that the German offensive was grinding to a halt, and that Hitler had neither the men nor the arms to take Moscow. Some companies were down to twenty or thirty men, and German morale was shot. The Russians had also suffered heavy losses, but morale was high, in the knowledge that they had stopped the enemy.

In the twenty days of the second German offensive they had lost 155,000 men, 800 tanks, 300 guns, and 1,500 aircraft. The vaunted "invincibility" of the Wehrmacht had been tested and found to be a myth.

There were many excuses and much shucking off of the blame for the German defeat. The generals put it on the shoulders of Hitler, who had halted the center drive on Moscow in August and diverted forces to the Ukraine. Generals Guderian and Hoth blamed the Russian winter. Russian propagandists denied this, saying that their forces had to operate under the same conditions. The fact is that the Russians had proper winter clothing and the Germans did not, and the Russians made much of the heroism of their forces.

Many German heads fell in the aftermath of the failure. Field Marshal von Brauchitsch was dismissed as commander of the German ground forces. Field Marshal von Bock was fired as commander of Army Group Center, General Guderian was sent on leave from the Second Tank Army, General Hoeppner was fired as commander of the Third Tank Group.

But the most radical change was that Hitler took over personal command of the armies of the Eastern Front. Operation Barbarossa had failed in every way. From this point onward, it would be a new war.

CHAPTER

9

Moscow Counterattack

STALIN HAD NO REAL MILITARY EXPERIENCE OUTSIDE the Revolution, and he was anything but the great military genius depicted in official soviet history of the time. Nor did he have the powers of prognostication attributed to him. He came to strategic wisdom only through trial and error. Many of his orders were so half-baked or wrong that they were never carried out.

For example, on August 28, 1941, he had ordered the air force on two fronts to smash some German tank formations with about 500 aircraft, the operation to begin at dawn the next day. This order showed how little he knew about fighting a war: it was patently impossible to carry out the order in such a short time.

In the beginning of December 1941, the German attack had fizzled out, the troops of the Wehrmacht were exhausted and half-frozen, and it was the Russians' turn to move. The Western Front had been reinforced by the First Shock Army, and the Tenth Army and a number of other units had been combined to create the Twentieth Army.

Stalin ordered the counterattack by General Koniev's Kalinin Front and Marshal Timoshenko's Southwest Front combined with the Western Front. General Zhukov telephoned Stalin and was asked to assess the enemy, "He is exhausted," Zhukov said, and it was true. The effect of heavy losses, partisan activity against the long supply lines, and the severe winter for which the Germans had not prepared brought the generals to urge Hitler to countenance withdrawals.

Zhukov continued, "But without the help of the First Shock Army and the Tenth Army our troops will be unable to eliminate any dangerous salients. If we don't eliminate those salients now, the enemy may be able to reinforce his groups in the Moscow area, bringing in large reserves from the north and south."

Stalin said he would discuss the matter with the General Staff. Zhukov did not want to telephone the General Staff because he and Shaposhnikov had a running battle about strategy; so he did not. Stalin then asked to see his plan for use of those armies, and shortly afterward transferred the two armies to Zhukov's command.

His aim for the counteroffensive was to eliminate the two wedges on the northern and southern flanks of the Western Front. The Western Front was held by Zhukov; he did not have the resources to do more than this. He spoke to Stalin several times in the next few days, and on December 4 they had a conversation about air power and tanks.

"We can't give you any more tanks," Stalin said. "We don't have any. But you'll get your air support. Arrange it with the General Staff. I am going to call them now. Just remember that the Kalinin Front offensive begins on December 5, and the operational group around Yelets on the sixth."

✳ ✳ ✳

The offensive had the modest aim of driving the invaders back twenty to thirty kilometers. But on the night it began General Guderian had issued an order to the Second Panzer Army to withdraw to positions about eighty kilometers southwest of Moscow.

Stalin's Error

The Supreme Command still insisted on the big encirclement, even after Vyazma had shown the futility of it. Stalin decided to drop a large number of paratroops in the German rear, to cut communications and serve as a link between the pincers. He planned to enclose the Germans near Smolensk. Yet German resistance was increasing everywhere, and as noted, the failure at Vyazma should have been a warning.

It is clear that Stalin overrated both the Russian driving force and the breakdown of German morale. Nor did he pay much attention to the exhaustion of the Russian troops. The plan to encircle and smash all the German troops between Moscow and Smolensk and capture Orel and Bryansk was much too ambitious, given the state of his reserves and ammunition and equipment. Thus, Stalin's order that Bryansk be taken and a rein of reinforcements sent to that area, diverted the Red Army from its main aim, which was Vyazma. The whole series of orders issued in the Smolensk area during that early spring was totally unrealistic.

The Western Front offensive began on December 6, along with the Kalinin Front and Yelets moving in bitter cold, with deep snow hampering the troop movements. The offensive began with a bombardment, and then the troops moved out. The First Shock Army reached the outskirts of Klim on December 13 and, with the Thirtieth Army, surrounded the town and broke through the enemy lines on the next day. By December 16, the town was cleared of the enemy.

Altogether the counteroffensive was effective and raised Stalin's spirits so much that he was ready to plunge into a more dangerous move—a general offensive. On January 5, Zhukov was summoned to the Kremlin. Marshal Shaposhnikov reported on the situation at the front and presented a plan for the offensive.

"The Germans seem bewildered by their setback at Moscow and are poorly prepared for the winter," Stalin said. "Now is the time to go over to the general offensive."

Attacks were to be made in the north and in the south, but the major assault would be in the center. The combined forces of the Northwest, Kalinin, Western, and Bryansk Fronts would form pincers that would trap the main forces of the enemy around Rzev, Vyazma, and Smolensk.

Stalin then asked for the opinions of his generals

"We should continue the offensive on the Western Front," said Zhukov. "There the enemy has not had time to restore the fighting capacity of his forces. But a successful continuation of the offensive will require reinforcement, especially of tanks, without which we cannot expect to make much progress. As for offensives near Leningrad and in the southwest, our forces there face formidable enemy defenses. Without powerful artillery support, our troops would be unable to break through. They would be worn out and suffer completely unjustifiable losses. I would favor reinforcing our troops on the Western Front, and waging a stronger offensive there."

N. A. Voznesensky also spoke out against the general offensive, arguing that they did not have the resources to wage a general offensive on all fronts.

Then Stalin spoke again: "I've talked to Timoshenko and he favors the attack," he said. "We must quickly smash the Germans so that they cannot attack when spring comes."

Stalin was supported by Beria and Malenkov, who said that Voznesensky was always finding difficulties. No one else wanted to speak so Stalin said, "This then ends the discussion."

It was obvious to Zhukov that the decision had been made earlier, and that Stalin had simply wanted "to nudge the military," as he liked to put it. Shaposhnikov confirmed Zhukov's feeling.

"It was foolish to argue. The chief had already decided. The directives have already gone out to the fronts and they will launch the offensives almost immediately."

"Then why did Stalin ask my opinion?" Zhukov asked.

"I just don't know," Shaposhnikov answered with a sigh.

✳ ✳ ✳

Shortly before Christmas 1941, the Army Group Center decided to establish a winter line of resistance from Velev through Yuknov on the Ugra River, to Gzhatsk, and then north. Field Marshal von Kluge had already mobilized a division to cover the retreat of the Fourth Army. He called a meeting of his staff at his headquarters, a cottage in Maloyaroslavets. Maps were distributed and the staff prepared to move men out. Then came a telephone call from General Hans von Greiffenberg, chief of staff of Army Group Center. He spoke to General Guenther von Blumentritt, chief of staff of the Fourth Army.

"You'd better make yourself comfortable," von Greiffenberg said. "A new order has just arrived from Hitler. Fourth Army is not to retreat—not a single yard."

And so the great retreat was stopped before it got started.

Back at Fuehrer Headquarters at Rastenburg, Hitler had been fuming all day. His soldiers were retreating. Didn't they know that if they withdrew only a few miles, they would sacrifice most of their heavy equipment? The tanks, guns, and heavy trucks were all irreplaceable. Didn't they know the value of munitions?

He had to return to Berlin; affairs of state were calling. He had to manage a new war against the United States. Admiral Doenitz was calling for more submarine production. The Reichstag was about to go back into session. But before he left, he issued a new order to the Eastern Front.

"Stand fast," the order said. "Not one step back."

A few hours later Field Marshal von Kluge telephoned. Colonel General Erich Hoeppner, he said, had ordered his army front to withdraw, in defiance of the Fuehrer's order. The Second Army retreat could cause the destruction of the Fourth Army.

Hitler flew into one of his rages. He ordered the immediate dismissal of Hoeppner from command and his discharge from the army for disobedience. That night, Hitler spent in the OKW Headquarters reading room, alternately studying his maps and cursing his generals.

Handicaps

The Germans were handicapped that winter by a severe shortage of warm clothing. This prompted a Soviet caricaturist to picture the German soldier as a comic character—"Winter Fritz"—wrapped up in women's shawls and feather boas, with an icicle hanging from his nose. On December 13, the Soviet Information Bureau published a communiqué announcing the failure of the enemy to encircle Moscow and describing the early results of the first Russian counteroffensive. The newspapers published photos of the generals who had become famous overnight in the defense of Moscow: Zhukov, Lelyushenko, Kuznetsov, Rokossovsky, Govorov, Boldin, Golikov, Belov, and Vlasov.

The successes of the Russians were quite spectacular: they liberated nearly every place between twenty and forty miles from Moscow: Kalinin, Klin, Ystra, Yelets, and Tula were the bigger ones. But there were reminders of the cost: when the Red Army recaptured Volokolamsk they found a gallows in the main square with eight bodies hanging from it—seven men and one woman executed by the Germans as partisans to terrorize the civil population.

The Red Army's serious handicap was a shortage of transportation. There were only 8,000 trucks available on the Moscow Front, a totally inadequate number. Not even half the required supplies could be delivered by motor transport. Hundreds of horse-drawn sleighs were used. And these had limited capacity. It was not for another year, until the Lend-Lease Program of America was in full swing, that the transport problem was solved.

But the big problem of the first Russian offensive was that Stalin bit off more than he could chew. He was planning a vast encirclement of the German forces opposite Moscow, but he did not have the ammunition, supplies, and men to carry it out. Besides, Stalin underestimated the strength of the German resistance fuelled by propaganda, disciplinary measures, and reinforcements from the west.

On January 25, the Russians suffered their first setback of the campaign—their failure to take Gzhatsk by storm. In this sector the Red Army came to a screeching halt at the end of January. Stalin wanted to break through to Vyazma, but despite a high degree of heroism and sacrifice, they just couldn't make it. The tale of one squad of soldiers tells it all. They were called the Panfilov men, and their monument was a cartridge case embedded in a tree trunk. The thirteen men had been sent to stop German tanks from advancing along the Minsk highway. At the end of the day there were only three of them left, Alexander Vinogradov of Frunze and two others. "We shall stand firm," he wrote, "as long as there is any life left in us."

A few hours later there was only Vinogradov, "Now I am alone, wounded in the arm and in my head. The number of tanks has increased. There are twenty-three. I shall probably die. Somebody may find my note and remember me. I am a Russian, from Frunze. I have no parents. Goodbye dear friends. Your Alexander Vinogradov, 22.2.42."

And then there was only the cartridge case, embedded in the tree trunk, in the silent forest.

Only hours later, a new crisis developed involving Heinz Guderian, one of Hitler's favorite generals and commander of the Second Tank Army, which was now frozen in solid at Tula. Army Group Center had ordered Guderian to withdraw west into the gap created by Hoepner's action, the object being to sacrifice the Second Tank Army, if necessary, to save the Fourth Army. Guderian was not interested in being sacrificed; he wanted to save his troops. He proposed to withdraw along his line of advance, stage by stage, abandoning and destroying equipment as he went, including tanks that were frozen into the ice.

Von Kluge argued with Guderian, but got nowhere. The panzer general said the Hitler order was impossible and could not be obeyed. Von Kluge complained to Hitler, who relieved Guderian of command and ordered him to Rastenburg to explain.

When Guderian appeared, Hitler started by telling him he could have his command back if he would only listen to reason

It was not reason, Guderian replied, but lunacy and suicide. He would not obey. He was interested only in saving his men.

For once Hitler did not explode, perhaps because he had already blown his top at several generals. He was all sweet reason. Guderian must be tired. He prescribed a rest, somewhere quiet to convalesce "from this enormous strain on his nerves." So Guderian went back to Germany, not in disgrace, but in limbo. And the tension on the Eastern Front continued.

Hitler had his way. Field Marshal Keitel agreed with him that to hold was the only solution, expensive as it would be. It was with heavy hearts that the OKW staff celebrated a cheerless Christmas amid rumors that this unit and that was about to rebel. Some did rebel. The commander of the Sixth Army Corps, General Foerster, flatly refused an order that would have cost him half his men. He was sent home to Germany in disgrace. Hitler would have no rebellions. Not even at the divisional level. He personally cashiered a division commander for refusing to obey an order. And ultimately he won. The army held. The decimation was awesome. In January, Fourth Army took stock: its headquarters artillery strength had been forty-eight heavy howitzers, thirty-six mortars, forty-eight 100-mm guns, nine 150-mm guns, eighty-four assault guns, and 252 tractors. It was now down to five heavy howitzers, eight mortars, seventeen 100-mm guns, two 150-mm guns, twelve assault guns, and twenty-two tractors. This was the sort of attrition that no army could stand for long. But had Hitler not demanded that they hold, it would have been worse. Germany's war on the Eastern Front had developed into a no-win situation.

✳ ✳ ✳

The general offensive turned out to be another of Stalin's military disasters. On January 13, the attack was opened on the Leningrad Front. It led to a dreadful winter of fighting in frozen bogs and marshes, no successes, and extremely heavy Russian losses.

On the Western Front, by January 17, the Russians had cut the Moscow-Rzhev railroad. But instead of reinforcing the front to exploit the success, Stalin ordered the First Shock Army back to the reserves. Zhukov telephoned headquarters to protest and was told

---

America Enters the War

On December 7, 1941, a Japanese carrier fleet attacked the U.S. naval base at Pearl Harbor, Hawaii, and precipitated the entrance of the United States into World War II. The Japanese attack came as a complete surprise to Adolf Hitler, whose mind was wrapped up in the Eastern Front, and he made the considerable error of declaring war on the United States. Had he not done so it might have been difficult for Prime Minister Winston Churchill to persuade President Roosevelt to declare the war against Germany to be paramount. The American military and naval commanders wanted to fight Japan. Reluctantly, they turned their faces and efforts to the war against Hitler and the Pacific War took a back seat in logistics. That accounts for the fall of the Philippines, for with a minor effort General Douglas MacArthur could have saved it. But he got no reinforcements and no encouragement except to go to Australia and fight his way back.

Field Marshal Keitel and General Jodl were in the OKW Headquarters at Rastenburg that night of December 7, when Hitler came bursting into the conference room with a wireless message in hand.

"I gained the impression that the Fuehrer thought that the war between Japan and America had suddenly relieved him of a nightmare burden; it certainly brought us some relief from the consequences of America's undeclared state of war with us," Keitel wrote.

Like most of the world, Hitler expected the Americans to strike first against Japan. But there he played into the wily hands of Churchill, who found it easy to persuade Roosevelt that the greater threat was Hitler. And so one of the major beneficiaries of Hitler's decision was Stalin's Russia, which immediately became the recipient of vast supplies of American aid.

---

that the order came from Stalin. He telephoned Stalin and was told "Don't argue, just send the army."

When Zhukov protested that this order would leave him short of troops, Stalin barked, "You have plenty of troops. Just count them."

And then Stalin hung up the phone.

Zhukov protested to Shaposhnikov.

"My dear fellow," the marshal said. "There is nothing I can do. It is Stalin's personal decision."

So the offensive on the Western Front also failed, General Yefremov's Thirty-Third Army was cut off at Vyazma with Belov's cavalry corps and surrounded by the Germans. Belov finally fought his way to the lines of the Tenth Russian Army, but the Germans

---

That First Winter

That first winter, the German people were surprised to learn that the *Wehrmacht* would not, after all, reach Moscow by the end of the year. That shock (for Germany had been assured by the Nazi leaders that victory had already been attained) was followed by Dr. Goebbels' call for furs and warm clothing for the troops of the Eastern Front. Expecting easy victory before the snows, the supply section of the *Wehrmacht* had failed to deliver winter clothing, and the soldiers at the front were still dressed in summer cotton uniforms with Russian temperatures below the freezing mark. The mud of Russian autumn had frozen into the ice of Russian winter. Even when the German public responded nobly to the appeal, most of the soldiers still wore their cottons, with perhaps a greatcoat and a single woolen blanket. When a Russian prisoner was captured he was first stripped of his warm winter clothing, furs, and felt boots.

The water froze in the boilers of the railway locomotives as the temperature fell to −40°. The oil in the artillery pieces froze and they would not train. The machine guns froze and would not fire, but the gunners could not open the breaches to repair them; when a man touched a piece of steel his skin immediately froze tight to it. The answer was glycerin, which the Russians had but the Germans did not. Tank engines began to freeze up and the tankers built fires under them at night to keep them warm or ran the engines all night. In operations, if a tank slipped off the road into a ditch, there it remained until the thaws. If other tanks were sent to dislodge it, they, too, were at risk. In this frozen atmosphere, the Russians launched their Moscow counterattack. Marshal Zhukov's offensive began north of Moscow, striking at the left flank of the German Third Panzer Group.

---

anticipated Yefremov's effort to break out, it failed, and he was killed in battle along with the majority of his troops.

In February and March 1942, Stalin insisted that the Western Front armies carry out further offensive operations. But Zhukov replied that the troops were exhausted and they had not received promised deliveries of ammunition so they could advance no further. They were reduced to one or two shells per gun per day.

Stalin kept insisting on attack.

"If you don't achieve results today," he said, "you will tomorrow. If you attack, you will at least tie down the enemy and results will be felt on other parts of the front."

But operations on all fronts failed to achieve their objectives because the Russians lacked superiority in manpower and arms.

"Events demonstrated the error of Stalin's decision calling for a general offensive in January," Zhukov said. "It would have been wiser to have concentrated more strength in the western sector."

But despite Stalin's serious errors of judgement, he could not be faulted on personal courage. He stuck to his post in Moscow at the height of the German threat.

When his son Yakov was transferred to a camp in Nuremberg and then one in Luebeck—where the Germans denied Russian officers the privileges granted under the Geneva convention and Stalin was apprised of his son Yakov's situation—he said nothing. All Russia was suffering. His determination was encouraging to all the people.

Stalin's second son, Vasily Iosifovich, was a spoiled product of the Soviet system of toadyism. Sent to the best schools, given the best privileges, raised by Vlasik, the head of Stalin's security guard, he lived in a climate of flattery and permissiveness. By the time he was grown he was spineless, capricious, and weak. He took ruthless advantage of his position as the dictator's son. While Yakov used the family name Dzhugashvili, Vasily used Stalin.

Even as a youth he was profligate and dissipated, with an eye for women. Lavrenti Beria, commissar of Internal Affairs and chief of the

Security Police, kept a house on Katchov Street with an extensive collection of pornography, liquor, and girls on request. Vasily was a frequent visitor and sometime drinking companion. He often borrowed money from Beria, which he never repaid. He became a pilot and was a fair one, though not great. He did nothing to merit the captain's rank with which he began the war. On February 19, 1942, he was promoted to colonel and given command of a fighter squadron. Later that year Vasily was appointed commander of the Air Division of the Moscow Military District. He soon became infamous for his dissolute behavior, but the toadyism continued. Was he not the son of the leader of the Russian people? And were not the Russian people determined to win the war?

The battle of Moscow marked the changeover from defensive to offensive Russian operations.

The Germans had lost the key battle and they would go on to lose the war.

Prelude to Stalingrad

Operation Blau succumbed almost immediately after the firing of Field Marshal von Bock. First and Fourth Panzer armies reached points on a radius of within twenty-five miles of Millerovo, but they sliced through the Russian columns rather than surrounding them and at the end of several days the First Army had taken only 22,000 prisoners, about one-tenth of what was expected. The problem was that they were fighting air; the Russian forces evaporated before them. The most significant capture of the First Army was twenty-two trainloads of American and British tanks taken on the railroad out of Millerovo. Hitler shifted his headquarters from Wolfsschanze in East Prussia to Vinnitsa in the Ukraine, and General Halder and the staff of OKH moved into prefabricated quarters in a pine forest a few miles from the city.

Hitler's reason for the move was obviously to be able to say that he had taken personal control of the army. And he had a new plan—Operation

---

Bluecher—which meant invasion of the great bend in the Don, and encirclement of the vast Russian armies located there.

For Russia, the German entry into the Great Bend of the Don meant the opening of the battle for Stalingrad. The official Russian history of the war says, "Comrade Stalin immediately sensed the plan of the German high command." This is doubtful (Stalin had his own hand in the writing of the history) and the allusion supports the vision of Stalin, the all-wise all-seeing leader.

On July 12, Stalin created the Stalingrad Front, but when General V. I. Chuikov visited the front headquarters not long afterward he was impressed by its instability. It seemed to be "living on wheels," prepared to move out at a moment's notice.

For the moment, the Stalingrad Front had as little bearing on current events as the Voronezh Front had the week before. Hitler's attention was diverted elsewhere.

Bitter Spring

FROM THE OUTSET OF THE WAR UNTIL AFTER STALINGRAD, Stalin's meddling with the military command of the Russian armies cost millions of lives, losses for which scapegoats had to be found, beginning with General Pavlov. But somehow the Germans were stopped by December 6. Operation Barbarossa had failed.

The Russian counteroffensive, ordered by Stalin, bogged down and stopped because the Russians did not have the men or material to push on.

When winter broke over the Eastern Front in the first week of December, German Army Group South was better off than Army Group Center and Army Group North. The southern group had completed the retreat from Rostov and taken up a defensible front on the Mius and Donets Rivers. When the attack phase became defense, Hitler left Army Group South with two missions: to occupy the whole Donets Basin and retake Rostov, and to capture Sevastopol.

General von Manstein's Eleventh Army was given the task of taking Sevastopol. He had nearly taken it in the fall, but was prevented by General Petrov, commander of the Russian Maritime Army. General von Manstein had a new plan of attack, one that was supposed to go into effect in the last days of November. But this timetable was prevented by the rains. When the weather improved in the second week of December, von Manstein decided to launch the attack. The Eleventh Army's seven divisions, all at least 25 percent under strength, could not guard the coast adequately and attack at the same time. This was the rub.

The assault began on the morning of December 17, along the twenty-seven-mile front of the outer perimeter, the first defense line. Inside lay the main line, the rear line, and the thickets of forts, pillboxes, and antitank obstacles. The Russians, through their partisans and agents in the mountains, knew how short von Manstein was on strength and supply, but he gambled on the surprise factor and very nearly brought it off.

General Oktyabriskiy, commander of the defense, was in Novorossisk, planning the landings on the Kerch Peninsula when the attack began. On the first day the Germans pushed through the outer perimeter, and in the next two days reached the main line. But Stalin put the fortress under the Transcaucasus Front and sent in reserves and several warships of the Black Sea Fleet; the line held at the rear line.

The Russian Kerch landings were scheduled for December 21 but were delayed because of the crisis at Sevastopol. The Germans knew they were coming, but there were far more potential landing sites than the Eleventh Army could cover. The landings began in a gale before first light of December 26. The Russians had no landing craft so the troops had to wade ashore from the ships' boats, meaning that they had no vehicles or artillery upon landing. Instead of requiring one or two days, the landings took five days—even then the 20,000 troops lost many of their heavy weapons.

The German Forty-Sixth Division began methodically wiping out these bridge heads, but the Russians brought in more troops and

Three Russian Defeats

The three defeats at Kerch, Sevastopol, and Kharkov brought bad news and concern to the Russians. Two of them were unavoidable, and the third was a consequence of the Kerch tangle. Kerch itself was a consequence of bad planning and worse implementation. As the official history of the war put it, "Our forces proved themselves incapable of holding the Turkish Wall, and retreated to Kerch. The local command had shown itself incapable of using air force effectively, and our troops retreated under constant German air attack. By the 14th the Germans broke into the southern and western outskirts of Kerch and between the 15th and 20th our rearguard units fought desperately to enable our main force to cross the Kerch straits to Taman Peninsula on the Caucasus side of the five-mile-wide strait. Even so it proved to be impossible to carry out the evacuation in an organized manner. The enemy captured practically all of our equipment which was then used against the defenders at Sevastopol."

The defeat was attributed to Lieutenant General Kozlov, commander of the Kerch Army Group and his top commissar, Mekhlis. They and numerous subordinates were demoted, and Mekhlis was relieved of two high posts, vice commissar of defense and one of the chiefs of the political administration of the Red Army. He was accused of wasting hours arguing about the situation at Kerch instead of acting. Mekhlis was one of the villains of the 1937 purge of the Red Army. He had brought upon himself the hatred of many young generals. The Kerch disaster paved the way for an even greater one: the fall of Savastopol. This was a noble disaster, not a shameful one as was Kerch.

Kharkov was to become the subject of Nikita Khrushchev's indictment of Stalin after the dictator's death.

Stalin, the revised history of the Great Patriotic War reports, made many errors in planning the spring operations of the Red Army. The first error was to prepare for the German onslaught in the wrong place. Because of the concentration of German forces in the Moscow area, he expected the attack to be repeated on the capital city; so he strengthened the Bryansk Front, instead of strengthening defenses in the south and southeast.

Second, Stalin overrated Russian strength and underrated the Germans. In assessing the battles of the winter, he had not taken notice of the fact that the Germans had recovered much of their strength.

The Russian rout at Kharkov in May 1942 was concealed from the public. The fact was that Stalin played a leading role in conceiving and persisting in this disastrous operation. The revised *History* says so flatly; the operation continued at the demand of Stalin, while Khrushchev protested that these troops were walking into a trap. The tank reserves came too late to do any good. Finally, a large number of Soviet troops were encircled and in the attempts to break out, many brave men, including at least three general officers, were killed.

The offensive against Kharkov, which had begun so successfully, ending in the rout of three armies of the Southwestern and Southern Fronts. The only indication of the extent of the Kharkov disaster was the strange communiqué noted by the passengers on Alexander Werth's train from Murmansk: 5,000 killed but 70,000 missing.

three destroyers and two cruisers. The Germans brought in artillery and scored a hit on the cruiser *Krazniy Kavkaz*. The Forty-Sixth German Division and the Russians slugged it out on the Kerch Peninsula without definitive result.

That winter, with the German offensive stopped and the Russians unable to mount a sustained offensive, it was time for decisions. Hitler planned to resume the offensive in 1942. The intent was to destroy the Russian defensive strength and to deprive Russia of the resources necessary to carry on the war. The main effort would be in the south, where the Germans would take possession of the Caucasus. They would also press for the capture of Leningrad.

The further objective of the summer campaign would be to encircle and destroy the Russian armies in a series of small tight encirclements. Hitler knew that the German forces were in bad shape after the failure of Operation Barbarossa, but he and his generals thought the Russians were worse off. The Russians had lost nearly 10 million men killed and captured between June 1941 and April 1942. This meant they had only a manpower reservoir of 9 million men and could no longer withstand losses of the sort they took in the battles from Bialystok to Bryansk. The Russians, in Hitler's opinion, could not throw reserves in the way they did in the winter of 1941–42. Hitler no longer had any design on Moscow. He would go into the Caucasus and strike the Soviet Union at its most vulnerable point.

The Russians had suffered enormously in the first five months of the war. Their losses in men were matched by the economic damage. But, on the other hand, Stalin had converted the Russian economy to total war. War production had risen from 36 percent of the total in 1940 to 57 percent of all industry in the first half of 1942. Output of combat aircraft exceeded the German output 8,300 to 7,200. Russian tanks were built four times more rapidly than German tanks, and their output of T-34s was growing steadily.

In an order of February 23, 1942, Stalin definitely planned a new offensive. The Russians were inferior in terms of number of men under arms, with 5.5 million men in first line units, compared to the 6.2 million Germans and Axis troops. The most urgent task of the Russian government was to persuade the Western Allies to open a second front in 1942. President Roosevelt promised, but Prime Minister Churchill was noncommittal. The North African campaign was not regarded by the Russians as sufficient and the suspicion was very deep (particularly in Stalin's mind) that the Western powers were holding back deliberately, hoping that the Germans and Russians would exhaust themselves against each other.

The Russian offensives that spring failed one by one and it became apparent that the Germans would mount a new offensive. Stalin, precipitate as always, planned an "active defense" whose aim was to forestall the German initiative.

"Are we supposed to sit in defense, idling away our time, and wait for the Germans to attack first?" he asked. "We must strike several preemptive blows over a wide front and probe the enemy's readiness," he told Marshal Shaposhnikov and General Zhukov. This comment was followed by orders to prepare and carry out offensives in the vicinity of Kharkov, in the Crimea, and in other areas.

In the following weeks, Stalin ordered offensives along the whole front from the Barents Sea to the Black Sea. On the Crimea they were to clear the peninsula of all Germans. The Southwest Front was to strike toward Kharkov from the northeast and southwest. The Bryansk Front was to advance past Kursk. The West and Kalinin Fronts were to smash Army Group Center's Rzhev-Vyazma line. The Northwest Front would eliminate the Demyansk pocket, and the Karelian Front would attack west of Kandalaksha, while the Leningrad Front would break the Leningrad siege. Meanwhile, it was expected, the Soviet forces would be reorganizing and reequipping. The Russians would attack and defend simultaneously. That was Stalin's pipe dream. Like most pipe dreams, it became a cropper.

German Army Group Center stabilized its line along a ragged 900-mile perimeter between Velikiye Luki on the north and Orel in the south. At Agzhatsk the group's Fourth Panzer Army was within ninety miles of Moscow.

Liquidation of the Demyansk pocket was a logical objective. In April, Stalin gave the Northwest Front five rifle divisions, along with eight rifle and two tank brigades. General Kurochkin began attacks on May 3 and continued until late June, striking repeatedly in the same places. The Demyansk pocket remained.

This failure for the Russians was overshadowed by the disaster at the Volkhov pocket. That struggle ended on June 23 with the surrender of 33,000 prisoners, including General Andrei Vlasov, commander of the Russian Twentieth Army, who ultimately became commander of the German-sponsored Army of Liberation.

Early in March, Stalin asked for plans for a Southwestern theater offensive for the spring and on the night of March 30 he accepted a plan to drive against Kharkov. Marshal Timoshenko took command on April 8, a plan that envisaged the entrapment of most of the German Sixth Army. On the morning of May 12, the Russians again

---

The Anglo-Soviet Alliance

One of the bright spots in an otherwise dismal spring of 1942 was the Anglo-Soviet Alliance, signed in May. It was the result of a trip to Moscow in December 1941 by Foreign Minister Anthony Eden and delicate negotiations that skirted around the Atlantic charter's edges. Prime Minister Churchill took the view that Russia was an "expendable ally" (which Stalin knew very well), and Stalin in 1941 was pressing for a second front (which Churchill knew very well and resisted.) But Roosevelt and General Marshall were more positive about it. Also the United States signed a new Lend-Lease Agreement that promised Russia more aid.

The second front that Stalin wanted did not materialize that year. Quite frankly, the Americans were not prepared for it. But they did send troops to Africa and their efforts tied up a few divisions that otherwise could have supported the German efforts on the Eastern Front.

---

went on the offensive. That morning the German Sixth Army was hit by twelve rifle divisions and 300 tanks. Before noon they had cracked the German lines; by evening Russian troops were eleven miles from Kharkov. On May 14, Timoshenko still had tanks enough for the second stage, but he failed to send them in until May 17 and the initiative passed to the Germans.

The Germans had massed every aircraft the Luftwaffe could put together for their counteroffensive, named Fridericus. The Russian tanks drove five miles deep into the German line south of Kharkov, but the German Fourth Air Corps completely surprised the Russians with the fierce air attack of May 17. The Third Panzer Corps drove seventeen miles, two-thirds of the distance to Izyum.

At this point, the Russian General Staff wanted to call off the offensive, but Stalin was persuaded to continue. "Let everything remain as it is," he ordered. He then would not answer the telephone, so the disaster fell.

At the end of May 19, the German Sixth Army reported that, "The enemy's offensive strength has cracked, and the breakthrough to Kharkov is therefore prevented."

On the west and south, the Russian Fronts collapsed, sealing off the Izyum Bulge. Attempts to break out were made by the Russians on May 25 and 26, but these attempts failed. On May 28, the Germans found they had captured 240,000 prisoners, 1,200 tanks, and 2,600 artillery pieces.

Stalin said of the disaster, "Battles must be won not with numbers but by skill. If you do not learn to direct your troops better, all the armaments the country can produce will not be enough for you."

This from the man who was noted for his insensitivity to losses and his stubborn refusal to take advice.

✳ ✳ ✳

It was not until late June that the Russian high command decided on a strategic defense. Anticipating that the German attack would again be aimed at Moscow, the Russians wasted time and effort moving troops to the wrong places. Instead of concentrating forces on the South and Southwest Fronts, Stalin was responsible for most of this "geeing and hawing," particularly because he insisted on fortifying the central sector.

Early in April, Hitler designated Sevastopol and the Kerch Peninsula as targets for preliminary operations before the main summer campaign. By May 26, the final reports for the German victory in the battle of Kharkov were in and he wanted to strike fast, while the Russians were still in shock. The Germans would trap the Russian Twenty-Eighth Army and prepare cover on the south for the Sixth Army's main thrust, called Blau I.

On the Russian side, Marshal Timoshenko, commander of the Southwestern Front, and Commissar Nikita Khrushchev both expected trouble, but they still thought the major effort would be against Moscow.

By the end of June, the Russian situation everywhere on the Eastern Front had grown worse. Spring operations had failed and the

Morale

In the spring of 1942, writer Alexander Werth returned to Russia as a passenger on a liberty ship in Convoy PQ 16. He came as a correspondent for the *Sunday Times*. He spoke Russian so was in an unique position to observe the people around him on a week journey by rail from Murmansk to Moscow in a third-class hard sleeper. Werth found morale surprisingly good, allowing for the facts of the hard war, hunger, deprivation, and tragedy in nearly every family. He was impressed by a ten-year-old girl named Tamara who marched up and down his carriage singing a song she had learned at school.

Hitler is cursing his luck,
He can't take Leningrad,
He can't take Moscow.
He can see the Nevsky and the gardens but he's stuck.
Then the thief tried Moscow, but again he got thrown back.
All his efforts are in vain;
He's stuck, he is stuck again.

Enormous areas of the USSR were still occupied by Germans, but the fact they had failed to capture either Leningrad or Moscow was very cheering. The people on Werth's train seemed to have recovered self-confidence, although the degree depended on how well-fed they were. The old ladies in their black gowns were the most lugubrious, worrying still about the coming of the Nazis. The railwaymen, who had undergone a difficult winter with almost daily bombings, were still grim. All the Murmansk-Moscow railway stations had been destroyed, and rolling stock and rusting locomotives littered the rail yards. Morale among the officers and soldiers was considerably better. Some of them spoke admiringly of the British Hurricane fighter pilots that were operating out of Murmansk. Others spoke lovingly of the *katyusha* rockets, which had taken so high a toll on the enemy.

In that part of Russia, Leningrad was almost an obsession. The people on the train all knew of the starvation in that city. One thing that impressed Werth was that in the week he had spent on this train, no one mentioned the name Stalin. Werth wondered at the time whether it was because they took his name for granted or there had begun to be some doubts about the quality of his leadership. Later he discovered that the people had indeed had doubts—these doubts were beginning to resolve themselves with his masterly performance of staying put in the Kremlin when others fled.

It was not until he reached Moscow that Werth saw any evidence of Stalin worship. Stalin *was* Moscow. Stalin was given credit for saving the city, his bumbling forgotten in the euphoria of salvation.

Moscow had a lean, hungry look about it. Rationing was severe and no one seemed to have quite enough to eat. Compared to the starving in Leningrad, however, they were well off. What the Germans had not appropriated from the countryside had been taken by the military and consumer goods were almost unobtainable except on the black market. A heavy worker like a railwayman got 1 1/2 pounds of bread per day, 4 ounces of cereal, 3 1/2 ounces of meat, 3/4 ounce of fat, 3/4 ounce of sugar, 1/2 ounce of tobacco, 1 ounce of tea per month, 2 1/2 ounces of fish per day. Moscow itself was empty, nearly half its citizens absent. Many of its workers were still in the east, where their ministries had moved in fear that Moscow was lost. There had been considerable bombing—the Bolshi Theater, for example, had taken a 1,000-pound hit and was not operating, but other theaters were and tickets were surprisingly easy to obtain.

"The great skedaddle" of October was a source of much emotion, shame by those who had run, and pride by those who had stuck it out and liked now to remind others of it. The Germans were still too close for comfort, at Gzhatsk, Viazma, and Rzher, and that spring of 1942 there were serious rumors: something had gone wrong at Kharkov. The Germans were reported to be preparing a new offensive in the south.

Stavka, Stalin concurring, had resumed the strategic defensive. But, of course, with their eyes fixed on Moscow, the Russians made their buildup in the wrong places.

On April 29, Field Marshal von Bock wrote in his diary that the first draft of the directive for the German summer offensive had been put together. The first phase was to begin on June 15. Army Group South expected to complete the first phase during the second week of July. Then Blau II would begin with the First Panzer Army striking east of Kharkov along the north side of the Donets and the Fourth Panzer Army south along the Don River. They would meet midway between, at Millerovo. Blau II would be completed in the second week of August, with its center about 180 miles west of Stalingrad. Army Group A would take control of the First and Fourth Panzer Armies. It would use the Eleventh and Seventeenth Armies to take Rostov and occupy the eastern Donets basin and develop the thrust toward Stalingrad.

When Blau III was completed, Army Group South, which by that time would be known as Army Group B, would dig in with Sixth Army on a front from the Army Group Center Boundary to Voronezh to Stalingrad. Army Group A would head south across the Lower Don to the Caucasus. The German troops thus involved numbered close to a million men with another 300,000 Axis soldiers. The Panzer VI tanks with their 88-mm guns were supposed to be ready but they were not, although the output of 75-mm antitank guns had turned out to be unexpectedly high.

In the first week of May, General Greiffenberg, who would be Marshal List's chief of staff, began assembling the Army Group A staff in Zeppelin, the OKH compound at Zossen, which was south of Berlin. Two weeks later he began to move to Stalino, which would be the Army Group A Headquarters. Until it took command of the front, the staff would go under the name Coastal Staff Azov; there would be no new unit symbols or other identifying markings. Other staffs coming in were also assigned cover names. The Fourth Panzer Army became Superior Special Purpose Staff Eight.

Between March and late June, arrivals from the west brought Army Group South strength to sixty-five divisions—forty-five infantry, five light infantry, four motorized infantry and eleven Panzer. Twenty-five Axis divisions brought the total to ninety. The German troops now numbered close to a million men and the Axis added another 300,000. The German tanks carried the 50- and 75-mm guns that were capable of knocking out T-34 tanks.

The major Russian commands in the Blau area were General Golikov's Bryansk Front, Marshal Timoshenko's Southwest Front, General Malinovsky's South Front, and Marshal Budenny's North Caucasus Front. The four fronts had a total of seventeen field armies. Each had an air army and the Bryansk Front had a tank army.

The Bryansk Front was now under Stavka control. The Germans estimated that they would have to contend with ninety-one Russian rifle divisions with thirty-two rifle brigades, twenty cavalry divisions, and forty-four tank brigades.

In Stalin's view—which was also the view of the Stavka and the General Staff—the Bryansk Front was the most critical. The Russians considered two possible German lines of attack—one from Orel toward Tula and the other from a point northeast of Kursk toward Voronezh. The Tula drive was considered to be the most likely.

The Germans were well aware that their readiness for battle that summer did not compare with their readiness for Operation Barbarossa in 1941. Many of their troops, particularly the eighteen- and nineteen-year olds, had only eight weeks of training under their belts. General Panzertruppen Frederick Paulus, commander of the Sixth Army, wrote a chiding letter to his corps commanders, "The personnel and material deficiencies afflicting the divisions are well known to the higher leadership. Nevertheless, the higher leadership is determined to carry out its intentions in the eastern theater of war to the full. Therefore, it is up to us to get the most out of the troops in their present condition."

The role of Army Group Center in Operation Blau was most important. With the failure of the Russian offensive at Karkhov, the strategic initiative had passed to the Germans. But it was essential

A. M. Vasilievsky

A. M. Vasilievsky was the son of a priest and attended a theological seminary. During World War I, he was an officer in the Czarist Army. When the war ended, he became a battalion commander with the rank of captain. In 1919, he entered the Red Army. He fought in the civil war as a deputy regimental commander. He then attended the divisional school and became a regimental commander in 1921, a post he held until 1930.

In 1931 Vasilievsky went to the General Staff in Moscow as section chief in the department of combat training. In 1931, he became a Communist Party member. He was chief of combat training in the Volga Military District in 1934–36. From 1936 to 1938 he attended the academy of the General Staff. After graduation he was appointed to work in the General Staff. In 1940, he was promoted to deputy chief of operations and from August 1941 he was chief of operations. Concurrently, he was made deputy chief of the General Staff.

In June 1942, he replaced Marshal Shaposhnikov as chief of the General Staff. In this position, almost until the end of the war, he divided his time between work in Moscow and lengthy field trips on which he supervised preparation and execution of major operations and coordinated large formations. Of thirty-four war months in the post of chief of the General Staff, twenty-two were spent at the front. In February 1945, he replaced General Cherniakhovskii as commander of the Third Belorussian Army Group, leading the assault on East Prussia. In the August campaign against the Japanese he led the Soviet Far East Armies in Manchuria and Korea. In 1946, Vasilievsky again assumed the post of chief of the General Staff and simultaneously first deputy minister of the armed forces. From 1953 until 1957 he was first deputy minister of defense. Vasilievsky retired from active service in December 1957.

that secrecy be maintained and the true situation not be revealed to the Russians. With that objective in mind, all new headquarters were established well away from the front line, disguised as elements of permanent rear echelons. It was hoped that Russian attention would be diverted from the southern flank. This mission was given to Army Group Center. Because of its proximity to Moscow it was high in potential for attracting Russian attention.

On May 29, Army Group Center Headquarters issued a top-secret directive.

"OKH has ordered the earliest possible resumption of the attack on Moscow. Under the code name Kreml (Kremlin)." All subsequent correspondence regarding the operation was to be handled under the Operation Kreml name.

Operation Kreml was strictly a paper operation—a deception—but it had the substance to make it a masterpiece. Coinciding with Russian thinking, its premise was solid: to simulate a repeat of the 1941 drive on Moscow. The front was close to where it had been in November 1941, and Second and Third Panzer Armies were in relatively the same positions north and south of Moscow as they had been when the advance stopped.

In the first week of June, sealed Moscow area maps were distributed down to the regimental level with orders that they were not to be opened until June 10. At the higher headquarters they began to hold planning conferences, with a target date of August 1. Security was tight, only the chiefs of staff and branch chiefs knew they were working on a deception. Air force flights were increased over and around Moscow, and prisoners of war were asked questions about Moscow's defenses. But despite all German precautions for Operation Kreml, Russian counterintelligence got wind of it, and it failed. The Russians were not fooled.

Operation Blau was possibly compromised on June 20 when a light plane carrying Major Joachim Reichel, a staff officer with the attack

The Russian Soldier

They say that everyone who has seen action has a battle that was especially memorable. When the battle I want to tell you about was being planned, a hundred versions were contemplated. But, as happens too often during war, it was played out according to the 101st version, which no one had foreseen.

When we received orders in the evening that the attack was to be launched under cover of darkness, I realized it was to be a New Year surprise for the fascists—a surprise attack to get the enemy out of their well-appointed dugouts and trenches so that they would have a chance to see what the Russian frosts were like in the open fields.

Well, we got them out of the first line of defenses, but they laid on such a wall of machine gun and artillery fire before the second line that we had to hug the earth.

I glanced at my watch, it was 11:20 PM. I wondered if I would live to see 1943. I was clinging to the side of a freshly made shell hole, which was slowly filling with water. It was a swampy area. When the hole finally filled up I'd have to get out and face those bullets. The icy water was not for me.

Half an hour until the new year, somewhere people were celebrating, exchanging good wishes. I had no one beside me to whom I could wish a happy New Year. I remembered the tradition that a wish offered on New Year's Eve was sure to come true.

I hope I stay alive, I thought, but realized at the same moment everyone on both sides was making that same wish. So that was a lot of nonsense. I should wish for something more realistic . . . that we should take the second line of defenses? But we'd do that anyway, if not today . . . then tomorrow. So what then could I wish for? College? To see my wedding day? Whatever I thought hinged on victory. Then only could it become a reality.

Suppose we do win, I kept on thinking, what would I like to start my postwar life with? My dream was to return to my hometown, Tashkent, where Mother and Father and She were waiting. And after the first hectic moments of greeting I wanted to be left alone, to walk in the evening down Pushkin Street, alone under the street lamps, and I wanted the pavements to be crowded with girls in light summer frocks and boys in well-pressed trousers.

A mortar bomb landed nearby, showering me with earth and splinters. Involuntarily I pulled in my head and looked down. At that moment I discovered another world at the bottom of the shell hole. The circle of water was a transparent lens, in it I saw what I had been dreaming of—a peaceful fathomless sky, a moon, stars, and gossamer clouds. Then I saw a dark spectre staring out at me. Although I realized it was my own face, I was terrified. Was the apparition an omen that I was about to die?

I moved warily to take a closer look. To see if the face in the water were dead or alive. In that instant, I felt my hair standing on end and the blood in my veins turning to ice, for in the water I saw reflected a German helmet. He was peering into the shell hole and took me for a corpse because I was lying head down. I shot first, and didn't miss. I leaped out of the shell hole to see if any more were coming. After firing a few rounds I was forced back into the shell hole by the heavy fire. I looked at my watch. We were five minutes into the New Year. My fortune-telling had come true. In another second I would have been a corpse.

My fear turned to exhilaration. Not a bad New Year's present: to be alive. I looked at the body of my enemy. He must have been someone before I killed him. Was he wishing a few minutes ago that he would stay alive to return to his Gretchen? One thing was certain he had not been thinking of death.

And that was his mistake. Anyone who steps on our soil should think of death.

plans, landed on the Russian side of no-man's land. The staff officer's body and that of the pilot were found two days later, but with no plans. Field Marshal von Bock decided that they would move according to schedule and, after some hesitation, Hitler agreed. Blau was put on alert and on June 28 it finally kicked off.

By that time, General Golikov and Marshal Timoshenko believed that they were ready. Timoshenko had the German staff officer's papers. But when Stalin had that information, it aroused his conspiratorial nature and he ordered it to be kept secret, even though the Germans were already moving.

On June 26, Golikov was summoned to Moscow, where Stalin told him he did not believe the Blau plan was plausible and that it was a trumped-up bit of work by German Intelligence. It was necessary, Stalin said, to beat the Germans to the punch, and he ordered Golikov to be ready to attack toward Orel by July 5.

At daylight on June 28, the German barrage began. The Russian answer was slow and ragged. After half an hour the German guns paused and the tanks began to move.

The morning was cloudy and warm, promising rain. Most other action was not visible to German observers on a hill nearby. The spearhead, the Fourth Panzer Army, had reached the Tim River by noon, where it captured an undamaged railroad bridge. That afternoon it moved another ten miles to the Kshen River. There, they were on the land bridge to Voronezh, where Russian resistance was spotty. Before dark, the vanguard of the Fourth Panzer Army, the Forty-Eighth Panzer Corps, had moved another ten miles through heavy rain. By then the Twenty-Fourth Panzer Corps had reached the Kshen River. Paulus' Sixth Army was still not moving.

The rain lasted until 12:00 the next day. The Sixth Army then surveyed its situation and found all the roads for the various corps were passable. Field Marshal von Bock ordered the Sixth Army to start moving the next morning.

On June 30, Sixth Army made a breakthrough to the Korocha River, moving twenty miles. A blunt German wedge was driven into Golikov's line. He conferred with Stalin that day and was warned that he had more than 1,000 tanks to the enemy's 500. "Everything now depends on your ability to lead these forces," Stalin said.

On the morning of July 1, von Bock conferred with General Hoth of the Fourth Panzer Army. They agreed that the army would have to head straight for Voronezh, without looking to the right or left. By late afternoon, the Sixth Army had smashed the whole right half of the Southwest Front west of the Oskol River and had a bridgehead across that river.

On July 2, the road to Voronezh was open to the Germans. Golikov went to the front to take personal command of the Russian Sixth, Fortieth, and Sixtieth Armies. He would not have much time, Army Chief of Staff Vasilievsky said, because conditions had deteriorated drastically in the Voronezh area.

At 7:00 on the morning of July 3, Hitler's Condor transport plane landed at Poltava, carrying Hitler, Field Marshal Keitel, General Halder, and others of Hitler's retinue. There seemed to be no reason for the trip, except that Hitler was annoyed with Marshal von Bock. If so, at the last minute he lost his nerve, and to von Bock he seemed to be in high good humor, joking with his generals and laughing. At 9:00 he boarded the plane again and by noon was back at *Wolfsschanze*.

It was a good day for the Germans. The Sixth Army was pursuing an enemy who was not even making a pretense of hard resistance. At the end of the day, von Bock sent a message to Paulus and Weichs that read, "The enemy opposite Sixth Army and Fourth Panzer Army is defeated."

On the ninth day, July 5, the offensive was rolling. The Forty-Eighth Panzer Corps had three bridgeheads across the Don River, one reaching to within two miles of Voronezh. Von Bock was jubilant and it showed in his dispatches. "At no point thus far in the campaign in the east have such strong evidences of disintegration been observed on the enemy side."

But, that night, a different picture was painted by the OKH liaison officer with the Fourth Panzer Army. He radioed OKH that "the *coup de main* at Voronezh has failed; Twenty-Fourth Panzer Division opposed by strong enemy south of the city; *Grossdeutschland* also opposed in its bridgehead. Concerted attack being planned for tomorrow."

At Fuehrer Headquarters the liaison officer's message raised visions of streetfighting and a hard battle for the city. Von Bock and Hoth were instructed to leave Voronezh to less valuable divisions than the panzers.

The next day brought a superficially glorious conclusion to the assault on Voronezh. The city was taken by the Germans without a shot being fired. Late in the day, in an acrimonious conversation, von Bock asked for permission to occupy the city, which was granted.

While the Germans were finding their success a little awkward, the Russians were in deep trouble. The Bryansk Front had gathered 600 tanks, but Golikov's departure to Voronezh and a drop in confidence in him caused the Stavka to begin issuing orders directly to the Fifth Tank Army. So the days between July 4 and July 6 were days of crisis in the Russian high command. Stalin saw himself and the Stavka as having to deal personally with dangerous tactical problems confirming their previous estimates that the drive on Moscow again had now begun.

Thus, Operation Kreml had really succeeded in its diversionary aim.

General Zhukov hurled three armies against the Second Panzer Army, which was shaken but managed to stop the attack. In the south the situation was so confused that Stalin ordered a strategic retreat for the first time in the war. South and Southwest Fronts were to retreat to the Don River, sixty miles away, and dig in there.

On July 7, Golikov's three armies became the Voronezh Front while General Rokossovsky was appointed to command the Bryansk Front. Zhukov's Orel offensive ran for five days and then stopped. But Operation Blau was dead in the water because the Russians had outguessed the Germans and switched over to a flexible defense. Von Bock was fired as commander of Army Group B as Hitler got rid of a rival who might receive the credit for victory. Von Bock went home to Germany, where he spent the rest of the war on his estates, never to be employed again.

Stalingrad

THE APPEARANCE OF THE GERMANS ON THE CHIR
River on July 17, 1942, signaled the beginning of the battle for
Stalingrad. A German encirclement was formed on the lower Don,
but an eighty-mile stretch of the river was still open. To reach the
crossings the Russians had shorter distances to travel than the
Germans. Hitler was determined not to let the quarry escape.
Disregarding General Halder's protest that it would only pile up the
armor again as at Voronezh, Hitler sent all of List's armies to Rostov
by the shortest routes.

Hitler also expanded the mission of the German Sixth Army.
General Paulus now was to occupy the whole northeastern quarter
of the Don River bend and, by gaining ground in the direction of
Stalingrad, to build a defense west of the Volga River.

Even while the orders were being written at the new Werwolf
Headquarters in Vinnitsa, a continuous heavy downpour had begun in
the bend of the Don. The rain came down in buckets for the next night
and day. No vehicles moved. The Panzer divisions were paralyzed.

Stalin's Associates

The older ones, like Molotov and Voroshilov, had been with Stalin since his rise to power. They were his creatures and they had no higher aspirations. Their loyalty was absolute, although it was mixed with a good deal of fear. They had no dignity or self-respect. If Stalin kicked them, they would lick his boots.

The attitude of the younger ones was more complicated. Either, like Khrushchev and Voznesensky, they did have ideas of their own. Or, like Beria, they were cynics who, like Stalin, believed only in power. Among Stalin's close associates there were scoundrels, like Zhdanov and Kaganovich, and more able ones, like Kalinin and Mikoyan, who in other surroundings might have been perfectly decent public officials. Kalinin wept when he signed many orders for arrest, but he signed them nonetheless. Mikoyan is known to have protected a few people, but he was head of the Politburo subcommittee that signed the order for Bukharin and Rykov (and many others) to be arrested, tried, and shot. He knew that they were innocent. He could have opted out of giving orders to kill. But the price was too high for him; he preferred his own survival to the survival of others.

Most of Stalin's associates were quite blameless in their private lives. They had no vices and loved their wives and children. They lived well, not extravagantly like Goering, and the others did not keep expensive cars, except Brezhnev. Molotov was a model citizen in private life, but so was Himmler.

Stalin's men worked very hard, but with exceptions of a few like Zhdanov and Sherbakov, who died relatively young, and those who were shot, they were distinguished by longevity. In their nineties Molotov and Kaganovich could be seen walking in the streets. Budenny died in his ninetieth year and Voroshilov was only a few months younger. Mikoyan, Bulganin, Malenkov, and Suslov all died in their eighties; Krushchev and Poskrebyshev in their seventies.

The wages of sin were not death, but a long life as an old age pensioner.

Hitler's mood matched the weather. He snapped at Halder, keeping the officer on the phone to express Der Fuehrer's impatience. Two days earlier Hitler had coldly ignored Halder's advice to hedge on the Rostov encirclement—to send four other divisions to cross the Donets as fast as possible, then strike east and cut the Salsk-Stalingrad railroad, positioning themselves to move either southwest or west. The Sixth Army was ordered "to take possession of Stalingrad by a daring high-speed assault." The stage was set on the twentieth for the last act in the battle of Rostov, but when the Germans arrived the Russians were gone, having pulled out during the night. The Rostov pocket was empty. The First Panzer Army's entire take of prisoners on the 200-mile journey was 83,000, not enough to have cut decisively into the Russian manpower supply. Halder's warning of a traffic jam at Rostov was fulfilled. On July 25, twenty divisions were standing within a fifty-mile radius of Rostov—all stuck tight. The Germans were also beginning to feel the effects of trying to operate simultaneously in two directions.

That day General Paulus submitted his plan to capture Stalingrad. He proposed to sweep to the Don on both sides of Kalach, then drive a wedge of armor flanked by infantry across the remaining thirty miles. At the Fuehrer's situation conference that day, General Jodl predicted that the future of the Caucasus Operations lay in Stalingrad.

East of the Don almost the entire able-bodied population of Stalingrad was at work building four concentric defense lines around the city.

On July 25, the battle for the Don was joined almost everywhere downstream from Serafimovich. So confident was Hitler of success that the Grossdeutschland Division was to be detached and shipped to the Western theater, while five of Eleventh Army's seven divisions were shifted north for attack on Leningrad.

Hitler then split his forces, sending them off at right angles to each other, so that they would have to operate separately, each having to be sustained independently.

The Sixth Army was the first to feel the pinch. Short on fuel and ammunition it had to pull back on July 26. By July 28 the Twenty-Fourth Panzer Corps was down to a hundred rounds of artillery ammunition per battery and half a load of ammunition per tank. Army Group A was no better supplied.

But the Russian forces were in worse shape. They did not have a front anywhere south of the Don bend. By the end of the July 28, there were huge gaps between the armies and the strategic retreat was in danger of becoming a rout. That day Stalin signed his famous Order No. 227.

"Not a step back! Every commander, soldier, and political worker must understand that our resources are not unlimited. After losing the Ukraine, Belorussia, the Baltic, the Don Basin, and other areas we now have a much smaller area, fewer people and factories, and less grain and metal. We have lost more than 70 million people, over 14 million tons of grain per year, and more than 10 million tons of metals per year. We no longer have superiority over the Germans either in manpower reserves or in grain stocks. To retreat further is to cast oneself and the homeland into ruin. Every clod of earth we give up strengthens the enemy and weakens our defenses and our nation. Not a step back! Such must be our highest purpose now."

Not all the terms of the order were revealed to the Russian people, then or later. But the Germans got hold of a copy. From the German records came, "The people of the Nation, who have looked upon the Red Army with love and respect, are disillusioned. They are losing faith in you. Many of them curse the Red Army because it is abandoning our people to the yoke of the German oppressors and is itself fleeing to the east."

Stalin then listed the punishments. In each front area one to three punishment battalions of 500 men would be created. Into them would go the soldiers, including senior commanders and political officers, who had shown cowardice or failure. They would be committed in especially dangerous situations so that they might expiate their crimes against the homeland with their blood. In each army area, special blocking detachments would be stationed directly behind unreliable divisions. It would be their duty to shoot spreaders of panic or cowards on the spot.

In its general outline that summer, Hitler's political and military strategy called for the defeat of Soviet forces in the south, the conquest of the Caucasus and advance to the Volga River, and the seizure of Stalingrad and Astrakhan, setting the stage for the political destruction of the USSR.

The Germans still maintained a superiority over the Russian armed forces in manpower and material, but they had to take into account that this year they were no longer capable of launching three offensives simultaneously, as they had done in Operation Barbarossa. The plan this year was to take the south, then launch drives against Leningrad and Moscow.

It was plain that Stalin did not believe the assurances of Churchill and Roosevelt that a second front would be opened in Europe. He trusted Roosevelt more than Churchill, whom he knew to be anti-Russian to the core.

In assessing the military situation, Stalin proposed to conduct a number of separate offensive operations, a point on which Marshal Zhukov disagreed. He proposed to conduct one offensive on the Rhzev-Vyazma salient, a thrust that would weaken the Germans west of Moscow and cause them to abandon offensive operations there.

At the end of March, Stalin called a conference, heard Zhukov out, then ordered offensives in the Crimea and at Kharkov. The results could have been predicted by any responsible general—the Crimea offensive failed and the result was heavy losses. The Russians went on the defensive, but the Germans broke through on May 8 when General Kozlov had to abandon Kerch. Having seized Kerch, the Germans now concentrated their attack against Sevastopol. On July 4, after fierce fighting, which ended the nine-month siege, the Germans captured the fortress, freeing up an army for use elsewhere.

On May 3, the Russians launched an offensive at Demyansk, but it failed after a month. Zhukov spoke to Stalin on the telephone

The Missing Generals

One of Stalin's special interests in the war was to track the fate of his missing generals. He didn't believe in surrender; anyone who surrendered must have the makings of a traitor in him, Stalin said. In the first months of the war he issued special instructions to find Kachelov, Ponedelin, Vlasov, Potopov, and Rakutin. The first two were easy enough. Lietenant General Kachalov had been commander of the Twenty-Eighth Army. Beria's security agents reported that he had surrendered voluntarily to the Germans and was working for them. The same report was made on major General P. G. Ponedelin, commander of the Twelfth Army. Stalin ordered them to be tried in absentia. It was done and they were sentenced to be shot, deprived of all their property, and stripped of decorations.

The fact was that Kachalov was killed by a direct hit from a German shell. Still, his relatives had to live with the disgrace until 1956.

The fate of General Ponedelin was even more tragic, a blot on the soviet escutcheon. He was captured, wounded, and unconscious. He spent four years in German prison camps without agreeing to cooperate with the Nazis. On repatriation in 1945, he was arrested, tried again, convicted, and sentenced to five years in Soviet prison camp. He appealed to Stalin, and on August 25, 1950, the sentence was reversed. He was taken out and shot.

When General Yefremov disappeared, Beria was ordered to find him. Quite by accident his body was discovered in 1943 in the village of Slobodka in the district of Temkinsk. A woman reported she had seen some soldiers bury the body of a general. The corpse was dug up, identified, and it was determined that he had shot himself to avoid capture by the Germans.

Potopov's fate was not determined nor was that of Rakutin. But the truth about A. A. Vlasov was discovered. Stalin had promoted him himself to be commander of the Second Assault Army, which was cut off in the early days of the war on the Volkhov Front.

When Stalin investigated, General Vasilievsky told him that the Second Assault Army had become encircled and that General Khozin had not sent reinforcements in time. Stalin ordered Khozin cashiered and General Govorov appointed to command the Leningrad Front. The mystery of the fate of the Second Assault Army remained. The Germans claimed that many were killed and 30,000 captured.

Weeks after the event, Beria showed up in Stalin's office and handed him a file.

"What is this?" Stalin demanded.

"See where the missing commander of the Second Assault Army has turned up," Beria said. Stalin read and learned that General Vlasov was working for the Germans as head of the Russian Committee, which was dedicated to the overthrow of Stalin, signing of a peace with Germany, and creation of a new Russia. In 1943 Vlasov and several of his aides were tried in absentia and sentenced to be shot. The sentences were carried out in August 1946 after Vlasov and the others had been captured by Soviet forces and repatriated.

around that time, and Stalin demanded the severe punishment of Kozlov, Mekhlis, and Kulik for the failures in the south (which were in reality Stalin's failures). He asked Zhukov if he had changed his mind about offensives.

Zhukov said no. He still felt that they should harry the enemy in the south with air strikes and artillery fire, but they should go on the offensive only after the enemy had been worn down. Stalin was not listening. On May 12, the Southwest Command began a new offensive toward Kharkov, but they neglected to consider the possibility of a German thrust in the area of Kramatorsk. The Russian forces at first did very well and advanced thirty miles in three days. But then there they were stopped cold. On May 17, eleven divisions of the German Army Group Kleist began an offensive in the Kramatorsk sector. The enemy broke through the Ninth and Fifty-Seventh Russian Armies, advanced thirty miles in two days, and drove a wedge into the left flank of the Southwest Front at Petroskoye.

In the middle of May, Stalin expressed concern over the threat posed by the German Kramatorsk grouping. Marshal Timoshenko reported that his military council felt the threat was exaggerated and that he was supported by Nikita Khrushchev, the political officer. On the evening of May 18, General Vasilievsky, the acting chief of staff, urged Stalin to stop the Kharkov operation and use those forces to attack the German Kramatorsk grouping.

Stalin rebuffed Vasilievsky in his lordly way. He could be extremely harsh, even with his intimates. That month he fired his son Vasily as commanding officer of an air regiment. Beria had come to him reporting that Vasily's drunkenness was causing trouble. Furious because Vasily's behavior seemed to reflect on the family name, Stalin sat down and dictated a letter to Marshal Novikov, chief of the Air Force.

1. V. I. Stalin is to be removed at once from the post as commander of his air regiment and given no other command post without my orders.
2. Both the regiment and its former commander, Colonel Stalin, are to be told that Colonel Stalin is being removed from his post as regimental commander for drunkenness and debauchery, and because he is ruining and perverting the regiment.
3. You are to inform me that these orders have been carried out.

Then Stalin could turn back to the problems of the war.

On May 19, the Military Council of the Southwestern Command had begun to take steps to rebuff the German attack, but it was too late. By May 22, the Sixth and Fifty-Seventh Armies, parts of the Ninth Army and General Bobkin's group, were completely encircled. Many units broke out but others fought on until the end rather than surrender; several of the most competent generals were killed.

By August 30, the troops of the Southeast Front had been forced back to the inner defense ring. Lt. Gen. A. I. Lopatin, commander of the Sixty-Second Army, preserved that army for a stand within the city. He was later replaced by V. I. Chuikov, whom Zhukov did not like. A raging feud developed between the two.

In those crucial days Stalin ordered diversionary operations west of Moscow to tie down enemy reserves. A Russian offensive on the Western Front, where Zhukov was in command, made a successful offensive in August to drive the enemy from the Sychevka-Rzhev area. This offensive was halted after it broke through German defenses and reached the Rzhev-Myazma railroad, but the town of Rzhev was still controlled by the Germans. The German command used divisions that were intended for the Stalingrad campaign and the Caucasus.

Zhukov said that if he had only had one or two more armies at his disposal, he could have defeated the Germans in the Rzhev-Vyazma salient. But his forces were limited.

On August 27, Zhukov had a telephone call from Stalin, summoning him to the Kremlin. "You'd better put the chief of staff in charge," the dictator said. "Give some thought to whom should be appointed commander in chief in your place." Thus, and only thus, Zhukov learned he was scheduled for a new, more important assignment. Stalin was very careful on the telephone and never revealed any more information than was essential to the business at hand. He was supremely aware of eavesdroppers.

Zhukov left that afternoon for Moscow and arrived late in the evening. Stalin was at work in his office as he usually was at night. Several members of the State Defense Committee were with him, and his secretary, A. N. Poskrebyshev, who announced Zhukov's arrival.

Stalin said that the situation in the south was very bad, and that the Germans might take Stalingrad. The State Defense Committee had decided to appoint Zhukov to be Deputy Supreme Commander and to send him to Stalingrad. Army Chief of Staff Vasilievsky and Politburo Member Malenkov were already there.

"How soon can you take off?" Stalin demanded. Zhukov said he needed a day to study the situation and Stalin agreed, which he did not always do. Over tea, he briefed Zhukov on the conditions at Stalingrad

---

Staff Order No. 227

At Stalingrad, when the Russian troops were in retreat at the end of July 1942, General Vasilievsky went to see Stalin, who was pacing nervously in his office. Vasilievsky made a routine report while Stalin continued to pace. Suddenly he stopped in midstride.

"They've forgotten it!" he exclaimed. "Staff Order No. 270, August 16, 1941. Retreating without permission is a crime that will be punished with all the vigor of wartime. . . . Write a up a new one."

"When do you want it ready?"

"Today. Come back when it's ready."

That night he signed the notorious Order No. 227, which outlined the most stringent punishments for retreat without permission. It was to be known as the "not one more step backward" order.

It included establishment of special units within each division to shoot down any soldiers found retreating without permission. And the establishment of penal companies, which would be assigned to such dangerous tasks as clearing mine fields.

It was Stalin at his most brutal.

---

and said he had already decided to transfer three more armies to the Stalingrad Front. Under cover of an attack by the First Guards Army against the German Volga River wedge, the other two armies were to be moved into battle. "Otherwise," Stalin said, "we may lose Stalingrad."

Stalin made it clear to Zhukov that the battle for Stalingrad was of the utmost military and political importance. The German capture of the city would cut off the south of the Soviet Union from Russia. They might lose that great inland waterway, the Volga River.

Zhukov took off from Moscow's Central Airport on August 29. Four hours later his plane landed at an airstrip north of Stalingrad on the Volga.

He was met by General Vasilievsky, who told him the latest military development as they drove to the headquarters of the Stalingrad

Front at Malay Ivanovka, about fifty miles north of Stalingrad. They reached the headquarters at noon. General Gordov, the commander, was up front, so they talked with his chief of staff, General Nikishev, and the chief of operations, Colonel Rukhle. Marshal Zhukov had the impression that they were very unsure of themselves and of whether the enemy could be stopped at Stalingrad.

Zhukov reached General Gordov by telephone and arranged with him to remain at the headquarters of General Moskalenko's First Guards Army. When he and Vasilievsky arrived, Gordov and Moskalenko reported. They were very encouraging. The four officers agreed that the combined forces of the three armies could not be ready to attack before September 6. Zhukov informed Stalin by telephone of that fact. Stalin offered none of his typical objections.

Since General Vasilievsky had been ordered to return to Moscow, he took off. Zhukov had to report to Stalin that the First Guards Army was unable to get in position to attack as ordered on September 2, and he had postponed the attack until September 3. After an artillery bombardment on that day, the First Guards Army attacked but was able to progress only a couple of miles toward Stalingrad. Continuous enemy air strikes and counterattacks prevented further success.

Stalin wired Zhukov, "The situation at Stalingrad has deteriorated further. The enemy stands two miles from the city. Stalingrad may fall today or tomorrow if the northern groups of forces do not give immediate assistance. See to it that the commanders of the forces north and northwest of Stalingrad strike the enemy at once and come to the aid of the Stalingraders. No delay can be tolerated. To delay now is tantamount to a crime. [This was typical Stalinesque bluster.] Throw all your air power to the aid of Stalingrad; the city has few planes."

Zhukov telephoned Stalin and said he could order the offensive to start immediately, but the troops of the three armies would have to go into battle almost without ammunition, because that could not come up until evening. Further, it would take that long to coordinate the movement of tanks, infantry, artillery, and air support, and without that coordination the offensive could not succeed.

Digging Deep for Manpower

Hitler had to have oil and he had to have it fast. "If I do not get it," he told General Paulus one day, "I will have to end the war."

When the Germans counted noses in that spring of 1942, Hitler saw that their casualties, not including the sick, were almost 1.2 million for the year. Keitel was sent off to Romania and Hungary to find new divisions of Axis troops to help out. Goering went to Italy and persuaded Mussolini to commit Italian troops to the Russian Front. Hitler had commitments for fifty-two Axis divisions: twenty-seven Romanian, thirteen Hungarian, nine Italian, two Slovak, and one division of Spanish volunteers, returning Hitler's compliment of the 1930s when he sent "volunteers" to help Franco fight the Spanish revolution.

General Halder, the commander of the German Army, expressed grave misgivings about the employment of unknown and untried Allied troops. If nothing else, the differences in language and military tradition were going to create difficulties. But Hitler would not listen, so foreign divisions began to come into the line to stand shoulder to shoulder with the men of the *Wehrmacht*. Even more to the disgust of the German soldiers the *Waffen SS* was brought onto the scene. The *Waffen SS* was the despair of the regular army. At the top the men were Nazi party men whose loyalty was to Hitler and not to the army system. Therefore nothing was too good for the *Waffen SS* and the organization was skimming the cream off the manpower pool. With Hitler's support the *Waffen SS* had enticed the most intelligent and valuable segments of the nation's youth into its ranks by means of propaganda, bribery, and pressure tactics.

Therefore the best and brightest, who would have been eligible for high command in years to come, were lost to the army. So wrote Field Marshall Keitel, ever the army man, "Now in the spring of 1942, Hitler was encouraging the *Waffen SS* because he did not trust his generals. The *Waffen SS*, he said, was an elite corps being trained exactly in the way he wanted. Ultimately the *Waffen SS* consisted of thirty-eight divisions, and the army men hated every one of them."

Stalin was at first obdurate, "And you think the enemy is going to wait while you're getting organized?" he sneered. "Yeremenko insists that the enemy is going to take Stalingrad on his first try unless you strike from the north."

Zhukov said he did not agree and finally Stalin gave him permission to start the offensive, on September 5 as planned, "But if the enemy begins a general offensive against the city, attack immediately. Do not wait for the troops to be completely ready. Your main job is to keep the Germans from taking Stalingrad and, if possible, to eliminate the German corridor separating the Stalingrad and Southeast Fronts."

✳ ✳ ✳

At dawn on September 5, the assault began but the density of artillery fire was not enough and failed to yield positive results. The ground assault followed salvoes of Katyusha rockets. Zhukov watched from an observation post of the First Guards Army and could tell that the bombardment had failed.

Within two hours that opinion was confirmed by reports of commanders in various sectors—the enemy had stopped them cold in several areas and was counterattacking with infantry and tanks. Large formations of tanks were moving up from Gumrak, Orlovka, and Bolshoya Rossoshka, on the western side of Stalingrad. Enemy bombers were also attacking the Russian positions. By the second half of the day the Germans had pushed them back to their original positions in some sectors. The battle died down that evening and Zhukov could sum up the results. The Russians had advanced only a mile or two and the Twenty-Fourth Army had not advanced at all.

By evening more ammunition was coming up and they had fresh intelligence about the enemy. Zhukov decided to pursue the attack in the morning, regrouping his forces during the night.

Late in the evening he had a telephone call from Stalin. "How are things going at Stalingrad?" he wanted to know.

Zhukov reported on the day's battle and said that the Germans had shifted their forces from Gumrak to the front north of Stalingrad.

"That is very good," Stalin said.

"But our forces did not advance very far," Zhukov continued. "And in some sectors they did not advance at all."

"Why?" Stalin asked.

"Because we did not have enough time to prepare the offensive, and therefore could not aim our preparatory fire properly. When our forces attacked, the enemy stopped them with fire and counterattacks. Besides, enemy planes had air superiority and bombed our positions all day long."

"Just keep up the attack," Stalin said. "Your job is to divert as many of the enemy forces as possible from Stalingrad."

✳ ✳ ✳

That night the Russians bombed the German positions and the next day the battle was renewed. On September 6, the Germans were reinforced and dug in with tanks and self-propelled guns, which could only be eliminated by heavy artillery fire. The Russians were short on heavy artillery. On September 10, Zhukov toured the battlefield and concluded that the Russians could not break through the German lines with the forces at their disposal. Generals Gordov, Moskalenko, Malinovsky, and Kozlov concurred in that opinion.

Reporting to Stalin that day, Zhukov said, "We will not be able to break through the enemy force and join up with the Southeast Front. The Germans have strengthened their northern front with units brought up from Stalingrad. Further attacks with the present forces are useless and will result in heavy casualties. We need reinforcements and the time to regroup. Thrusts by individual armies are not sufficient to dislodge the Germans."

Stalin ordered Zhukov to come back to Moscow and report in person. When he reached the Kremlin, Vasilievsky was also there to report on the fighting of German forces toward Stalingrad from Kotelnivko and the German drive on Grozny. When Vasilievsky had finished, Stalin said, "They want to get at the oil of Grozny at any price. Well, now, let's see what Zhukov has to say about Stalingrad."

Zhukov repeated what he had told Stalin on the telephone.

"What would it take to eliminate the enemy corridor and link up with the Southeast Front?" Stalin asked.

"At least one full strength field army, a tank corps, three tank brigades, and 400 howitzers. In addition we would need the support of a least one air army during the operation."

Vasilievsky expressed his agreement and Stalin reached for his map showing the disposition of Supreme Headquarters reserves and studied it. Vasilievsky and Zhukov stepped away from the table, talking in low tones about the need to find another way out.

"What way out?" Stalin suddenly demanded, surprising Zhukov with the acuity of his hearing. The meeting turned out to be inconclusive and they agreed to meet again at 9:00 the following evening.

Vasilievsky and Zhukov spent the next day studying alternatives. They knew that Soviet production of weapons and the organization of strategic reserves was improving and that by fall they would be ready to go on the offensive.

They submitted a plan to Stalin: first, to continue to wear down the enemy by active defense; second, to prepare a counteroffensive of such magnitude against the enemy at Stalingrad as to shift the strategic situation in the south decidedly in the Russian favor. It seemed clear to them that the main thrusts would have to be against the Rumanian-held flanks of the Stalingrad grouping. Such a counteroffensive could not be prepared before mid-November.

All the forces the Germans had sent into the Caucasus toward Stalingrad had been worn down and weakened. The enemy would have to go over to the defensive in the south, just as it had in the Battle of Moscow.

Zhukov knew that Paulus' Sixth Field Army and Hoth's Fourth Tank Army had been so weakened in the fighting for Stalingrad that they would be unable to complete the capture.

Leningrad

Operation Barbarossa was begun with three ends in view—the capture of Leningrad, the capture of Moscow, and the capture of the Caucasus. The capture of Leningrad was to be accomplished by a thrust through Pskov, Luga, and Gatchina, while the Finns were expected to strike from the north. A second enveloping movement was to be carried out around Lake Ilmen and then on to Petrozavodsk and Lake Ladoga.

The Wehrmacht smashed through to Ostrov and Pskov. The Russians were in great disarray. Of the original thirty divisions on the northwest front, only five were now fully manned and fully armed; the rest were left with 10 to 30 percent of their complement. To slow down the German advance, some regular reserve troops were thrown in, but also some improvised opolcheniye units, workers' battalions, and student and even schoolboy battalions. Several hundred thousand civilians had been mobilized to dig three lines of trenches, antitank ditches, and other rudimentary defenses on the approaches to the city. No fortifications existed in that part of Russia, for it had never occurred to anyone before the war that Leningrad might be threatened from the south or the southwest.

The Germans pushed on relentlessly and reached the Luga River before the Russian defenses were complete. But by July 10, a long stretch of the Luga line had been manned by the Luga operational group consisting of four regular infantry divisions and three divisions of Leningrad opolcheniye.

The Germans had also forced the Narva River and were advancing on the former Russian capital from the Narva area and also from the Luga area, but also to the east of Leningrad, with the obvious purpose of isolating Leningrad and joining the Finns on the east side of Lake Ladoga. It was not until the Russian armies had fled to the immediate vicinity of Leningrad that they began to contain the Germans with any success.

Voroshilov had lost his head completely and it was not until General Zhukov was rushed to Leningrad at the beginning of September that the defense of Leningrad began in real earnest. It was to become the greatest of all the great stories of human endurance. Never had any city of the size of

Leningrad been besieged for nearly two and a half years. By the beginning of September, Leningrad was completely isolated from the Russian mainland and nearly 3 million people were trapped there. Except for air, which was very dangerous because the Germans had air superiority, the only route of communication with the mainland was Lake Ladoga, which had no proper harbors.

How was it possible that so many people could have remained in Leningrad? And what hope was there of feeding this enormous population if Leningrad was encircled?

There had been a lack of foresight by the civic authorities, who had given almost no thought at all to provision of food within the city. On September 6, two days before the land blockade was complete, Popov, head of the Leningrad Soviet, cabled Moscow asking the State Defense Committee to send food by rail immediately. But the railway had already been cut. Two days later, all land communications had been cut as well. On September 12, it was established that food stocks were the following:

Grain and flour	35-day supply
Cereals and macaroni	30-day supply
Meat	33-day supply
Fats	45-day supply
Sugar and confectionary	60-day supply

The first sign of alarm was the decision, made on September 2, to cut rations to 22 ounces of bread a day for workers, 14 ounces for office workers, and 11 ounces for children and dependents. A second cut was made on September 12.

To economize on flour, the authorities made a search for substitutes. When several grain barges were sunk by the Germans in Lake Ladoga, a large portion of the grain was recovered by divers. Although moldy, this supply was to be used as a supplement to the slender supply of grain. In late October,

(Continued)

other substitutes were found. Cellulose was added and although the moldy flour and cellulose gave the bread a sour taste, it was palatable.

A stock of 2,000 tons of sheep guts was found, which was made into a very smelly jelly whose odor had to be neutralized with cloves. At the height of the famine, this jelly was used as a meat substitute, supplied to meat ration card holders.

There was some cheating—forged cards, stolen cards, and the cards of the dead used by the living. An employee of the printing plant that made the cards was found to have 100 of them. She was shot. The Germans also air-dropped false ration cards, which added to the confusion.

In the middle of October a re-registration of all cardholders showed that about 70,000 improper cards were in use, those belonging to the dead or the absent, some of them in the army.

At the height of the famine, there was an epidemic of lost ration cards. The authorities brutally refused to replace them unless the loser could prove his loss.

The shortage of foodstuffs worsened. The provision of six ounces of powdered eggs instead of two pounds of meat was no fair exchange, but that was all there was. In November and December the whole of Leningrad was living on starvation rations and people began to die, especially after the fourth ration cut in November.

Besides the hunger, in the winter there was extreme cold. Both coal and oil supplies were virtually exhausted by the end of September. The authorities began cutting the nearby forests. The electricity supply was almost exhausted. Use of electric light was limited to government offices and hospitals. Tramcars stopped running. No food, no light, no heat, and German air raids and constant shelling—this was the life of Leningrad in the winter of 1941–42.

The fifth cut in rations brought more deaths that winter. Calories were reduced to 1,087 for workers, 581 for office workers, 466 for dependents, and 684 for children. In December, 52,000 people died. And in January 1942,

4,000 people died every day. Altogether, an estimated 900,000 people died from hunger during the blockade. The blockade was lifted in January 1943 after troops of the Leningrad Front and those of the Volkhov Front joined forces and cut a ten-mile corridor through the German salient south of Lake Ladoga. Schluesselberg was recaptured, a rail link was reestablished, and a pontoon bridge built across the Neva so that trains could run and trains began to run from Moscow through the Schluesselberg Gap.

As for the Russian forces, they too had been so weakened that they were unable to defeat the enemy. The strategic reserves were not yet ready, but by mid-November Stalin would have at his disposal forces equipped with T-34 tanks that would do the job. Besides, the Russians, from senior commanders to the troops, had learned from experience how to match up against the Germans in any situation.

✳ ✳ ✳

On the evening of September 13, Vasilievsky called Stalin and said he and Zhukov were ready to report. As they were making their report, Secretary Poskrebyshev walked in and said General Yeremenko was on the telephone. Stalin interrupted to speak with the general and returned to say the Germans were expected to attack the next day with tank forces near Stalingrad.

Turning to Vasilesvsky, Stalin ordered him to have Rodimtsev's One Hundred Twenty-Fifth Guards Division cross the Volga and send other troops across the river the next day.

He told Zhukov to call generals Gordov and Golovanov and tell them to start air attacks immediately. Gordov was to attack first thing in the morning to tie down the enemy. Zhukov had better get back to Stalingrad and size up the situation around Serafimovich and Kletskaya. Vasilievsky would have to visit the Southeastern Front and see how things were going on the left wing. The plans for the counteroffensive would have to wait. No one was to be told of the existence of such a plan.

✳ ✳ ✳

The three days of September 13, 14, and 15 were hard days for the Russians at Stalingrad. The Germans continued to advance through the ruins of the city, toward the bank of the Volga, putting forth enormous effort. But the Sixty-Second and Sixty-Fourth armies stood their ground, turning the ruins into a gigantic fortress. The turning point was the coming of Rodimtsev's Thirteenth Guards Division, which crossed the Volga on September 15 and immediately counterattacked, recapturing the hill of Mamayev Kurgan. General Golovanov's long-range bombers and the Sixteenth Air Army also hit the Germans hard, and the troops of the Stalingrad Front attacked the German Eighth Army Corps.

General Yeremenko visited the First Guards Army command post and met with Marshal Zhukov and General Golovanov. Yeremenko asked whether a more powerful counterattack was coming. Zhukov, having been sworn to silence by Stalin, could only mumble that something was afoot, but it would have to come later. At the end of the month, Zhukov and Vasilievsky were summoned back to Moscow to continue the discussions of their plan. Stalin asked Zhukov what he thought of General Gordov. Zhukov replied that Gordov seemed to be skilled enough but could not get along with his staff and his commanders.

"In that case," Stalin said, "we had better get another commander." Zhukov suggested Konstantin K. Rokossovsky, and Vasilievsky backed him up. Rokossovsky was the son of a Polish locomotive engineer and had been in military service since 1914. He had entered the Red Army in 1918 and risen to command a cavalry regiment and then a division—and finally a corps. He had been caught in the Stalin military purge of 1937, arrested, and jailed for nearly three years but released from prison in March 1940 and given a cavalry corps again. In June 1941, he was given command of the Ninth Mechanized Corps in the Ukraine and in July he commanded an operational group near Smolensk. In the battle for Moscow he commanded the Sixteenth Army. He would be given command of a front known as the Don Front. General N. F. Vatutin would command the newly created Southwest Front.

Zhukov and Vasilievsky returned to Moscow for more discussions until Stalin finally put his seal of approval on the plan. Six reconstituted divisions crossed the Volga in October to reinforce the Sixty-Second Army and the Don Front. Hitler ordered Paulus to seize Stalingrad in the immediate future, and shifted German forces from the flanks, replacing them with Rumanian troops. In mid-October the Germans launched one more offensive to finish off Stalingrad, but the Russian troops stood fast as the battle raged around the islands in the German stream. On October 19, Rokossovsky's Don Front began an offensive; at the same time the Sixty-Fourth Army began an offensive against the enemy flank in the Kuporosnoye area, just south of the center of Stalingrad.

At the beginning of November, the Germans tried desperately to eliminate the islands of resistance in the city, and on November 11 began one final offensive, which failed because they were at the end of their strength. During the months from June through November the Germans lost 600,000 men, 1,000 tanks, 2,000 guns, and 1,400 aircraft in the region of the Don, the Volga, and Stalingrad.

Stalin was invariably pitiless in his decisions over personnel. In the matter of the final push against Stalingrad, Beria proposed Yeremenko, while Zhukov preferred Rokossovsky. Stalin made the decision.

"I would assess Yeremenko below Rokossovsky," he said. "The troops aren't fond of Yeremenko. He is boastful and bragging."

"Yeremenko will be terribly hurt," Zhukov said.

"We're not high school girls," Stalin rejoined. "We're Bolsheviks and we must put worthy leaders in charge."

And although Stalin had not hesitated to fire his own son Vasily when he thought Vasily's behavior was tarnishing his reputation, later, when friends of Vasily's reported that "Colonel Stalin has come to his senses," the dictator approved of Vasily's promotion to the command of an air division.

✳ ✳ ✳

By November 1942, the battle for Stalingrad was in its fourth month, the defensive fighting marking the end of the first period of what the Russians called The Great Patriotic War. This was an especially trying time for the Russian people, for the Germans had driven to the outskirts of Leningrad and Moscow and occupied 700,000 square miles and a population of 80 million people.

But in so doing the Germans had lost more than 2 million dead, wounded, and missing men; the best elements of the German air and ground forces had been lost, and the German high command had no way of replacing them.

In November 1942, the Germans believed that the Russians would not be able to carry out a major offensive in the Stalingrad area and the Russians encouraged that belief with a disinformation campaign. They conducted offensive operations in the Moscow area that fall to give the impression that they were planning a winter offensive against the German Army Group Center.

Meanwhile, the Russian High Command was planning Operation Uranus, the great Stalingrad counteroffensive, which involved eleven armies (and several lesser forces), 13,500 guns, 1,100 antiaircraft guns, 115 detachments of rocket artillery, 900 tanks, and 1,115 planes.

It had been assumed that the plans were laid by Stalin in August 1942, but the fact is that the plans were made by the General Staff and that Zhukov and Vasilievsky had a major hand in them. At dawn on October 6, with General Voronov and General Ivanov, Zhukov visited the Fifty-First Army near Lake Tsatsa and discussed a counteroffensive. They drafted a report to the General Staff that night, and the next day Zhukov asked Rokossovsky for a similar report to be sent to General Headquarters. Since the General Staff was the working arm of the Supreme Command throughout the war, no strategic operation could be carried out unless the General Staff had organized it.

Zhukov had his hand in all the details—supply questions and even the recognition signals to be used when Southwest Front and Stalingrad Front soldiers met after encircling the Germans. Secrecy was so intense that Zhukov would not write any orders lest the secrecy break down by that writing. The troops moved into position only at night and were dispersed into villages. No reference to the coming attack was permitted, even in telephone conversations.

The main role in the first phase was played by General Vatutin's Southwest Front. Zhukov and Vasilievsky spent the end of October and the early days of November at the front, going over the operations plans with the commanders and their staffs.

Zhukov arrived at the command center of the Fifty-Seventh Army at Tatyanovka on the morning of November 10. Before the conference they took a final look at the terrain over which their troops would attack. On the evening of November 11, Zhukov sent Stalin a message rounding up last details. The operation was to begin on November 15. Stalin replied with a message about air power.

If air support for Yeremenko and Vatutin proves unsatisfactory the entire operation will fail. Our air forces must concentrate on the following:

1. Attack in the area of operation of our shock troops; harass the German air units and cover our forces.
2. Open the way for advance of our forces by systematic bombardment of German positions.
3. Pursue the retreating enemy with systematic bombardment and harassment to disorganize him and prevent his making a stand at another defense line.

Talk this over with Novikov and Vorozheikin, and let me have your opinion.

— Stalin

* * *

On November 12, Zhukov and Vasilievsky telephoned Stalin and asked permission to come to the Kremlin to talk over several matters. They received permission and the next morning were there. They found Stalin in a good mood. They pointed out that the Axis forces facing both the Southwest and Stalingrad Fronts were Rumanians and not of high fighting caliber. General Paulus's Sixth Army and the main force of the Fourth Tank Army remained in the Stalingrad area, where they were tied down by the Russian troops of the Stalingrad and Don Fronts.

As far as they could tell, the Germans had not detected the massing of the Russian armies. The formation of the fronts that were to encircle the German forces trapped in Stalingrad had been reviewed. Everything would be ready on November 19. Zhukov set this as the day for the attack and Stalin approved the decision. To prevent the buildup of forces in the area west of Moscow, they proposed an offensive in the Vyazma area.

"That would be a good idea," Stalin said. "But which of you would handle it?"

Vasilievsky and Zhukov agreed that Vasilievsky would take over coordination of operations around Stalingrad, while Zhukov handled the Kalinin and Western Fronts.

On November 17, Zhukov was summoned back to the Kremlin, ostensibly to work out some problems but actually to set him and Vasilievsky up as scapegoats in case anything went wrong with the Stalingrad operation.

* * *

The offensive began on the morning of November 19 and within four days the Twenty-First Field Army and the Fifth Tank Army took 30,000 prisoners. Stalin was worried about operations on the right flank of the Don, and sent orders to General Rokossovsky demanding greater activity by all his armies. By December 5, the noose had been drawn tight around Stalingrad and the German Sixth Army was caught in the trap. Now the Russian problem was preventing a breakout.

Paulus found himself cut off with 300,000 men in an area thirty miles long and twenty miles wide, with its front still in Stalingrad but its rear sticking out over the Russian steppe.

Paulus was now prodded by his generals to persuade Hitler to give him freedom of action. He finally asked the Fuehrer. Hitler responded on November 24 with an order: "Create a pocket. Present Northern Front and present Volga Front to be held at all costs. Supplies coming by air."

Supplies?

The supplies had slowed to a trickle. Goehring had bitten off more than he could chew and had flubbed the job. The men were now literally boiling their boots and cracking the marrow bones of dead horses for whatever sustenance they afforded.

One of Paulus' generals told him frankly, "The complete annihilation of 200,000 fighting men and their equipment is at stake. There is no other choice [but to break out]."

Hitler knew his man—a staff officer, not a man of action. He played Paulus like a fiddle, and Paulus quoted his orders that there was to be no surrender, that they would be supplied by air until they could be honorably extricated—"facts," neither of which turned out to be true.

On January 9, the Russians offered a real choice: honorable surrender or annihilation. Paulus again refused to surrender. The Russians advanced from west to east, pinning the Germans back into the ruined city. Again the Russian High Command offered surrender; again Paulus refused. The situation of the Germans had now become hopeless. The last wounded to be evacuated were evacuated by air on January 24.

Even Hitler must have known what was coming, but he tried to stave it off. He honored Paulus with the oak leaves to the Knight's Cross on January 15. Then he promoted Paulus to field marshal, knowing that no German of that rank had ever surrendered.

The Russians entered the last German defense area, and the building in which Paulus had his headquarters. A young officer entered the building and demanded Paulus' surrender. He was taken to a room where the field marshal was lying listlessly on a bed. He demanded surrender. Paulus nodded. The battle was over.

Field Marshal Erich von Manstein had been chosen by Hitler to try to effect the relief of Stalingrad and launched an offensive on December 12. In three days the forces advanced twenty-five miles toward Stalingrad. Soon the relief forces were only twenty-five miles from the beleaguered city and it looked as though they had succeeded. But the key was that Paulus would have to fight his way out and link up with von Manstein, and this Paulus could easily have done, even at this late date. But Hitler refused to permit Paulus to make a breakout with his Sixth Army. Meanwhile Stalin interfered, holding up reinforcements for the Russians.

✳ ✳ ✳

Luckily for the Russians, Stalin's interference was brief and not too costly, 300,000 German troops were caught in the trap, and on December 28 it was all over. The responsibility for wiping up was given to Rokossovsky, and on January 31 Field Marshal Paulus surrendered to Rokossovsky's troops.

Rolossovsky described the surrender:

> On January 31, General Paulus was taken prisoner with his staff and brought to us at Staff Headquarters.
>
> Marshal N. N. Voronov and an interpreter and I were in the building. The room was lighted with electricity and we were sitting at a small table. I awaited this meeting with interest. At last the door opened and the duty officer reported the arrival of the Field Marshal and ushered him into the room. He stood stiffly before us.
>
> His manner betrayed great tension, which he could not conceal. A tic contorted his face, and he was obviously upset. It was apparent that he was expecting something frightful to happen. This

was painful to observe, and, glancing at Marshal Voronov, I invited Paulus with a quiet gesture to sit at the table. Looking to the right and left, he timidly sat down. There were cigars and cigarettes on the table, I was smoking and invited Paulus to do the same. He promptly did so and just as promptly drank a glass of strong tea but because of his feverish state, the twitching of his hands and face did not stop. To the very end of our conversation he was unable to bring himself completely under control.

A few German units held out until February 3. Of the original garrison, 42,000, mostly wounded, were evacuated by air. The Russians counted 107,000 prisoners, 16,000 in the fighting and 91,000 in the surrender. There were twenty-four generals. The number killed was around 200,000. And only two men escaped to reach the German lines.

Of the prisoners taken, only 6,000 ever reached Germany again, several years after the end of the war.

Paulus was held by the Russians for eleven years, and finally released in East Germany. He lived in Dresden until his death in 1957 from motoneuron disease.

Spring 1943

AFTER THE DEFEAT OF THE AXIS FORCES ON THE
Volga and Don Rivers, the enemy pulled back and a period
of quiet set in along most of the fronts. To prevent further deteriora-
tion of its position, the German high command had launched
an offensive against Belgorod. This was to be a precursor to elimina-
tion of the Kursk salient. This offensive brought about the loss of
Belgorod, Kharkov, and a large part of the northern Don Basin, a dis-
appointment to the Russians to end the glorious winter of Stalingrad.
In his Red Army Day Order of February 23, Stalin spoke of the winter offensive, saying that "the mass expulsion of the Germans from
the Soviet Union has begun," but at the same time, he warned of
future setbacks for the Russian forces.

The German Army was more experienced at war than the Russian
Army was, at first, but this was no longer true, Stalin said. The Russian
armies had grown in strength and skill, while the German High
Command was now drawing low-quality men into the army.

This did not mean that the Germans were finished, Stalin added.
"The German Army has suffered a defeat, but it has not yet been

smashed. It is now going through a crisis; it does not follow that it cannot pull itself together. The real struggle is only beginning. It would be stupid to think that the Germans would abandon even one kilometer of our country without a fight."

Of all Stalin's wartime statements this was the least pro-ally. Stalin did not mention North Africa where a second front had been launched by the British and Americans. He said that the Soviet Union was "bearing the whole brunt of the war." He did not mention lend-lease, although supplies were beginning to arrive in the Soviet Union.

Marshal Zhukov was on the Northwest Front, commanded by Marshal Timoshenko, when he received a telephone call on March 14. Zhukov reported that because of the early spring the Russian troops here might have to halt their offensive temporarily. Stalin asked some questions and then agreed with this assessment. He asked Zhukov to return to Moscow and discuss the situation on other fronts. That same evening Zhukov was in Moscow and when he arrived at the Kremlin he found a large group there discussing the problems of industry. He joined the discussions. The meeting went on until 3:00 in the morning. When everyone had left, Stalin asked Zhukov to stay for dinner. While they were eating, a staff officer brought a map of the Voronezh area and reported that the situation there had deteriorated in recent weeks and that enemy forces had launched a new offensive.

Dinner became breakfast, and they finished at around 5:00 AM. Two hours later, Zhukov was on his way to the Voronezh Front to find out what the situation was and to take appropriate action. He arrived and spoke to Stalin over a high security line. He told Stalin that it was essential to move all available troops from the reserves and neighboring fronts into the Voronezh Front to stop the Germans. An hour later he learned that Stalin had already ordered the transfer of three armies to the Belgorod area.

On March 18, the Germans entered Belgorod but were unable to advance farther to the north. A Russian detachment ambushed the

Death's Head Tank Division near Shapino and took prisoners. Thus, the Russian high command learned of the German drive on Oboyan.

By March 20, the Twenty-First Army had established a defense north of Belgorod and the First Tank Army was massed south of Oboyan. At the end of the month the Germans made repeated but unsuccessful attempts to break through along the Northern Donets River, where the Sixty-Fourth Army was deployed. After suffering heavy losses the Germans stopped to fortify their lines. From that time until the summer, the situation was quiet along that front.

To strengthen the Voronezh Front, Stalin appointed General N. F. Vatutin as the new front commander. He and Zhukov began to visit all the Russian units. Zhukov was specially concerned about the Fifty-Second Guards Division, which he knew would have to take the brunt of an attack. Vatutin and General I. M. Chistyakov, commander of the division, agreed and they took steps to strengthen the position with artillery.

In this lull, each of the front commands took steps to strengthen aerial and ground reconnaissance of the enemy. By mid-April they

---

The Tiger That Became a Pussycat

The surrender of General Paulus occupied Hitler's mind briefly, but he was soon off on another tangent. The tiger tank had gained quite a reputation in the war in the west, and he wanted to see how they would do in the severe Russian climate. The place for the demonstration was a bit of no-man's land, a long road that lay between the Russian and German armies.

Six tiger tanks were chosen and moved out onto the road in a column. The Russians let them go until they were well into no-man's land. Then they targeted the front and rear tanks and stopped them with armor-piercing shells. The four tanks in the middle were also stopped, unable to maneuver to escape. The Russian gunners picked them off, one by one. Next day, General Zeitsler related the story of the test in the morning situation meeting. Hitler did not bat an eye, but he did not mention the tiger tank again.

had obtained much information about enemy forces in the Orel, Sumy, Belgorod, and Kharkov areas.

On April 8, 1943, at 5:30 AM, Zhukov sent an appreciation of the military situation to Stalin, using the dictator's code name Comrade Vasilyev.

1. Having suffered heavy losses during the winter the enemy will apparently not be able to assemble sufficiently large reserves by spring to renew his advance into the Caucasus and toward the Volga River in an attempt to outflank Moscow.

   In view of the lack of large reserves the enemy will have to limit his energies in the spring and first half of summer 1943, he will have to make his plans as he moves, stage by stage, with the ultimate aim of seizing Moscow in 1943. Given the enemy's disposition of forces opposite the Central, Voronezh, and Southwest Fronts, I hold that he will direct his principal offensive operations

---

No More Field Marshals

The surrender of General Paulus at Stalingrad was a very sore point with Hitler and at Rastenburg, Stalingrad was ostentatiously removed from the map. On February 2, the Russian radio blared the story of the surrender all day long. Hitler talked back to the radio, accusing Paulus of cowardice, ingratitude, and treason. General Jodl suggested that Paulus had not really surrendered; it was a Soviet propaganda trick.

"No," said Hitler. "He really surrendered. How can one be such a coward?"

Jodl repeated his doubt that Paulus had really surrendered.

"No," Hitler said. "The man is a coward. I don't believe those tales that he was wounded several times, either. He is a traitor. Mark my word, soon you will see him broadcasting for the Russians." It was true. A few months later Paulus was doing just that.

"What hurts me most is that I promoted him to field marshal," Hitler said. "That is the last field marshal I will appoint in this war."

---

against these three fronts hoping to defeat our forces in the area, and thus achieve enough room for maneuver to outflank Moscow closer to the city.

2. In the first stage the enemy will apparently attempt mass maximum force, including up to thirteen or fifteen tank divisions with a great amount of air support, and strike with his Orel-Kromy Group to bypass Kursk on the northeast, and with his Belgorod-Khakov group to bypass Kursk on the southwest. An auxiliary strike aimed at cutting up our front may be expected from the west near Vorozhba, between the Seim and Psek Rivers, directed against Kursk from the southwest. The ultimate aim would be a line running through the Korocha River, the town of Korocha, the town of Tim, the Tim River, and Droskovo.

3. In the second stage, the enemy is likely to strike against the flank and rear of the Southwest Front in the direction of Valuiki and Urazovo. He may try to join this drive with another from the area of Lisichansk north toward Svatovo and Urazovo. The enemy may also be expected to drive toward a line running through Livny, Kastornoye, Stary Oskol, and Novy Oskol.

The German Soldier's Friend

One day when Hitler was taking a rare break to visit Obersalzberg his train stopped on a siding so he could send the latest batch of messages to *Wolfsschanze*. A troop train consisting almost entirely of boxcars came up alongside. Hitler was in the dining car, sitting at a table covered with fresh white linen and set with gleaming silver. The soldiers began pouring out of the boxcars on the next siding, wounded men, bandaged in rags, skinny, hungry mean with cracked boots and stained greatcoats.

Hitler took one look and ordered the shade pulled down. This was the leader who had told his generals that he would not come to their victory party in Poland because he ate only at field kitchens when he was with the troops.

---

4. In the third stage, after regrouping the enemy may attempt to reach a line running through Liski, Voronezh, and Yeletz.

5. We can expect the enemy to put greatest reliance in this year's offensive operations on his tank divisions and his air force since his infantry seems far less prepared for offensive operations than last year. Opposite the Central and Voronezh Fronts the enemy now has up to twelve tank divisions so that, by moving three or four tank divisions from other sectors, he may be able to throw as many as fifteen or sixteen tank divisions with a combined strength of 2,500 tanks against our Kursk Grouping.

6. In view of this threat we should strengthen our antitank defenses of the Central and Voronezh Fronts as soon as possible, assemble thirty antitank artillery regiments, in the Supreme Headquarters Reserve for use in the threatened sectors, concentrate all self-propelled artillery regiments to a line through Livny, Kastornoye, and Stary Oskol, placing some of the regiments at the disposal of Rokossovsky and Vatutin, and concentrate as much air strength as possible in the Supreme Headquarters Reserve so that massed air attacks in conjunction with tanks and rifle units can strike at the enemy's shock forces and thus disrupt his offensive plans.

I am not familiar with the final disposition of our operational reserves, but in my view they should be assembled in the areas of Yefremov, Livny, Kastoprnoye, Novy Oskol, Valuiki, Rossoshh, Liski, Voronezh, and Yelets. Deeper reserves should be positioned at Ryahzk, Ranenburg, Michurinsk, and Tambov. One reserve army should be stationed in the area of Tula and Stalinogorsk.

I consider it unwise to launch a preventive attack in the next few days. It would be better if we first wore the enemy down with our defenses and destroyed his tanks, and only then, after having moved up fresh reserves, went over to a general offensive and finally destroyed his main force.

—Konstantinov (Zhukov's code name)

What Was Permitted

After the war when famous Russian leaders wrote their memoirs, Dmitri Volkogonov tells us, they wrote only what Stalin permitted. Volkogonov knew whereof he spoke. For twenty years he had worked in the political adminis- tration of the Soviet army and navy, and one of the main tasks was to censor published materials. Glavlit, the Main Administration for Protection of State Secrets in Print, made certain that only the approved versions of events found their way into print.

Approved by whom?

Stalin, of course.

Such matters as the war records of Stalin's favorites were rigorously cen- sored. You would look in vain, for example, for any report critical of L. I. Brezhnev. In 1942, his regimented political commissar, Sinyanskky, reported that Brezhnev "was incapable of bringing about the desired improvement in behavior and mood among political workers of the front." He was said to be a boozer. Such reference never appeared in print.

On September 16, 1942, Secretary Poskrebyshev handed Stalin a spe- cial report from Soviet Intelligence about a radio intercept from Berlin.

"Stalingrad has been taken by brilliant German forces, Russia has been cut in two parts, north and south, and will soon collapse in her death throes."

He mulled over that for awhile, then dictated a telegram to be sent to General Yeremenko and Commissar Nikita Khrushchev: "Report some sense about what has been happening in Stalingrad. Is it true Stalingrad has been captured by the Germans? Give a straight and truthful answer. I await your immediate reply."

For Stalin the only important matter was the goal. Conscience or grief never tormented him. There is not a single document in the archives that shows his concern for human life.

Glavlit existed all Stalin's life and far beyond. It was abolished only in July 1990.

* * *

Vasilievsky arrived a few days later and he and Zhukov went over the plans again. They drafted a document that they sent to Stalin. As of April 12, Stalin had not arrived at a concrete plan of action. No offensive out of Kursk was planned. Then Stalin telephoned Zhukov at Bobyshevo, the Voronezh Front Headquarters, and asked him to come to Moscow to plan for the Kursk salient. He and Vasilievsky met with Stalin at Supreme Headquarters on April 12. By mid-April Stalin had approved a preliminary defense plan. Many improvements had been made in weaponry. The air force had the new Yak-9 fighter, and the Russian air force now exceeded the Germans in number of planes. Each front had its own air army of 700 to 800 planes.

The artillery was converted entirely to motorized traction. By the summer of 1943, before the Battle of Kursk, the Russian armies were superior to the German armies both in quantity and quality.

The Battle of Kursk

IN THE EARLY MONTHS OF THE WAR, STALIN'S PRESTIGE hit a new low. For months after the signing of the Nazi–Soviet Pact, propagandists had drummed into the Russian people the idea that the alliance had been an act of wisdom. Russia had regained her old frontiers. People were saying that "the boss"—Stalin—knew what he was doing.

The shock of the German invasion seemed at first like an apocalyptic disaster. Millions began to question: why had Stalin—the great all-wise leader—allowed this to happen? References to Stalin were few and far between and his picture virtually disappeared from the pages of Russian publications.

Then, the victory in the Battle of Moscow, and particularly Stalin's undisputed courage in electing to remain in the capital when the Germans seemed sure to capture it, restored much of his prestige.

Another bleak period came in the Black Summer of 1942, the losses of Kerch, Kharkov, and Sevastopol, and the German breakthrough into the Caucasus. Alibis had to be found and scapegoats punished for these dreadful developments—and they were—but the Russian people began to lose confidence in Stalin.

After the Russian salvation of Stalingrad, Stalin was treated with a new respect, verging on adoration by sycophants. Many new terms crept into the official Soviet histories: "Stalin's strategic leadership," "Stalin's brilliance," "Stalin's military genius" are but three of them. But the shallowness of this "savior of the nation" was to be seen in his treatment of his eldest son, Yakov, the prisoner of the Germans. Rather than suffering over Yakov's fate, Stalin feared that this son's will would be broken in prison camp and that he would work for the Germans. His concern was that this would embarrass him.

Yakov turned out to have a much stronger will than his father credited him with. The thought that he might crack was to him worse than death, as he passed through lesser hells—Hammelburg, Luebeck, and Sachsenhausen—his strength was failing. On April 14, 1943, Yakov threw himself on the electrified barbed wire fence of the prison camp and was shot by a German guard.

One reason for the new adoration of Stalin, encouraged by the men around him, was that after Stalingrad the Russian people sensed that they were going to win the war.

Stalin's relations with his generals changed, and a degree of trust was established, as much as was possible with a paranoid dictator who saw danger to himself in every relationship. Zhukov, particularly, benefited from this new relationship, but so did others among the bevy of experienced and brilliant commanders produced by the war. The General Staff, under Vasilievsky's expert leadership, was working efficiently, unlike the early days when Mekhlis and Kulik exercised the baleful influence of police generals on the affairs of war. Beria, head of the hated Secret Police, the most venal of them all, continued in power, but only because Stalin found him indispensable in casting aside rotten wood in the ranks of party and the military.

Privately, Beria detested Stalin and plotted against him and his family, while publicly prostrating himself before the dictator. Only after Stalin died would he make his move to seize power. That attempt at coup would be frustrated by the cabal of other aspirants and Beria would go the way of almost all who were once close to Stalin, to the oblivion of an obscure death.

Hitler had already decided by the summer of 1941 that the Crimea would become a German colony. From Hitler to Goering, to Himmler and Erich Koch, Reichskommissar for the Ukraine, the Ukrainians

---

Remaking the Ukraine

In July 1941, Hitler had decided that the Ukraine was to be recast as a German colony. The Crimea was to be a playground, from which all "foreigners" were to be excluded. Robert Ley, the chief of the German Labor Front and leader of the Strength through Joy movement, chose the Crimea as his playground for Nazi youth. Hitler played with the idea of settling the South Tyrol problem with Mussolini by resettling in the Crimea the German-speaking people of the Italian part of the Tyrol. Marshal von Manstein, the German "Hero of the Crimea," was to be presented with one of the former imperial palaces on the Crimean Riviera. It was also proposed that the name be changed to *Gotenland*. But the immense Ukraine was a different story, a land of 40 million people, a bread-basket and source of iron, coal, steel, and oil. The Ukrainians were never happy with their inclusion in the Soviet Union and were prepared to greet the Germans as liberators. But within weeks the German policies had turned this land of 40 million people from potential allies to deadly enemies. The Ukraine was to the Germans first a source of food, second of coal and iron, and third of slave labor. The racist policies made the land much less valuable and productive than Hitler had hoped. Ultimately, the Germans found themselves importing coal to the Ukraine! The cause of the downfall was the massacre of the Jews and the deportation of millions of young Ukrainians to Germany as slave labor, a policy that began in the first months of 1942.

As early as 1919 Adolf Hitler propagated the idea of *Lebensraum* (Living Space) as justification for the cut-throat expansion of German sovereignty. In order to build a lasting empire, he believed, Germany would have to attack countries to her east—Poland and Russia. Hitler also maintained that the Communist Party and its own attempts at world revolution had been engineered by Jews. (Copyright © *Presse-Illustratlonen*)

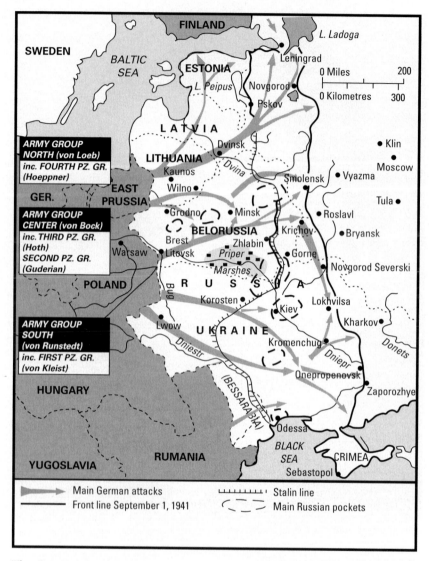

The Germans employed three army groups for Operation Barbarossa—North, Center, and South—and planned to destroy all Soviet resistance in swift advances on Leningrad, Moscow, and Kiev. Hitler threw 183 divisions into the assault, while the Nazis faced 170 Russian divisions, which represented 54 percent of the Red Army's total strength.

Gerd von Rundstedt, German Field Marshal. The important Nazi official who was dismissed from his post after disagreeing with Hitler over strategic matters is here pictured defending himself and his crimes at the Nuremberg Trials. (*National Archives, courtesy of USHMM Photo Archives*)

Germans guard prisoners at Rovno, one of the Poland camps for Soviet prisoners-of-war following the initial victories that marked the June 22, 1941, campaign. (*Main Commission for the Investigation of Nazi War Crimes in Poland*)

Alfred Rosenberg, Nazi ideologue and newly appointed Reich Commissioner for the Occupied Eastern Territories, is welcomed by Ukrainian representatives upon his arrival at a train station in July 1941. (*State Archives of the Russian Federation, courtesy of USHMM Photo Archives*)

A June 1935 portrait of three-year-old Anna Glinberg, a Jewish child from Kiev who was later killed during the mass execution at Babi Yar, where an estimated 33,771 unarmed men, women, and children were slaughtered over the course of two days (September 29 and 30, 1941). (*Yelena Brusilovsky, courtesy of USHMM Photo Archives*)

Soldiers of the *Waffen-SS* and the Reich Labor Service look on as a member of an *Einsatzgruppe* (death squad) prepares to shoot a Ukrainian Jew kneeling on the edge of a mass grave filled with corpses. (*Library of Congress, courtesy of USHMM Photo Archives*)

Leningrad inhabitants, including women of all ages, use shovels and picks to help construct antitank ditches in answer to the call to defend their city to the last during the Siege of Leningrad. (*Office of War Information Collection* #BO-530)

Sergeant P. Dorzhiev, a Russian sniper who killed 181 Germans on the Leningrad front, looking through binoculars and holding a rifle, circa 1942. (*British Ministry of Information*)

A first-aid instructor, Nina Kuranova, tends a badly wounded soldier in the thick of the fighting on the Leningrad front. (*British Ministry of Information*)

Two Soviet machine gunners in their firing position on the Leningrad front, circa 1942. (*Office for Emergency Management*)

Soviet parachutists board a plane during drilling practice, circa 1942. (*Office of War Information Collection* #BO-1571)

Waffen-SS troops and SD officers force Soviet Jews to dig their own mass grave before being executed in 1942. (State Archives of the Russian Federation, courtesy of USHMM Photo Archives)

Joseph Stalin in the conference hall of the Kremlin addresses a meeting of the Moscow Soviets held in October 1942 in celebration of the Twenty-fifth anniversary of the revolution. (*Library of Congress Prints and Photographs Division*)

Three German soldiers walk down a desolate street amid the ruins of Stalingrad in
September 1942. (*Rothkopf & Heine #227*)

Stalingrad, December 1942. (*Maltry*)

Stalingrad, Russia, September 1942. Solitary walls and chimneys stand amid the total destruction. (*Rothkopf & Heine* #226)

Marshal Georgi Zhukov, Deputy Supreme Commander of all Soviet Forces, circa 1942. (*Office of War Information Collection* #BO-1565)

In a cornfield near Stalingrad, Russian troops wait to ambush advancing German troops in 1942. (*New York World-Telegram and the Sun Newspaper Photograph Collection / Library of Congress*)

Joseph Stalin, Franklin D. Roosevelt, and Winston Churchill on the portico of the Russian Embassy in Teheran, during their *second* meeting from November 28 to December 1, 1943. (*U.S. Signal Corps*)

By 1945, Soviet munitions production had quadrupled from its 1941 output. Here workers, maintaining day-and-night schedules, assemble tanks at a plant in the Urals. (*Sovfoto / Encyclopedia Britannica*)

An oil painting of Stalin. The cult of Stalin was well-entrenched by 1944. Most supporters viewed him as the mastermind behind the looming Soviet victory. (*Yanker Poster Collection / Library of Congress*)

Stalin and Roosevelt seated at a table during the Yalta Conference in February 1945. (*Associated Press / U.S. Signal Corps*)

Dwight D. Eisenhower, Supreme Allied Commander, Admiral Sir Harold M. Burrough, Allied Naval Commander-in-Chief in Europe, and Marshal Georgi Zhukov at the Supreme Headquarters, Allied Expeditionary Forces (SHAEF) on June 10, 1945. At right is Lt. Col. O. Pontuhoff, interpreter. (*U.S. Army*)

This caricature of Joseph Stalin by artist Justin Murray, circa 1945, portrays the Soviet dictator as a bird of prey smoking a pipe and waiting on a branch. (*U.S. Copyright Office* #K59561)

American and Soviet soldiers pose in front of a portrait of Stalin in Berlin in 1945. (*Aviva Kempner, courtesy of USHMM Photo Archives*)

Wehrmacht and SS defendants sit in the dock during their 1945 trial in Smolensk, Russia, for perpetrating war crimes against the Soviet people. (*Central State Archive of Documentary Film and Photography, courtesy of USHMM Photo Archives*)

were *Untermenschen.* Goering said, "The best thing would be to kill all the men in the Ukraine and then to send in the SS stallions."

The Ukraine was portrayed as a vast reservoir of food, strategic materials, and labor for Germany, but actually the Germans received very little benefit from their occupation. For two major factors turned what promised to be a German ally into an implacable enemy: the massacre of the Ukrainian Jews and the deportation of millions of young Ukrainians to be slave laborers.

The next major development in the war on the Eastern Front was the battle of Kursk, which Historian Alexander Werth has billed as "Hitler's last chance of turning the tide." After Stalingrad, Hitler badly needed a victory to regain his lost prestige, and the opportunity seemed to present itself in a salient captured by the Russians between Orel on the north and Belgorod on the south. The Russians looked upon this Kursk salient as their springboard for the reconquest of Orel and the Bryansk country to the northwest and the Ukraine to the southwest. Since March 1943, they had been fortifying the salient with thousands of miles of trenches, gun emplacements, and other defensive positions, and the defense in-depth had assumed a perimeter of defense that extended around the north, west, and south sides of the salient.

In the spring of 1943, Hitler had decided to hold a line running down from the Gulf of Finland to the Sea of Azov and inflict a major defeat on the Russians in what he called Operation Citadel in the Kursk salient.

As German historians tell the story, "It was also to be hoped that the reserves the Russians would throw into battle could be smashed. The smashing of this salient would shorten the front. To be sure, some argued that the Russians would expect an attack in precisely this area and there was danger of losing more German troops than they could kill or capture on the enemy side. Hitler, however, held that Operation Citadel could succeed "if it was held early enough."

The problem that developed was delay. The terrain was difficult and the German divisions were being replenished slowly after

Stalingrad. So the operation was postponed until the middle of June, when many tiger and panther tanks would be available and Ferdinand self-propelled guns would be coming from the armament factories in Germany.

Zhukov and Vasilievsky had not wasted the spring months. In about three months, half a million railroad cars had been brought to reinforce the Kursk salient. The Germans had 2,000 tanks but the Russians had more than 3,000, along with nearly 2,000 aircraft.

Zhukov had emerged from Stalingrad as Stalin's deputy in the conduct of the war. He was now constantly on the move in his role as deputy Supreme Commander, traveling from the fronts to Moscow and working out the strategies of the campaigns. All signs pointed to the Kursk area as the next battleground. The main German concentrations were here and as the spring wore on it became apparent that Zhukov had read the German intent correctly. The question on the Russian side was whether they should strike first or wait until the Germans attacked and then strike back?

Zhukov proposed to let the Germans strike first. Then he would grind them down and destroy their ability to conduct any future major offensive.

The Imagination of the World

The Kursk operation was delayed and delayed again. The German divisions were replenished very slowly. General Model, commanding the troops north of the salient, declared the operation could not succeed without strong reinforcement by heavy modern tanks, superior to anything the Russians had. The attack therefore, was postponed until the middle of June. Meanwhile, numerous tiger and panther tanks and Ferdinand mobile guns were rushed from armaments works in Germany straight to the front. But there were other delays. Hitler feared that Mussolini was about to drop out of the war. When he had satisfied himself that Mussolini was not giving up, he decided to stick to his original plan. The Kursk victory, he said, would fire the imagination of the world.

Stalin was fearful of this plan, and as the moment of engagement neared he became ever more fearful. As Zhukov knew, Stalin need not have been so worried; by that summer of 1943, the Russians had amassed forces superior to the German and in addition 200,000 guerillas were operating behind the German lines.

For the operations against Kursk, the Germans would use fifty divisions, 10,000 guns, 2,700 tanks, and 2,000 planes.

Toward the end of June it became apparent that the Germans would strike within the next few days,

At that time Zhukov was at the Central Front with Rokossovsky. On June 30, Zhukov had a telephone call from Stalin instructing him to remain in Orel and coordinate the activities of the Central, Bryansk, and Western Fronts. Vasilievsky would be in charge of the Voronezh Front, Stalin said.

The Russians had amassed a high density of artillery in the Thirteenth Army sector where they expected the main enemy blow to strike—148 guns and mortars per mile of front line. The antitank defense was deployed to great depth on the Central and Voronezh Fronts.

✳ ✳ ✳

Russian Intelligence estimated that the German air force under the command of Field Marshal von Richthofen had 2,000 planes operating against the Central and Fronts. Beginning in March, the Germans had blasted rail junctions, highways, Voronezh cities, and key objectives in the area. In June, air attacks concentrated on troops and support units along the front. Russian cover was provided by the Second, Fifth, and Sixteenth Air Armies and two fighter divisions of the Soviet air defense forces. Antiaircraft defenses were increased.

On July 4, Zhukov was at Central Front Headquarters when he learned of an engagement with advanced enemy detachments near Belgorod. A captured soldier of the German One Hundred and Sixty-Eighth Infantry Division revealed that the enemy attack would be launched at dawn on July 5.

✷ ✷ ✷

By July 5, the Central Front had deployed five antiaircraft divisions from the Supreme Headquarters Reserve and twenty-eight regiments of artillery. The Voronezh Front had four Supreme Headquarters divisions, twenty-five antiaircraft divisions, and five antiaircraft batteries. The fortified area was more than a hundred miles deep and they were prepared to counter the enemy's offensive.

At about 2:00 on the morning of July 5, General Rokossovsky asked Zhukov if they should not inform Stalin of the coming attack.

"We can't waste time," Zhukov replied. "Give the order and I will call Stalin and report." He was put through to the commander in chief at Supreme Headquarters. Remarkably, without complaint, Stalin approved the move, and asked only to be kept informed.

✷ ✷ ✷

Zhukov and Rokossovsky were at the office of the chief of staff Malinin when at 2:20 AM the ground began to shake and the preliminary bombardment began. The boom of the heavy artillery and the explosions of the M-31 rockets were clearly discernible.

In the midst of the bombardment, Stalin called, "Well, have you begun?"

"Yes, we have."

"What's the enemy doing?"

"Attempting to return the fire with a few batteries."

"All right. I'll call again."

✷ ✷ ✷

The German attack began at 5:30 AM but it was not well-coordinated, suggesting that the Germans had taken heavy casualties from the shelling. Still, the Germans advanced four miles that first day. The Russian aerial support was ineffective, the dawn strikes at the enemy airfields came too late, and the German planes were already in the air in support of their ground forces. But as the battle developed, the Russian air support became much more effective.

"The Tigers Are Burning"

There was tremendous tension in Moscow when it was learned that the German offensive had begun. What was being fought in the very heart of Russia, in Turgeniev country, was a modern battle of Kulikovo, in which Prince Dmitri Donskoi routed the Tartars in 1380.

On the first day of battle two things were clear: the Germans had thrown tremendous forces into the battle, and they were suffering losses on an unprecedented scale and not getting much in return.

The Russian communiqué after the first day's fighting read: "All the attacks were repelled with heavy losses to the enemy and only in some small places did small German units succeed in penetrating slightly into our defense lines. Preliminary reports show that our troops have crippled or destroyed 586 enemy tanks."

It was the figure of 586 tanks that captured the Russian imagination. There had never been anything like it. By July 9, the four days of anxiety came to an end: "The Tigers Are Burning" was the title of a report from the front. On July 15, the Russian communiqué announced that the Russian counteroffensive against Orel had begun and that the Russians had broke through the German lines and advanced between fifteen and thirty miles in three days. On July 24, there was a Stalin order to Generals Rokossovsky, Vatutin, and Popov announcing the liquidation of the German summer offensive and the recapture of all the territory the Germans had gained since July 5. German losses were put at 70,000 killed, 2,800 tanks destroyed, and commensurately satisfactory figures for guns, planes, and motor vehicle.

The Germans began their offensive with three tank divisions and five infantry divisions in their first line of assault, striking at the Russian Thirteenth Army and the adjoining forces of the Forty-Eighth and Seventieth Armies. That day the Germans carried out five fierce attacks, in attempting to break through the Russian line, but almost everywhere the Russian stood fast and only at the end of the day did the Germans succeed in driving wedges into the line in the Olkhovatka and two other sectors.

An especially fierce fight was put up by the soldiers of the Thirteenth Army, particularly General A. B. Barinov's Eighty-First Division. An artillery battery under Captain G. I. Igishev took the brunt of the attack and destroyed nineteen tanks during the day. All the men of the battery died, but they did not let the enemy pass.

Still, the enemy succeeded in advancing six miles by the end of July 6. After regrouping his shock forces, he then attacked again on July 7 against Ponyri, but the Russian forces held. By July 9, the Germans had not advanced further. During the battle that day Stalin called Zhukov at the Central Front Command Center and suggested, "Isn't it about time to throw the Bryansk Front and the left wing of the Western Front into action as we planned?"

"The enemy no longer has the strength to break through on the Central Front. Unless we want to give him time to organize his defenses we must go on the offensive with all the forces of the Bryansk Front and the left wing of the Western Front," Zhukov replied. "Without these, the Central Front won't be able to carry out the counteroffensive."

"Well, in that case," Stalin said, "go see Popov and throw the Bryansk Front into action. When do you think the Bryansk Front will be ready to start?"

"On the 12th," Zhukov said.

"All right," Stalin said. He had learned a great deal about war in the last few months.

✳ ✳ ✳

On July 9, Stalin ordered the offensive to begin. Zhukov was at the Bryansk Front Headquarters with General Popov and his staff. He became directly involved with the operations of the Eleventh Guards Army under Gen. I. K. Bagramyan. They decided to use a new artillery technique: to begin the attack in the middle of the bombardment. It worked very well—the offensive began on the morning of July 12 and on the first day they broke through the German defenses and began to advance toward Orel. They had fully expected the enemy to scramble to keep control of the Orel bridgehead and they were not disappointed.

* * *

The Germans began reinforcing the Bryansk Front, giving the Russian army the respite it needed to go on the offensive on July 15. The Germans began moving troops from the Central Front.

And so, the German offensive on the Orel Front collapsed. Now the Germans were to feel the might of Russian arms that had been prepared for the specific purpose of victory over this hated enemy.

On July 12, Stalin called Zhukov and ordered him to fly to the Prokhorovka sector north of Belgorod, where the largest and most fierce tank battle of the war was in progress, more than 1,500 tanks and self-propelled guns taking part. On July 13, Zhukov reached the area, the day of the turning point of the battle. The German forces had lost hope of victory and taken up defensive positions. On July 16 they began to pull back toward Belgorod. On July 18, with General Vasilievsky, Zhukov watched fierce fighting near the Komsomolets State Farm, where the Eighteenth and Twenty-Ninth Russian Tank Corps were facing counterattacks from German units.

General I. M. Chistyakov's Sixth Guards Army had been in action since July 4, with no rest and was virtually exhausted. So were the First Tank Army and the Seventh Guards Field Army. Because of this the enemy was able to pull Field Marshal von Manstein's troops back to the Belgorod defense line by July 23. The troops of the Voronezh and Steppe Fronts had to be replenished, and their activities coordinated. Zhukov approached Stalin about this delay and received the usual abuse from the dictator, who did not understand that the forthcoming operation required ample supply and careful preparation. Reluctantly, he agreed to delay, but kept pressing for haste.

Why Kursk?

The Kursk salient seemed to the Germans particularly favorable for attack. A simultaneous German offensive from the north and south would trap powerful Russian forces. It was also to be hoped that the operational reserves the enemy would throw into the fray could be smashed. Moreover, the liquidation of this salient would greatly shorten the front. True, there were some who argued that the enemy would expect an attack in precisely this area and that there was therefore danger of losing more German forces than destroying Russian forces. But Hitler would not be convinced and thought Operation Citadel would succeed, provided it was undertaken *soon.*

On July 23, the Russian forces reached lines north of Belgorod and restored the defensive positions of the Voronezh Front. Stalin was finally convinced to halt the advance and prepare for counterattack.

The counteroffensive at Belgorod began on the morning of August 3, 1943. The Voronezh Front led the way and two tank armies were able to advance twenty miles, breaking through the German entire line of defense. The Steppe Front, which faced tougher German opposition, also advanced ten miles that first day. The second day the German defenses stiffened and the Steppe Front advance was slowed down. At 6:00 on the morning of August 5, the Two Hundred and Seventieth Guards Rifle Regiment broke into the city of Belgorod. That evening, Moscow fired a salute honoring the troops for the capture of Orel and Belgorod. It was the first such salute of the war, and raised morale considerably.

Having gained control of Belgorod, the Russians began to develop their offensives on Kharkov and the Germans retreated to avoid being trapped. On August 23, the Russians entered Kharkov, freeing it from the German yoke.

Troops of the Steppe, Western, Bryansk, and Central Fronts continued their offensives, and by August 20 they had reached a line run-

---

Kursk: The Military Turning Point

Stalingrad was the political and moral turning point of the war in the east, but Kursk was the military turning point. After this the Germans had no chance to win. The authority for this statement is the postwar German historians, particularly Walter Goerlitz, who wrote in *Paulus and Stalingrad* "the German defeat at Kursk and Belgorod was the military turning point."

---

ning east of Lyudinovo, east of Bryansk, and through Dmitrovski Orlovsky. This completed the operations in the areas of Kursk, Orel, Belgorod, Kharkov, Bogodukhov, and Akhtyrka, resulting in the complete defeat of the German forces that Hitler had so confidently sent to capture the Volga and the Caucasus.

This confrontation of German and Soviet forces had lasted fifty days, and resulted in the defeat of thirty of Germany's strongest units, including tank divisions, which lost more than half their strength. The German losses were 500,000 men, 2,000 tanks and self-propelled guns, including many tigers, panthers, and Ferdinands, as well as 3,000 field guns and 2,000 planes. Those losses could never be made up by the German leadership. This significant defeat caused Hitler to transfer twenty-four divisions and other reinforcements from the Western Front, which showed how the German forces were weakening. Ultimate defeat was now only a matter of time.

From Kursk
to Teheran

FOLLOWING THE GREAT VICTORY AT KURSK THE RUSSIANS
began to advance on every front toward the Dnieper River and
beyond. Meanwhile, the Russian people began to believe that the war
was won, although there was much fierce fighting to come and
Leningrad was still within the range of German guns.

Moscow, however, was now completely out of danger, and so
safe that the diplomatic corps, which had evacuated to Kuibyshev,
came back to the Soviet capital.

On August 22, 1943, Stalin announced an urgent program of
reconstruction to put the liberated territories on their feet. It provided
for seed for the autumn's sowing, the return of livestock and machinery that had been evacuated, reconstruction of railways, and building of dwellings for the railway men.

Two conflicting tendencies arose, both of them expressive of the
character of Stalin. On the one hand, he wanted to return to "Leninist
Purity," but he also indulged in Great Russian ultranationalism, to the

Achtung! Minen!

The capture of the ancient Russian city of Orel and the liquidation of the Orel salient were the results of the Russian victory at Kursk. The fighting had been vicious, and for months afterwards the victors and the farmers kept encountering mines in the whole area. Correspondent Alexander Werth visited the salient shortly after the victory. Here is part of his article written for the London *Sunday Times*:

> *Achtung, Minen, Achtung, Minen . . .* "They're the devil," said the colonel who met us at Mtsensk. Along only 100 yards just off this road we dug up 650. There was very tough fighting around here. German Jaeger—tough troops, very good troops, can't deny that. But the mines are bad, very bad. Every damned day something happens. Yesterday a colonel came down this road on horseback; the horse kicked an antipersonnel mine—and there you are, horse and colonel both *phut!*

He talked of new delayed action mines found in German dugouts. Contraptions in which the acid eats through the metal; some take two months to blow up. And there were also booby traps, plenty of them. These mines and booby traps had become one of the Germans' most important weapons in 1943, and were the Russian soldiers' greatest worry and chief topic of conversation. Mines had caused terrible casualties to the Russians in the Orel fighting and were going to cause more at Kharkov and elsewhere. As Werth talked to the colonel, a horse-drawn cart drove past and in it were two moaning soldiers with blood streaming from their heads.

They had just been blown up by a mine.

extent that some people were completely turned off. Typical was the film *Ivan the Terrible* made by Serge Eisenstein, on Stalin's orders, depicting that cruel but wise Tsar as the forerunner to Stalin.

Meanwhile, the Red Army was making spectacular advances in the Ukraine and elsewhere. Kharkov was captured on August 23. Then, General Tolbukhin captured Taganrog, which the Germans had held since the autumn of 1941. On August 31, Rokossovsky captured Glukhov and penetrated deep into the northern Ukraine. Further south, the Donbas (Don River Basin) was being overrun and the Germans were pulling out after wrecking coal mines and factories. On September 8, the whole front page of every newspaper, by Stalin's order, trumpeted the news of the liberation of the whole of the Donbas. On September 10, Tolbukhin and Malinovsky captured Mariupol on the Sea of Azov. The last two German strongholds in the far south were taken—Novorossisk on September 16, and the Taman Peninsula on October 7, most of the Germans escaping to the Crimea across the Straits of Kerch.

On October 21, Rokossovsky captured Chernigov, which was almost totally destroyed by German bombing in 1941. Koniev took Poltava, then Kremenchug, breaking through to the Dnieper.

On October 25, Rokossovsky took Smolensk, and Stalin announced that the Red Army was advancing on Kiev in the Ukraine and Vitebsk, Gomel, and Mogilev in Belorussia.

The German hope of holding the Dnieper line vanished.

The Crimea was about to be cut off from the mainland. And on October 25 the Dnieper line cracked at the bottom when Dniepropetrovsk fell to the Red Army. The Russians were winning victories day after day.

The Western Allies were now seen as committed to the war, but with minimal loss of life to themselves and maximum shedding of Russian blood. Some twenty-five German divisions were pinned down in France awaiting the invasion of Normandy, and twelve divisions were tied up in Italy.

This was the backdrop of the Moscow Conference of foreign ministers in mid-October, the first Big Three meeting of its kind. It came at an excellent time for the Russians, after three months of uninterrupted victories.

The conference was held in Moscow because Stalin would not travel and he forbade Molotov to do so, either. The Russians were bearing the weight of the war, Stalin said, and so let the Western powers come to them.

Japan

In August 1939, the Japanese launched an assault on Kalkin Gol in Mongolia, Nomonhon, a trial balloon for the Strike North policy that then governed the Imperial Army's plans for expansion of empire.

The attack was met by General Zhukov with immediate and superior forces. Russian aircraft and tanks proved overwhelming to the Japanese. The Kwantung Army, which had launched the attack, lost 50,000 men in one month and retreated back into Manchuria. Tokyo immediately switched its policy from one of Strike North to one of Strike South. In March 1941, Japanese foreign minister Yosuke Matsuoka went to Berlin to sign the Rome–Berlin–Tokyo Treaty of Alliance. He stopped off in Moscow on his way home and signed a five-year treaty of neutrality with the Russians. When Matsuoka was ready to leave, Stalin entertained him and they spent so long over the vodka bottle that Matsuoka's train had to be held for him at the Moscow station. Stalin took Matsuoka to the station. When they were about to part company, Stalin enfolded the little Japanese in an immense bearhug and gave his blessing.

"We are both Asiatics. Now Japan can move south," he said.

South, he meant, not north.

✳ ✳ ✳

On August 9, 1945, Russia entered the war against Japan, hoping to get part of the loot that would result. Soviet troops marched into Manchuria and captured the Kuriles and southern Sakhalin, but that was all. General MacArthur rudely pushed them away from the occupation of Japan.

As of 2002 no peace treaty had yet been signed between Russia and Japan.

The number one question for the Russians was the cross-channel invasion of France, which the British had been resisting. The bigger question was how long the war would last.

The Moscow Conference lasted twelve days, and produced some positive results: the joint demand for unconditional surrender of the Germans and Japanese and the foreshadowing of the United

Nations organization. Finally, the conference published a Roosevelt–Churchill–Stalin declaration on war criminals, establishing the principle that the accused would be returned to the country where the alleged crimes were committed.

✳ ✳ ✳

Next came the Teheran Conference, where the final decision to launch the cross-channel invasion was made. The partition of Germany was discussed and Stalin promised that Russia would take part in the war against Japan, which had been carried mostly by the Americans.

The war was about to enter a new phase.

Russia Enters
Eastern Europe

B Y THE END OF 1943, TWO-THIRDS OF THE TERRITORY occupied by the Germans had been liberated and the Russians were moving toward the final expulsion of Germans from their lands. The Red Army was going to find itself in non-Russian territory, and this was going to create new political and diplomatic problems.

1944 would be known as The Year of the Ten Victories. In January the siege of Leningrad was finally lifted. The Russians broke through the ring of German pillboxes and minefields. Within a week the Germans were on the run, and did not stop until they reached the borders of Estonia.

In February, Koniev's and Vatutin's troops encircled several German divisions in the Korsun salient, then launched their famous Mud Offensive, which crashed through into Rumania.

In April, Odessa was liberated and in May the Crimea was completely cleared. In June, Finland was knocked out of the war, but the Red Army stopped the German advance on the 1940 Finnish border

Victory Salutes

On August 5, 1943, the Era of Victory Salutes began. The Red Army had just captured Orel and Belgorod and Stalin wanted to commemorate this change. First came Stalin's special announcement that the cities had been liberated. Then came the deep voice of Levitan, Radio Moscow's star announcer:

Order by the Supreme Commander in Chief to Col. Gen. Popov, Col. Gen. Sokolovsky, Army General Rokossovsky, Army General Vatutin, Col. Gen. Koniev . . .

Today, August 5, the troops of the Bryanks Front, in coopera-tion with the Western and Central Fronts, as the result of bitter fighting captured the city of Orel. Today also the troops of the Steppe and Voronezh Fronts broke the enemy's resistance and captured the town of Belgorod. The first units to break into these two places will now be named "Orel Regiments" and "Belgorod Regiments."

Tonight at 24 o'clock on August 5, the capital of our country, Moscow, will salute the valiant troops that liberated Orel and Belgorod with twelve artillery salvoes from 120 guns. I express my thanks to all the troops who took part in the offensive. Eternal glory to the heroes who fell in the struggle for the freedom of our country.

Death to the German Invaders!

The Supreme Commander in Chief,
Marshal of the Soviet Union—STALIN

With some slight variation in text, these were the words that Russia was to hear more than three hundred times before the final victory over Germany and Japan.

The Era of the Victory Salutes had begun.

and did not move against Helsinki. Also in June, Belorussia was liberated, with nearly thirty German divisions trapped around Minsk, and the Russians advanced nearly to Warsaw, where the Warsaw uprising had begun. The Russians liberated much of Poland, including the provisional capital of Lublin, nearly all of Lithuania, and reached the borders of East Prussia.

That summer of 1944 Stalin interfered directly in Polish affairs on behalf of the Lublin Committee for National Liberation formed when Lublin was freed by the Red Army. Prime Minister Churchill recognized what Stalin was up to and became alarmed at the prospect of Russian domination of the Poles. He urged the Polish government in exile in London to join the Lublin committee before it became a communist fait accompli. On July 26, the Soviet government recognized the committee as the legitimate political force in Poland and Marshal Nikolai Bulganin was made the Soviet liaison.

In July, the Red Army took the western Ukraine, including Lwow, crossed the Vistula, and tried and failed to break through to Cracow. There the offensive bogged down because the concentration of German forces was at its heaviest.

Early in August, Zhukov and Rokossovsky made vigorous efforts to destroy the enemy's grouping on the outskirts of Warsaw. In London the Polish government in exile had decided in July to launch an uprising against the Germans, believing that the Red Army would come to their assistance. On July 25, Gen. Tadeusz Bor-Komorowski, commander of the Polish Home Army, reported to London, "Ready at any moment for the battle of Warsaw."

That army tried every way to isolate Warsaw. Rokossovsky informed Moscow that the Home Army had refused to make contact with the Russians. Stalin thought the whole uprising was a Western plot to reestablish a bourgeois government in Poland. When the uprising began, the Home Army had only 16,000 troops, of whom only 3,500 were armed. General Bor-Komorowski knew that his army was

---

The Bear Growls

By Christmastime 1943, the Russians went over onto the offensive, and from this time on their offensives were no longer designated by seasons. The offensive was almost constant. Hitler had dreamed of destroying Leningrad to prove to the world the futility of trying to resist the German juggernaut. But without fanfare the siege of Leningrad was lifted. Resistance was not futile after all. No German had set foot in the city. Hitler fired von Manstein, the fair-haired von Manstein, next to Rommel the most darling of his generals.

In the summer while Hitler's attention was focused on Normandy, Marshal Zhukov launched a new drive near Bobruick and captured most of the twenty-five divisions there in two weeks. By the end of July 1944, the Russians reached the sea at Riga, isolating Army Group North, which would hold out for months and ultimately have to be rescued by sea from the Kurland Peninsula. Hitler's Thousand-Year Reich was crumbling before his eyes.

---

not strong enough to capture Warsaw. He expected the Russians to move and take the city. The Russians did not appear. Surprisingly, the people of Warsaw joined the rebellion against the Germans, pushed by their hatred for the Germans after five years of unmitigated terror. They began to build barricades and joined military detachments. But the Germans held all the key points in the city and when the Red Army did not appear, quickly the insurgents were forced to go on the defensive. From the outset, the position was hopeless; the rebels had few guns, little medicine, and they got no help from the Russians.

Rokossovsky said that on August 2 he received an intelligence report that an uprising had broken out in Warsaw, but claimed that none of the Polish elements of the Red Army knew anything about it.

In August, the Red Army struck south, in Moldavia and Rumania, trapping sixteen German divisions and several Rumanian divisions in pockets, charged into Rumania, which surrendered, overran Bulgaria, and reached the borders of Hungary.

In September, Estonia and most of Latvia were liberated, but thirty German divisions holed up in the Kurland Peninsula, where they remained until the German general surrender in May 1945.

In October, the Red Army broke into Hungary and eastern Czechoslovakia, joined up with the Yugoslav partisans, and took part in the liberation of Belgrade. At the end of the year, fighting began in Budapest, and continued until February 1945.

Also, in October, the Red Army threw the Germans out of Petsamo, crossing into northern Norway. The Russians' halt outside Warsaw at the time of the Warsaw uprising was viewed with deep suspicion outside Moscow; it was believed to be a deliberate withholding of aid to the Polish Resistance, which had strong ties with London.

The Germans were at last outnumbered in the field, and deserted by almost all their allies except for a few Hungarian divisions. Yet the Germans continued to resist at any cost, much less strongly than they resisted the Western powers because they considered the Russians to be savages.

✳ ✳ ✳

At Warsaw on August 2, the Germans launched a strong counterattack against the Russian First Tank Army and the Forty-Seventh Army, and for a time the issue was in balance. As the Russians struggled to force the Vistula, they could see Warsaw burning. The Russians stood by and watched.

It is significant that there is no mention of the Warsaw uprising in Volkogonov's biography of Stalin, although the incident lasted for sixty-two days and resulted in the complete destruction of the city. Stalin claimed that the Polish underground, supported by the vast majority of the people of Warsaw, was an invention of the London Poles. When the Western Allies pleaded with Stalin to allow their aircraft—which were supplying the Polish uprising—to land in soviet

---

Tragedy at Warsaw

In the summer of 1944, the Red Army entered Poland and Stalin made sweeping promises to the Polish people. One July 23, the left flank of Rokossovsky's First Belorussian Front moved toward the Vistula River after capturing Lublin. On July 31, the spearhead reached the outskirts of Praga across the Vistula from Warsaw, and there Rokossovsky stopped. The next day the Polish Uprising of General Bor-Komorowski began. But Bor-Komorowski was not the right color of Pole; he was not a Red. And so Rokossovsky sat by and watched the Polish uprising batter itself to death against the Nazis.

Stalin wanted Poland within the orbit of his postwar empire and he would have it no other way. His behavior was characterized by Churchill as "strange and sinister." The Red Army occupied Praga, but stopped there and waited. Under pressure from the Western Allies, Stalin authorized some airdrops and bombing of the Nazis, but it was a farce. On October 2, the Polish army surrendered to the Germans. The uprising had failed. The path was clear for Stalin to have his way with Poland. Western indignation was immaterial. Stalin never counted the consequences of his actions, but headed straight for the object in view. This was to be his undoing and the cause of the downfall of his empire.

---

territory, Stalin refused, "Sooner or later," he said, "the truth about the group of criminals who have unleashed the Warsaw adventure will become known to everybody."

But when he saw that Western goodwill toward Russia was wanning, and that the unpleasant fate of the Polish uprising was inevitable, Stalin changed his tactics. Soviet planes dropped some supplies to the rebels, a Polish unit attached to Rokossovsky made an unsuccessful attempt to cross the river, and American and British planes running supply service were finally allowed to land in Soviet territory.

When the insurgents surrendered to the Germans on October 2, the destroyed Warsaw was evidence of another of Stalin's victories.

He had again, as biographer Adam Ulam put it, "displayed savage determination not to be swayed in the pursuit of his goals, no matter what moral pressure was brought on him. It became evident to most Poles that the only hope of saving some shred of Polish independence lay in submission to Stalin's will, lessons that would be repeated in Czechoslovakia, Hungary, and Bulgaria."

After the failure of the Warsaw uprising, the Russians took their time in capturing the city and turning their attention to Eastern Poland, where their Voiso Polskoye was operating. A second Russian-sponsored Polish Army was formed in the Lublin area, with 50,000 men, and then a third; together the three armies were made into the Polish Front. By war's end this front boasted 450,000 men with all the implements of modern warfare. The liberation of Warsaw was finally accomplished by the First Polish Army, attached to Marshal Zhukov's First Belorussian Front, on January 17, 1945, and Polish soldiers went on to fight in the Berlin area. They liberated vast areas of Poland before participating in the battle of Berlin, where 185,000 Polish soldiers fought beside the Russians against the vestiges of the Nazi armies.

✳ ✳ ✳

Stalin was impatient that fall to stake his claim to Eastern Europe, so two entire army groups were diverted to that end. He telephoned Marshal Malinovsky and ordered that Budapest must be taken forthwith. There must be no delay. Malinovsky pleaded for time and reinforcements and Stalin hung up the phone on him. The resulting premature offensive cost the Russians enormous and needless casualties in what was a secondary theater of operations.

Finland was the great exception, largely because of President Roosevelt's affection for that country (the Finns were famous for having been the only country to pay its World War I debt). It was Stalin's plan that all of Eastern Europe be subjugated to the Soviet yoke.

Churchill's Ploy

Besides Poland, the Red Army had other fish to fry in the summer and autumn of 1944. Hitler's satellites were collapsing one after the other and it was important to stake claims to their future. There was rivalry between Stalin and his Western Allies and he thought it necessary to occupy Bulgaria, Hungary, and Rumania as soon as possible. Some Russians attributed Churchill's pressure for Russian capture of Warsaw to a desire to slow down Red Army progress in Eastern Europe.

Roosevelt did not recognize this, but Prime Minister Churchill did, and in October 1944 he went to Moscow to try to work out a diplomatic business deal with Stalin. Roosevelt demanded that the Churchill-Stalin meetings be chaperoned by U.S. Ambassador Averill Harriman.

Churchill proposed that Eastern Europe be divided into spheres of influence, Britain and Russia. In Rumania, for example, Russia was to have 90 percent influence, Britain 10 percent. In Greece the percentages were reversed. Stalin did not reply in words to these overtures, he took the paper with these figures and made a large tick on it, and then handed it back to Churchill. The Prime Minister chose to believe that this was a sign of assent.

The Churchill visit failed, and Stalin went on his jolly way to impose Soviet might on all the countries of Eastern Europe—save Yugoslavia, which resisted successfully under Marshal Josip Broz Tito.

Rumania

R USSIAN FORCES CROSSED THE RUMANIAN BORDER ON
April 21, 1944. Behind them came the Soviet military government. The Germans and Rumanian military put up strong resistance and the three Russian Fronts involved—the First, Second, and Third Ukrainian—went on the defensive. The Communist Party led in formation a United Workers Party, the first political step in the communization of Rumania. What Stalin was interested in was not communization but Soviet control, and soon he had it. The Rumanian government was organized with an Allied control commission supervising, but within weeks the American and British members found themselves virtual prisoners under Soviet control.

Stalin's justification was that Russia had to be compensated for its losses. Too often the Americans subsided in the arguments and let Stalin have his way, for they had no real feeling for Eastern Europe.

On August 20, the Second and Third Ukrainian Fronts began an offensive in the Iasi-Kishinev area. With some setbacks it went well until August 22. On that night a conference was held in the palace of King Michael of Rumania, a conference kept secret from Ion Antonescu, the

---

The Rumanians Welcome the Red Army

With some relief, the people of Bucharest welcomed the Red Army on August 30, for they feared a German counteroffensive and attempt to recapture Bucharest. The Soviet press reported that the Red Army aroused feelings of wonder and surprise in Bucharest; the Rumanians were amazed at the quantity and quality of the heavy equipment and could not at first believe that it had been made in Russia.

"The courtesy is overwhelming," one Soviet reporter wrote. "No sooner does one of our comrades produce a cigarette, than dozens of hands holding burning lighters are stretched out to light it for him."

Posters were displayed everywhere, welcoming *Maresalul genialul comandat al armatei rosei* and everyone was down on Antonescu, who was still locked up in the royal palace.

In all the Russian reports there was a note of condescension, sometimes of contempt, for all this cringing. But the reporters differentiated between the sincere joy of the ordinary Rumanian and the half-hearted relief felt by the "bourgeois loafers," in which Bucharest abounded.

Nazified dictator of Rumania. The king was meeting with representatives of the Communist, Social Democratic, Peasant, and National Liberal Parties. The communists had worked patiently for many months to form this group into an anti-Nazi bloc. The king, surrounded by his sycophants, set out to preserve the monarchy. A military committee, dominated by communists, was elected to overthrow Antonescu's regime, create an armed uprising, break off the alliance with Germany, and withdraw from the war. Antonescu's arrest should be made in the palace when he came to report to the king on military affairs.

On August 20, both Ukrainian Fronts struck out with forces estimated by the Germans at ninety infantry divisions and forty-one tank and three cavalry formations. The avalanche was set in motion and nothing could stop it on its way into the Rumanian interior. It was easy. Half the divisions of German Army Group *Sued-Ukraine* were

184

Rumanian and the Russians struck first at them. On August 22, the full extent of the disaster became apparent. Sixteen divisions of the German army were trapped in the Kishnev area and The Rumanian Third Army was trapped on the Black Sea Coast.

No one did anything to blow up the bridges across the Pruth River and the Danube, and the road was now clear for the Russians to speed to Bucharest.

Unlike the Rumanians, the trapped Germans fought like wolves, and 60,000 were killed, but in the end the Russians took 106,000 prisoners—among them two corps commanders, twelve division commanders, and thirteen other generals. Two corps commanders and five division commanders were killed. The Russians overran all of Eastern Rumania and on the thirtieth Malinovsky's men entered Bucharest and the oil city of Ploesti.

On August 21 and 22, Antonescu met twice with General Friessner, the German commander, at the latter's command post. Friessner said that political intrigues against the Germans were being hatched in secret in Rumania. Antonescu denied this and convinced Friessner of his loyalty to Germany. They planned a stout defense of Bucharest against the Red Army.

✳ ✳ ✳

On his return to Bucharest, Antonescu called a meeting of his cabinet, at which he announced the continuation of the war at Germany's side, and the mobilization of the country's resources to effect it. He then asked for an audience with the king at 4:00 PM on August 24. This meshed with the communist coalition's plans for the uprising and everything was prepared; the wheels were in motion.

At the appointed hour, Antonescu came to the palace and made a lengthy report on the conditions at the front. He was then dismissed and arrested. His foreign minister (also named Antonescu) had been arrested a few hours earlier and confined to the royal family's armored shelter. Antonescu was sent to join him. Next, the war minister, the minister of internal affairs, the inspector general of the

Guderian's Earthworks

Hitler's major errors in the east now came home to him as the Russians continued their advance. His underestimation of Soviet potential, the barbarism against the civil population, his contempt for his Balkan allies, and his destruction of the command structure of the German army all worked against a successful defense as the Russians came. General Heinz Guderian, his new chief of the army, saw that the only possibility to defend the German borders was to enlist troops unfit for mobile warfare—the disabled, overaged, and the young. He got Hitler to agree to a program of fortification. The defenses had to be built immediately if there was any chance of saving Germany from the Soviet drive.

Along the west wall the earthworks began to go up. Most of them were built by the volunteer labor of women, children, and old men—by summer 1944 this was the only untapped source of labor in Germany. Hitler had wasted his manpower by murdering the Jews and other minorities and by throwing men away in the east in one ill-begotten campaign after another.

Members of the Hitler Youth were also dragooned into the building of the fortifications and some into defending them. There were no military garrisons left in the east, all serviceable units had been rushed to the Western Front, where in August the Americans and British were dashing through France, bound for Paris and the low countries. General George Patton and General Bernard Montgomery had turned the Panzer tactics, many of them developed by Guderian, and now they were employing them against the Germans.

The only troops Guderian had for his defense in the east were the dregs left over from the western battle zone. So old and sick soldiers, and men who were not soldiers at all, rushed to Danzig, Königsberg, Breslau, and other cities along the east wall to defend it against the Russian onslaught. Guderian formed 100 fortress infantry batallions and 100 artillery batteries. But then, before he could get them into position, the greater need in the west caused

80 percent of them to be moved westward. This was done with Hitler's approval by OKW before Guderian knew about it.

The units were thrown willy-nilly into one breach after another and slaughtered instead of having that little time for training that might have made partial soldiers of them. And when Guderian asked for weapons for the eastern fortress, Hitler, Keitel, and Jodl said there were no weapons. They did not know what they were talking about. There were plenty of weapons left over from the western campaign early in the war, before Hitler took into his own hands all decisions regarding the armed forces.

That summer the management of the war was sharply divided. Guderian was commander of OKH, but effectively he was commander of the war in the east. OKW, which was Hitler, concerned itself only with the war in the west. The war against the Russians had ceased to exist in Hitler's mind. The eastern war was hopeless so Hitler had given up thinking about it.

The only thing that would save Germany from the Russians was for the Western Allies to get to Berlin first. Yet Hitler did not see that, and resisted them firmly. He still believed in miracles and the miracle that would turn defeat into victory for Germany. He was planning to throw his last resources into a sudden strike against the west that would turn the war around.

Guderian found weapons for his eastern garrisons and ordered them shipped there. Keitel and Jodl stopped the shipments and ordered everything larger than a 50-caliber machine gun shipped west. The guns arrived too late to do any good and without the gunners to use them. They would have been invaluable in the east, Guderian said. Even in the defense of the east, Guderian had trouble with Hitler. He suggested that a people's land army be formed under direction of the old SA. Hitler at first agreed but later changed his mind. He would establish a *Landssturm*, he said, but it must be under someone he could trust. So he appointed his secretary, Martin Bormann, as head of the *Landssturm*. The Volkssturm was built on the Nazi

(Continued)

pattern—more attention paid to how to give the proper Heil Hitler than to weapons training.

Besides all this, Guderian had to contend with the growing power of Heinrich Himmler, who had emerged after the Hitler assassination attempt more powerful than before. Hitler had placed Himmler in command of the replacement army, which was thoroughly Nazified.

Every day the war grew worse for Germany. All the troop units trained in Germany were sent west. But while Hitler was dreaming of victory in the west, Guderian was trying to shore up the decaying east.

gendarmerie, and the Bucharest prefect of police were summoned by telephone to the palace and arrested.

The rebels worried about the king's safety, so that night he was taken to a safe place far from the capital where he would remain for a time.

On August 23, shortly after 5:00 PM, the leaders of the communist coalition sent their military committee to the palace, picked up Antonescu and took him to one of the Communist Party safe houses. At the same time, representatives of the Communist and other parties gathered at the palace to form a new government. They formed a government that was mainly pro-monarchist, with General Constantin Sanatescu as its prime minister. In this government the four parties of the National Democratic bloc (the communists and their allies) each had only one representative, a minister without a portfolio. The intent of the government was to stop the process with the arrest of Antonescu. In particular, the man named as chief of the Rumanian General Staff, General Mihail, was very close to the king.

The communists learned what was going on and insisted that they and their allies have a piece of the action.

The new government proceeded to call on the country to surrender to the United Nations, leave the Nazi coalition, and struggle for the liberation of northern Transylvania. Shortly before midnight the king went on the air and read a declaration of peace, calling for armistice and peace and for the formation of a new government.

* * *

The military command in Bucharest, which was dominated by communists, began the uprising in Bucharest and detachments of armed workers filled the streets and squares, seizing the most important installations and institutions.

Alarmed, the German ambassador rushed to the palace. He was informed of the arrest of Antonescu and was told that the Germans must get out. He was told that no obstacle would be put in the way of the German withdrawal.

As he left the palace, the ambassador swore that he would drown Rumania in blood.

Now the Nazi general came to the palace, and promised to move the forces. But the next day, Hitler announced the suppression of Rumania, and German planes began to bomb. German military forces were moved into Bucharest. The People's Militia attacked the Germans and disarmed the German military units in the city.

The Rumanian army did not lay down its arms but continued to fight at the side of the Germans. On August 24, the KPR (the communist-led coalition) published an appeal to the people to take up arms against the Germans. So the uprising spread throughout the country. The next day, the Soviet government repeated a pious statement made in April to the effect that it had no intention to seize part of Rumanian territory or change the country's social order or infringe on its independence.

Stalin then ordered the offensive to destroy Germany and its allies.

The Red Army concentrated on two regions in Rumania, Bucharest, and Ploesti, the oil center. General Malinovsky ordered General Kravchenko to send his Sixth Tank Army against both places. Kravchenko sent two corps to Bucharest and one to Ploesti. On August 31, the troops entered Bucharest and an Allied control commission was established. Malinovsky was promoted to marshal.

Stalin had to decide what line to take toward the king of Rumania. He decided to treat him leniently because of the favorable effect it would have on Russia's allies. But only for the moment. The wind was already blowing the seeds of communism throughout the country, and soon the Soviets would supervise the takeover of the Rumanian government. Then the king and his family would go into exile.

At first, the Russians raised no objections about the composition of the Rumanian government, but before long it began to put pressure on the "doublecrossing elements" of the democratic bloc. General Sanatescu was replaced by General Radescu and later by Petru Groza. The young king was given a Soviet medal; but things changed and soon the terrible Mr. Vyshinski was sent to Bucharest to bully the king.

But that came later. Early in September the Rumanian Armistice delegation arrived in Moscow, where it was received in style and lived in luxury in the government guesthouse in Ostrovsky Lane. It was significant, however, that most of the talking was done by the new Minister of Justice, Mr. Patrasceanu, a man of great charm and whose even more charming young wife was a product of the French culture in Rumania. She would come to tea with the British and American foreign correspondents and would bring a whiff of Guerlain into the dingy Hotel Metropole.

At his press conference, Minister Patrasceanu described in detail how the coup d'etat of August 23 had come about and how "our king" had trapped dictator Antonescu. He also told how heroic the Rumanian troops had been when Bucharest was being shelled and bombed by the Germans. But of the difficulties that were likely to arise among the various parties of the coalition, Minister Patrasceanu said nothing.

✳ ✳ ✳

That month, Armistice delegations were queuing up in Moscow. No sooner had the Rumanians concluded their armistice than the Finns were waiting in the wings. The Rumanian armistice was signed on September 12 and the delegation made its way back to Bucharest. Mr. Patrasceanu continued to exercise his charms, until later, when the perfidy of Titoism spread through the Balkan states and Patrasceanu was arrested, tried, and shot as a Titoite.

—ᴍ—

17

Bulgarian Adventure

THE SITUATION OF BULGARIA WAS QUITE DIFFERENT. Britain and the United States were at war with Bulgaria but the USSR was not. There was a Bulgarian minister in Moscow throughout the war.

The Germans used Bulgaria as a source for raw materials and as a military base, but the Russians had shown tolerance of that country for a long time. This despite provocations, for example, when the Germans used Bulgarian ports to evacuate the Crimea. But by August 1944 the situation had changed greatly. When the Red Army overran Rumania, several armed German ships escaped to Bulgarian ports and were not interned. These ports also were reported to be hiding German U-boats.

On August 26, Bulgarian Foreign Minister Draganov declared Bulgaria's neutrality and promised that any German soldiers would be disarmed if they refused to leave the country.

The Russians said that was not good enough, and declared war on Bulgaria. On September 5, three days later, Russian troops invaded

Soviet Plans for Eastern Europe

In a paper to Eden written on May 4, 1944, Prime Minister Churchill set out "the brute issues between us and the Russians in Italy, Rumania, in Bulgaria, Yugoslavia, above all in Greece. Broadly speaking the issue is: Are we going to acquiesce in the communization of the Balkans and perhaps of Italy?"

Stalin at this stage was not interested in the form of government or economy in the countries the Red Army was about to occupy, or in building up a "Communist Bloc," as such. What he wanted was to stake out his claim to a Soviet sphere of influence in Eastern and possibly Central Europe. Within that, anyone in power would understand clearly that in the future their policies would have to be in conformity with Russian wishes, that their resources (especially after the losses the Soviet Union had suffered during the war) would have to be at Russia's disposal. And anybody who Stalin suspected of anti-Soviet tendencies (and he was a very suspicious man) would not be tolerated.

The tradition of complete subordination of communist parties everywhere to the interests of the "workers' Fatherland" made local Communist parties natural instruments for carrying out such a policy. But Stalin was also aware that too obvious a reliance on them could be counterproductive, arousing suspicion and opposition on the part of the British and American allies, who now had powerful armies of their own in Europe. He therefore preferred, where he could, to work through coalitions in which social democrats, peasant parties, and nationalists took part as well as communists—and the democratic anti-Fascist front was the current formula. Well-practiced communist techniques, such as infiltration, could be used to secure acquiescence while the multiparty facade was retained to reassure the west. Where communists, unaccustomed to Stalinist "doubletalk," took exception to such compromises on the grounds of Marxist principle, they could be expelled when they refused to accept the Moscow line without question, or could be excommunicated, as what happened in the case of Tito and the Yugoslav Communist leadership.

Stalin remarked to Anthony Eden when they first met in 1941 that Hitler's weakness was not knowing when to stop. Stalin did. Compared with

> Hitler's Utopian dream of a racist empire involving the movement of millions of people and the permanent enslavement of millions more, a modern Sparta on a gigantic scale, Stalin's New Order as it developed in the rest of the 1940s was a perfectly possible and practical scheme. This is proved by the fact that it lasted for thirty years after his death in 1953. Unlike Hitler, Stalin recognized that there were limits beyond which it would be dangerous to push one's luck. The most striking example of this is his retreat over Berlin in 1949.

Bulgaria. They met no resistance but were greeted as liberators. On the next day, after a coup, Kimon Georgiev formed the Fatherland Front that declared war on Germany. The two-day war was over. The Bulgarians showed a revolutionary enthusiasm that far surpassed that of the Rumanians.

Almost immediately, peoples courts were established to try war criminals, and the Bulgarian army was being purged of all its "Fascist elements." The armistice was signed in Moscow on October 28, and Bulgaria entered the Soviet sphere of influence.

After the defeat of the main forces of the German Army Group in southern Ukraine, the Russians were faced with finishing off the remaining German forces, which retreated into Hungary, Rumania, and Bulgaria. The Russian General Staff knew a lot about the Bulgarian people, a nation of bold warriors and courageous fighters against foreign aggression. On the other hand, the Nazis headed up a government that had brought Bulgaria into the war on the side of Germany.

The Russian General Staff hoped that the Bulgarian people would side with Russia in the days to come. They placed their trust in the Fatherland Front, which was led by Georgi Dimitrov, the head of the Bulgarian Workers Party. Dimitrov was actually in Moscow, and he had a long history with the USSR, having been secretary general of the executive committee of the Comintern before its dissolution in 1943.

The Fatherland Front was in control of the Worker Party, Agrarians, Social Democrats, and the intelligentsia (most of them), as well as the revolutionary youth.

Dimitrov was well known to the General Staff, so they had approved in 1941 the formation of an international unit of Spaniards, Czechs, Slovaks, Poles, Bulgarians, Greeks, and Rumanians, all under Dimitrov and his deputy, Ivan Vinarov, who had emigrated to the USSR and graduated from the Frunze Military Academy.

By 1944, the Fatherland Front had a national liberation insurgent army of 18,000 men and over 200,000 partisans in the countryside.

On August 6, the uprising began, with a statement by Dimitrov, "The Bulgarian people and its armed forces must go over to the side of the Red Army, which is Bulgaria's liberation from the German yoke, and at the same time purge the Bulgarian land of Nazi bandits and their vile minions."

For two days Bulgaria had no government; then on September 2, a new cabinet was formed under Kopsta Muravev, who announced the full restoration of the Bulgarian peoples democratic rights and liberties, including full amnesty for those who had fought against the dictatorial regime. Other promises were made but it soon emerged that the government was false. The enemy was threatening the Soviet Union on the Black Sea. And so this threat must be dealt with, Stalin decided, but first he needed more information. So he ordered Zhukov to visit the Second and Third Ukrainian Fronts and work with Marshal Timoshenko. He should also have a talk with Dimitrov and he called Dimitrov himself to make the arrangements for the meeting.

Zhukov, as usual, went off on his new assignment without delay. There was no time to waste in preparing for action. By early September the Germans knew the Russian forces were moving in that direction and to delay would mean loss of surprise. All they knew was that the Bulgarian army was in the center and northern part of the country. The operation plan was completed by September 4. The Germans were retreating across Bulgarian territory without hindrance. Several dozen German naval vessels had found shelter in

---

The Tale of Eighty-Eight Tanks

In August 1944, Marshal Antonescu of Rumania suggested the evacuation of the Germans of Moldavia and the establishment of a new line of defense in the Carpathian Mountains by Army Group Center. But, just then, came word of political difficulties in Rumania. Foreign Minister von Ribbentrop suggested sending a Panzer division to Bucharest. Guderian did not have one available but he suggested dispatch of the Fourth SS Polizei Division, which was fighting guerillas in Yugoslavia. Hitler said he would consider it but he did nothing. He could not make up his mind—a difficulty that was becoming more and more common.

At this time Guderian had serious reports about the situation in Bulgaria. Guderian got the impression that his Bulgarian allies were about to pull out of the war. He suggested that no more war materials be sent to Bulgaria and that the high command request the return of some that were in the pipeline. Keitel and Jodl scoffed and refused to act.

On August 20, the Russians launched a new attack against Army Group South Ukraine. The Rumanians began to desert in large numbers and turned against the Germans. In order to avoid a collapse of the front Guderian ordered a retreat and seizure of the Danube River bridges. But the Rumanians got to the river first, seized the bridges and thus left sixteen German divisions at the mercy of the Russians. Those divisions were entirely lost.

The Carpathian Mountain defense line that Guderian had wanted would not have prevented the Rumanians from deserting, but it would have saved those sixteen German divisions. As it was, the Southeastern Front had become a shambles. Early in September the Red Army moved into Bucharest; Bulgaria went over to the Russians, and Stalin's men took over the just delivered eighty-eight Panzer IV tanks and fifty assault guns that Guderian had tried vainly to prevent from being delivered.

Bulgarian ports and the Germans were concentrated in Sofia, Breznim, and Slivits. The German ambassador had announced that German troops had no intention of leaving Bulgaria. Stalin was worried that the Germans might pull off a coup and take Bulgaria into war with the USSR.

The Black Sea Fleet was called on for action and put under the control of the Third Ukrainian Front. Its task was to seize and hold the Bulgarian ports until the troops could arrive. The operation was scheduled to start on September 6.

Stalin approved the final plan on September 5 and that day the Soviet government sent a note to the Bulgarian government, a note delivered to the Bulgarian ambassador to Moscow at 7:00 in the evening.

When this became known in Sofia, the Central Committee of the Bulgarian Workers Party convened in special session with the staff of the Insurgent Army. They approved a plan for an uprising, the main blow to be struck against Sofia on the night of September 9. The head of the operation was Todor Zhivkov. The preliminary workers' strikes began on September 6.

Muravev's government was stunned, and on the night of September 6 its representatives asked the Russian charge d'affaires in Sofia to inform the Soviet government that Bulgaria was breaking off relations with Germany and asking for an armistice.

When that word reached Moscow, Stalin called Zhukov and told him that for the time being he should restrict the advance of the Third Ukrainian Front. A popular uprising was imminent, he said, and the time had come for the Muravev government to make some basic decisions. Meanwhile, the popular uprising was taking form and on Bulgaria's northern border the Red Army was poised to strike.

On September 7, the Muravev government, finding itself in a hopeless situation, broke off relations with Germany and the next day declared war on Germany.

Zhukov soon replied to Stalin. After reporting that Stalin's orders had been carried out, he said the advance units would begin to move on September 8 at 11:00 AM and the main forces would follow immediately. Zhukov would himself visit the armies and check on their readiness. This disposition of forces would assure the Second Ukrainian Front's operations against Hungary and help the Yugoslav

---

End of the Balkans' Defense

By mid-September it was apparent that the Balkans could not be defended. Hitler ordered a series of delaying actions but in order to make forces available for the defense of Germany this withdrawal was far too slow.

Field Marshal Keitel's trip to Finland had been useless. In mid-September Finland signed an armistice with the Russians and broke off diplomatic relations with Germany. This had a decided effect on Hungary. Hitler sent Guderian to Budapest to see Admiral Horthy, and assess the situation. Guderian returned to report that the situation there was far from satisfactory to Germany.

By the end of August, the Russians had reached Bucharest and were in Translyvania. The war was on Hungary's doorstep and so Guderian went to Budapest. After the fall of Paris, Hitler had to make a decision about the defense of Germany. Capitulation was out of the question because of the Allied demand for unconditional surrender.

Defense in the east would mean leaving the west unattended. Hitler opted for a defense in the west with a powerful blow to be struck against the Western Allies before they crossed the Rhine. Having done so, they would shuttle forces back east, to strengthen the defense, and shuttle again if the West struck. It was a desperate dream.

National Liberation Army. It would also compel the Germans to evacuate Greece.

The Third Ukrainian Front soldiers moved out at 11:00 AM on September 8. First to cross the border were the motorized units; the infantry divisions came an hour later. The Bulgarian border guards offered no resistance, and the Bulgarian infantry division at Dobriuch did not fire a single shot. The Bulgarian soldiers made many friendly gestures toward the Russians. The local inhabitants were equally friendly; people came out into the streets to greet the soldiers.

Meanwhile, the Black Sea Fleet started landing marines at the port of Varna. The Bulgarian uprising came on the night of September 9, in Sofia and other key cities. A new government was installed, headed by Kimon Georgev, who went on the air and announced the makeup of his cabinet. The government appointed a delegation to conclude an armistice with the USSR, civil liberties were restored, and the members of the government who had conducted an antipopular policy were arrested.

The cabinet contained one man who was no friend to Stalin. His name was Nikola Petkov, a member of the Agrarian Party and a foe of socialism. For the moment, he was lying low, but after the signing of the armistice with Russia on October 28 he protested against the Bulgarian Army's joint actions with the Red Army. Pro-Russian elements of the government ignored Petkov and his associates, and went on with their plans for the communization of the Bulgarian government. Soon 250,000 Bulgarian soldiers were serving as part of the Third Ukrainian Front, and in late December they were attacking the Germans in the area between the Drava and Sava Rivers, participating with Yugoslav and Russian troops in the crushing of the enemy as it tried to break through on the Drava.

Spheres of Influence

IN OCTOBER 1944, PRIME MINISTER CHURCHILL MADE his second trip to Moscow wanting to cut a deal with Stalin about the future of Eastern and Central Europe. During their very first meeting the matter was settled. He scribbled on a sheet of paper his proposal: Rumania—90 percent Russian predominance, 10 percent Western Allies; Greece—90 percent British and American, 10 percent Russian; Bulgaria—75 percent Russian, 25 percent Western; Yugoslavia and Hungary, 50:50. He pushed the paper across the table to Stalin, who took his blue pencil and made a big tick of approval on it and passed it back. Then Churchill had second thoughts, "Might it not be thought rather cynical if it seemed we had disposed of these issues in such an offhand manner? Let us burn the paper."

"No. You keep it" said Stalin.

And Churchill did.

The visit was a roaring success. When Stalin and Churchill appeared in the state box at the Bolshoi Theater they drew a rousing ovation from the crowd. At the end of the visit Churchill held a press conference.

Independent Tito

The difficulties that arose between Stalin and Tito stemmed from Tito's character. He was a communist, but more so an ardent Yugoslav nationalist who refused to subordinate Yugoslavia's interests to Russia.

After long hesitation, the three Allies agreed to accept Tito's National Liberation Army, not Draja Mihailovic's Royal Yugoslav Army, as the local military vehicle. But the Allies did not accept Tito's group as the government of Yugoslavia. Stalin was worried that Britain and the United States might think that he was using the war to spread communism. He was also angry with Tito and his Yugoslav companions for presuming that they could do independently what the Russians had done—and accomplish it in a handful of years.

Tito visited Moscow in September 1944 and met Stalin. The meeting was distinctly cool. At the end of their talks the Soviets agreed to leave Yugoslavia once their "operational task" was completed. Meanwhile, the civil administration would remain in Tito's hands and the partisans would be under Yugoslav command.

Stalin told Tito he would have to reinstate King Peter.

"The blood rushed to my head that he could advised us to do such a thing," Tito recalled. "I composed myself and told him it was impossible; the people would rebel in Yugoslavia. King Peter personified treason."

Stalin was silent. Then, "You need not restore him forever. Take him back temporarily and then you can slip a knife into his back at a suitable moment."

Tito was entertained at Stalin's dacha, as Djilas had been. Tito was also disgusted at the excessive eating and drinking there. He was used to a Spartan existence in the mountains. But Stalin was used to doing business in this fashion.

Each concealed his reservations about the other, and there certainly was nothing halfhearted about the offensive that the Russians launched in October, side by side with the partisans, to drive the Germans out of Yugoslavia. When Belgrade was stormed, Stalin kept his promise that the Yugoslavs would be first to enter the city. At the victory parade, Tito saluted the Belgrade batallion, which had started out from this place three and a half years earlier, fought over almost all of Yugoslavia, and returned with only two members of its original complement left. By the time of the Yalta Conference, in February 1945, there were no Soviet troops left in Yugoslavia where the National Liberation Army mustered 800,000 men for the final campaign against the Germans. This campaign continued even after the general surrender of May 9.

"When I last came to Moscow Stalingrad was still under siege, and the enemy was sixty or seventy miles from this city, and he was even nearer Cairo. That was in August 1942. Since then the tide has turned and we have had victories and wonderful advances over vast expanses. Coming back here I find a great sense of hope and confidence that the end of the trials will be reached. Some very hard fighting will yet have to be done. The enemy is resisting with discipline and desperation and it is best to take a sober view of the speed with which the conclusion will be reached on the Western Front. But there is good news every day, and it is difficult not to be over sanguine."

"We both have our armies in the field and I am glad that the Russians no longer have the heavy feeling that they bear the whole brunt. Unity is essential if peace is to be secure. Let us cast our eyes forward beyond the battle line to the day when Germany has surrendered unconditionally, beaten to the ground, and awaiting the decisions of the outraged nations who saved themselves from the pit of destruction that Hitler had dug for them."

He ended with a Churchillian peroration on Anglo–Russian–American friendship.

"This friendship in war as in peace, can save the world, and perhaps this is the only thing that can save the peace for our children and grandchildren. In my opinion, it is a goal easily attainable. Very good, very good are the results in the field, very good the work behind the lines, and hopes are high for the permanent results of victory."

Stalin's Ploys

The obvious intention of Stalin near the close of the European war was to establish in every Eastern European country occupied by the Soviets a regime that was solidly pro-Soviet. Prime Minister Churchill observed this with a sinking heart; Britain had gone to war in 1939 to prevent Hitler from taking over Poland, and now Stalin had even greater hegemony in the east and southeast than Hitler had achieved. Further in the process of establishing the United Nations, the Russians were posing many objections to American proposals, and the Americans did not know that these were no more than debating ploys—that Stalin was ready to give them all up at the proper time in exchange for American noninterference in Bulgaria or Poland. This had accounted for Churchill's second visit to Moscow and the deal he had cut with Stalin over Eastern and Central Europe.

Foreign statesmen were now eager to visit Stalin to use him for their own purposes. General DeGaulle came in December 1944 to try to make Roosevelt and Churchill take more notice of him, hoping to enlist Stalin's aid against "the Anglo Saxons," as he referred to them, to restore France to her rightful place in the world. Stalin paid no attention to DeGaulle's overtures. DeGaulle could do nothing for him and he knew that both Roosevelt and Churchill disliked the Frenchman. DeGaulle proposed a treaty of alliance with the USSR and Stalin agreed only after he had consulted Roosevelt and learned that the "Anglo-Saxons" had no objection. All DeGaulle might have done for Stalin was to recognize his Poles as the official government of the country and when DeGaulle refused to do this, Stalin became quite rude to him. If he were DeGaulle, he said, he would not shoot the French communist leaders, at least not right away. When Stalin said this, DeGaulle did not understand that he was being made the butt of a joke. Stalin was keeping the French communists under tight rein, to avoid antagonizing the British and Americans. Maurice Thorez, Jacques Duclos, and the others were chafing at the bit, hoping to take advantage of their enormous wartime prestige to seize power in Paris. But Stalin said no.

> Stalin made DeGaulle sit through a terrible Russian movie and when it ended invited the Frenchman to stay for another one. DeGaulle excused himself and made his own way to the door while Stalin remained at the table, eating a snack.
>
> Affairs of war were going Stalin's way at that time. The Red Army scored new victories, linking up with Tito's partisans in Yugoslavia, there were temporary setbacks in Hungary where the Germans were fighting for Budapest as though it were Berlin, but to offset this, the Western Allies took a hard blow at Christmastime with the sudden German explosion in the Ardennes.
>
> And to top it all, Stalin's generals were getting ready to begin the drive on Berlin. No wonder the Russian dictator was in such a jolly mood that on New Year's Eve he hosted a drunken brawl for his military leaders and the Politburo. Marshal Budenny brought out his accordion and performed the *gopak,* the famous squatting dance. The party did not break up until dawn.
>
> Everyone agreed that it looked like a good year had arrived.

* * *

The coming of the Red Army to Yugoslavia presented Stalin with a new situation and problem. Tito was an ally, not a dependent. He had, without Russian help, cleared most of Yugoslavia of Germans. He was a professed communist, and his government was communist, although extremely nationalistic. But this potential area of trouble did not appear in the war years. In spring 1944, he sent a military mission to Moscow. One member was Milovan Djilas, who recorded his impressions of Stalin when invited to the dictator's dacha.

"The room was not large, rather long, and devoid of any opulence of décor. Above a not-too-large desk hung a photograph of Lenin and on the wall over the conference table in carved wooden frames were portraits of Suvorov and Kutzov, looking much like the lithographs one sees in the provinces.

"But the host was the plainest of all, in a marshal's uniform and soft boots, without any medals except a golden star—The Order of Hero of the Soviet Union. This was not that majestic Stalin of the photographs or newsreels—with the stiff deliberate gait and posture. He was not quiet for a moment. He toyed with his pipe, which bore the white dot of the English firm Dunhill, or drew circles with a blue pencil around words indicating the main subjects for discussion which he then crossed out, and kept turning his head this way and that while he fidgeted on his seat.

"I was surprised at something else. He was of very small stature and ungainly build. His torso was short and narrow, while his legs and arms were too long. His left arm and shoulder seemed rather stiff. He had quite a large paunch and his hair was sparse. His teeth were black and irregular, turned inward. Not even his moustache was thick and firm. Still the head was not a bad one, it had something of the common people about it—with those yellow eyes and a mixture of sternness and mischief.

"I was also surprised at his accent. One could tell that he was not a Russian. But his Russian vocabulary was rich and his manner of expression vivid and flexible, full of Russian proverbs and sayings. As I realized later, Stalin was well acquainted with Russian literature—though only Russian.

"One thing did not surprise me; Stalin had a sense of humor, self-assured but not without subtlety and depth. His reactions were quick and acute—and conclusive, which did not mean that he did not hear the speaker out, but it was evident that he was no friend of long explanations."

Central Europe

A S STALIN KNEW WELL, THE LIBERATION OF HUNGARY would open a whole new avenue to his ambitions. Having conquered there, the Soviet forces could enter Czechoslovakia, which was on Germany's southern border, and could then move into Germany from the south. From the border it was only a few hundred kilometers to Berlin, and as Stalin and Churchill could agree, he who entered Berlin would be credited with having won the war against the Nazis. The Americans, whose geopolitical education was very scratchy, did not seem to be aware of this.

More, the conquest of Hungary would open the Southern Balkans to Russian influence. Italy, Greece, Albania, and Yugoslavia could be drawn into the Soviet net.

The next step of Stalin's campaign was indeed the liberation of Hungary from the Nazi yoke, for Hungary's geographic location—the center of Europe—put it at the crossroads of the continent's thoroughfares. It could come none too soon for the Russians, for they knew of Prime Minister Churchill's hopes of getting to Hungary first.

"The Hungarians," he wrote later, "had expressed their intention of resisting the Soviet advance, but would surrender to a British force if it could arrive in time."

Admiral Nicholas Horthy, the regent of the Hungarian kingdom, had made the country into a loyal satellite of Germany, sending oil for Hitler's tanks as well as bread and meat for Hitler's soldiers. Hungary also supplied troops for the glory of the great New German Empire, as the Russians were very much aware, having faced Horthy's divisions in the heart of their homeland.

Stalin ordered the Fourth Ukrainian Front, which was slogging up the foothills of the Carpathians, to go on the defensive, take a rest, and conduct mountain training exercises. The Second Ukrainian Front would swing around the southern end of the Carpathians. This was the last thing the Germans expected; they thought Stalin would go for the Bosphorus and the Dardanelles.

On September 14, 1944, Marshal Malinovsky's Second Ukrainian Front attacked on the approaches to Turda. After swinging to the north in the direction of Debrecen, the Second Ukrainian Front regrouped. But the Germans, stimulated by a standfast order from Hitler, counterattacked. After Stalin's generals reported that there was nothing to be gained by this approach in the Turda region, the offensive was shifted toward Debrecen, where it succeeded. The time had now come for an offensive against Budapest. Sensing this, the Horthy government made an attempt to negotiate with the Western Allies, but they sent his agent packing with advice to negotiate with the Russians. Horthy took that advice and late in September a delegation led by General Gabor Farago set out for Moscow and arrived safely there on October 1. Negotiations were begun, Stalin presiding, but they bogged down and Stalin became impatient. He demanded that the Hungarian government break off all relations with Germany and start fighting the Nazis. By 8:00 AM on October 16, they were to provide the Russian high command with full information about the disposition of Hungarian and German forces. The next day, Horthy made an appeal to the Hungarian people, warning of a German

---

Hitler's Daydreams

In these days of defeat and depression, Hitler found consolation in an illu-
minated model of the new Linz—his hometown—which he proposed to build
as soon as the war ended (in victory for Germany). The architect brought the
model to the *Reichskanzlerei* on February 9 and Hitler went frequently to
look at it and spin dreams—fantasies of the old Linz, which would now
become the finest city on the Danube, outshining Vienna and Budapest.

Linz, dear Linz; those were the days when young Hitler had been struck
by the vision that he was slated for some great destiny, which providence
would even now rescue him to perform. He still insisted, even at the beginning of 1945, that victory would come. He had only to hold out, as had
Frederick the Great when at the end of 1761 he, too, had been cut off in
Berlin with hostile armies advancing on him.

---

attempt at a coup, after which Hungary would become nothing but
a Nazi vassal.

When Hitler learned of Horthy's rebellion, steps were taken
immediately by the German Twenty-Fourth Armored Division in
Budapest. Horthy was removed from office, whereupon he asked for
asylum in Germany. He and his family were sent by special train to
Germany. Instead of an order to fight the Germans, the Hungarian
Army received an order from Ferenc Szalasi, the head of the new government, to fight the Russians. Hungary continued in the war as an
ally of Hitler.

Stalin took a personal hand in the effort to get the Hungarians
out of the war: he proposed that General Miklos, commander of the
Hungarian First Army, order his men to start fighting the Germans.
Miklos so ordered and ten Hungarian POW officers were sent
through the Russian lines to the Hungarian army carrying the order.
When they received this order, the soldiers of the First Army were dis-
oriented. They had Horthy's address of October 15, calling on them

Partisans

In Stalin's famous broadcast of July 3,1941, he called for a vast partisan movement in the German rear, and on July 18 the Party Central Committee issued a decree explaining that it was necessary to create intolerable conditions for the invaders to disorganize communications and transport. In the summer and fall of 1941, press, radio, and theater tried to cheer up the people with stories of partisan exploits.

Zoya Kosmodemianskaya, who had been publicly hanged by the Germans in the village of Petrishchevo near Moscow, became a heroine. But this was oversimplification. Very little was done to organize partisan movement before the German invasion and, generally speaking, the people of Belorussia and the Ukraine at first welcomed the Germans as liberators. But that changed when the people discovered that the Germans regarded them as *untermensch* and intended no good. Besides, there were some Russian officers and men who had been encircled by the Germans and had formed partisan bands to escape with the help of the peasants. The woods were also an escape for party officials and government officials who found it hard to conceal their identity. At the end of July there were 200 partisan groups in Leningrad province, in September there were fifty-four groups in Orel province, and thirty-six in Kursk province. Altogether, in the winter of 1941–42 there were 10,000 partisans taking part in the Battle of Moscow and they are credited with killing 18,000 Germans.

The year 1942 saw the development of partisan regions—*partizanskie kraya*—which were the supply bases for partisan groups.

On July 14, 1943, the Soviet Supreme Command ordered the partisans to start an all-out rail war. Coordinated blows were struck at railways in the Bryansk, Orel, and Gomel areas. During one night 5,800 rails were blown up. Altogether, in November 1943 in Belorussia 200,000 rails were blown up, 1,014 trains wrecked, 814 locomotives wrecked or damaged, and seventy-two railway bridges destroyed or damaged. Between 1941–44 the partisans in Belorussia killed 500,000 Germans, including forty-seven generals and Hitler's high commissioner, Wilhelm Kube, whose Belorussian girl friend put a time bomb under his bed. In the Ukraine, partisans in this period killed 460,000 Germans.

One of the obsessions of the partisans was the constant lookout for traitors and the need to kill them. At the height of the Partisan movement in 1944 there were at least half a million armed partisans in the USSR. About a million people in Belorussia alone were killed by the Germans in the course of the partisan war.

to stop fighting the Russians. Then on October 16, they had an order from the new head of the Hungarian government telling them to continue to fight for the Germans. Now came the Miklos order.

The result was thorough confusion and enormous efforts by the Germans to stop the rot and keep the Hungarians from getting out of the war. The Germans all but took over the Hungarian army, attaching special German offices to Hungarian units to watch them. The Germans succeeded and Stalin failed. Hungary stood fast on the German side in the war.

In the last ten days of October, the Russian General Staff had the whole story—the attempt by Horthy, Hitler's reaction, his punitive measures, and the orders to resist the Soviet forces.

On October 20, Marshal Malinovsky called on Stalin for more tanks so he could get his long-delayed offensive going.

There was no chance now of an armistice and Stalin realized it. He issued an order on the evening of October 24: "In view of the fact that the Hungarian forces have not ceased hostilities against our forces and are continuing to maintain a common front with the Germans, the Stavka orders that on the field of battle you act toward Hungarian troops just as you would toward German troops."

But, to make the pill more palatable, Stalin again ordered reiteration of the pious claim that the Red Army neither had territorial ambitions in Hungary nor of changing the social order. Their only purpose was to defeat Hitler. As General S. M. Shtemenko wrote:

"Not only was citizens' private property being preserved in Hungary; Soviet military authorities were protecting it."

All the false assurances given the Red Army then unleashed their full power against Hungary. On November 4, the General Staff reported to Stalin on difficulties with the offensive against Budapest. Stalin ordered more troops into action "to crush the enemy's Budapest grouping." Bitter fighting went on in the Budapest area in the first half of December. The main Soviet effort was to encircle Budapest. It was planned to create an outer ring, to beat off attempts to raise the siege of Budapest. This offensive was to begin December 20.

The Germans had transformed the beautiful capital of Hungary into a network of trenches without regard to monuments and buildings.

As of January 2, the Nazis launched a vigorous action on the outer front of the Budapest ring. For almost a month the fighting was brisk. Attacks by German tank formations striving to liberate the forces encircled in Budapest. Meanwhile, the Hungarian communists were active in fighting as partisans and politicizing the public. On December 21, a provisional national assembly was convened in Debrecen. It formed a government headed by Col. Gen. Bela Miklos and, of course, the government "reflected all the contradictory lines." This government continued until February 3, moving to the fortress of Vara in Buda, until February 13, 1945, when the violence ended. Stalin's eye immediately moved to Austria, where Vienna beckoned. After that, Czechoslovakia. The key to all this was the positioning of Soviet troops on the right bank of the Danube. Stalin and the General Staff agreed on that. When Marshal Tolbukhin telephoned Stalin on March 9 and asked permission to withdraw his forces to the left bank of the Danube, so as not to lose control, he got one of Stalin's most sarcastic replies.

"Comrade Tolbukhin, if you're thinking of dragging out the war for the next five or six months, then of course you should withdraw your forces beyond the Danube. It will be quieter there. So you should dig in on the right bank of the Danube. Which is where you and your headquarters belong. I'm convinced that the troops will do their difficult duty, if only they're well led."

Then the dictator went on, "Consequently, we'll have to go over on to the offensive as soon as the enemy is stopped, and crush him entirely."

He looked significantly at General Antonov, the chief of operations, and said, "The General Staff agrees with me."

Tolbukhin said he understood his orders and hung up.

That's how decisions were made in those days.

By April 4, the Nazis had been driven completely out of Hungary. That day was declared a national holiday and on that spring day "it is the custom for people to bring flowers to the common graves of more than 140,000 soldiers of the Second and Third Ukrainian Fronts who gave their lives. On that day the people do not think only of the military victory won on Hungarian soil," the Soviet propagandists said, "they also think of the great change in the course of Hungary's history. They recall that the heroic victories of the Red Army made it possible for Hungary's toilers to throw off the yoke of social and national oppression, and to put the nation on the broad highway of national progress—of a material and spiritual flowering."

✳ ✳ ✳

That spring, Eduard Benes' Czechoslovak government asked for assistance to bring about an armed uprising against the Germans in Slovakia. They had their own plan that involved operations in the Tatra Mountains, where they counted on the inaccessibility of the terrain.

The Stavka approved, and Stalin ordered that the Czechoslovaks be informed. The Russians planned to airlift two divisions of the Red Army into Slovakia to help.

By August 1944, great changes had taken place in Slovakia. Everyone could see that the war was going to end in an allied victory. The resistance movement was headed by the Slovak National Council. The communists were in the thick of it. The council prepared for an uprising.

Then Hitler decided to move in force in Slovakia and earmarked three SS divisions for the task to begin on August 27. On the night of

August 30, the Czechoslovak government called on the people of Slovakia to rebel. On the morning of August 31, the Russians had report that the Germans were beginning to occupy Slovakia.

Stalin ordered the Red Army to assist the Slovakians. He talked with Marshal Koniev and told him to use forces of the First Ukrainian Front. But on September 1 came reports that the Slovakian forces were involved in hard fighting with the Germans.

Konev reported to Stalin on his ideas of helping the Slovak uprising. He proposed to attack in seven days. The Thirty-Eighth Army jumped off on September 8, and the First Guards Army on September 9. The enemy reacted swiftly. On September 10 and 11, the Soviet forces broke through the second line of enemy defense, but only in a narrow salient. But on September 14, the enemy cut off the corridor. The fighting continued unabated and it would be another six months before Soviet troops and their Czechoslovak allies met in a liberated Prague.

20

On to Berlin

B Y THE AUTUMN OF 1944, THE GERMANS HAD BEEN expelled from almost the last of Russian territory and Stalin was beginning to think seriously of the postwar world. In October the planning for the Battle of Berlin was already underway in the Russian General Staff. Late in October and early in November the plan was complete. It provided for a rapid advance on the German capital with no halts in a forty-five-day period. During the November 7 holiday, the Soviet commanders came to Moscow. The armies were stopped and positioning took place for the final advance. Marshals Zhukov, Vasilievsky, Rokossovsky, Koniev, and Tolbukhin met with Stalin and the General Staff and it was agreed to launch the general offensive on January 20, 1945.

The November holiday ended. Then Stalin decided that Berlin would be captured by Marshal Zhukov.

When Rokossovsky protested, Stalin told him that Zhukov had been selected to command the First Belorussian Front and Rokossovsky would learn the details later.

Zhukov took over the First Belorussian Front on November 16 and that same day Rokossvsky moved to the Second Belorussia Front. That day, Stalin announced that he would personally coordinate the four army groups that would participate in the Berlin operation.

Stalin stopped to take stock. His war was progressing very nicely. The Western Allies had made concessions, in spite of Churchill's reluctance, that would assure him control of postwar Eastern Europe. To be sure, there had been some sticky moments over the abandonment of the Poles of the Warsaw uprising, but they had passed. Soviet troops had linked up with the Yugoslav army by the end of the year; Bulgaria and Rumania were safely in the Soviet bag; and Tito would make sure that Albania joined up.

> ### Eisenhower's Gaffe
>
> General Eisenhower had handed Berlin to Stalin on a platter. Prime Minister Churchill was aghast and General Montgomery was fuming. The British protested to Washington that such decisions were political in nature and should not be made by Eisenhower alone. But President Roosevelt was too sick to react, and members of his administration were preoccupied with his illness. General Marshall had always believed that military considerations came first, and he supported Eisenhower's decision. Thus the chance for the Western powers to take Berlin was sacrificed and a whole new can of worms was opened, which would haunt the Western powers for years to come, setting up the Cold War.

The Red Army was handling Hungary. Austria was proving difficult—the communists were not popular there—but the communist guerillas of Greece, Italy, and France were making certain that the Red presence would be known in the postwar world. Czechoslovakia was trying to avoid takeover by a determinedly neutral stance between east and west. Stalin had agreed to enter the war against Japan as soon as Germany surrendered, the Americans not knowing that they had already won that war. That would give him entry into Asia, a chance to bolster the Chinese communists and spread the revolution. Despite the disbandment of the Comintern in 1943, the international revolution was alive and well and Stalin had reason to be pleased.

Just before the Yalta Conference in February, Stalin inexplicably halted the drive of Marshal Zhukov on Berlin, much to the general's chagrin. The secret was that Stalin was having an attack of the jitters. What if the drive failed? Stalin knew that, above all else, he who captured Berlin would be known as the victor in the war against Hitler. Churchill was fully cognizant of that fact, but the Americans seemed blissfully unaware of the realities of Europe.

Yalta brought satisfying results for Stalin, beyond his hopes. The Allies accepted—albeit reluctantly—the fait accompli of the Lublin government. Poland was now anchored safely in the Soviet sphere of influence. Germany would be partitioned into Russian, British, American, and French zones of occupation. Berlin would be ruled by an Allied council. Now to secure the rest of Eastern Europe was to add Rumania and Bulgaria, which were already locked in. Hungary was not yet liberated from the Germans but the Communist Party was shaping up as one of the two most important elements—the other being the Smallholders Party made up of small landowners, which was in violent opposition to communism. Yugoslavia was firmly allied with Stalin, and it was dragging Albania along with it. In Greece the communist ELAS had become the leading political element, and the communists in Italy and France were the strongest parties, leading to hopes of a revolutionary postwar Europe.

The Russian offensive was resumed in February, and slogged slowly along toward Berlin. In the last week of March, Stalin had a gift from General Eisenhower, so surprising and important that he could not believe it. Eisenhower sent a message delivering Berlin to the Russians on a silver platter. The fact was that Eisenhower and General Bradley had both misread the strategic situation. There was much talk about the establishment of a "National Redoubt" in Bavaria, where the Nazis would hole up and carry on the war. It was

---

John Reed

Stalin moved from position to position during the revolution and ultimately betrayed the revolution and seized power, betraying Lenin and his closest associates—most of whom were shot.

The American John Reed died believing in the revolution with all his heart. He is buried in the Kremlin wall. John Reed believed in freedom; to him that was what the revolution was all about—freedom and the right of man.

John Reed, had he lived, would have been betrayed by Stalin, too. He was fortunate to have died still believing in his dream. He would not, even for a day, have accepted Stalin's dictatorship or the terrors to which the monster subjected the Russian people.

---

no more than—talk—but Bradley believed it and he convinced Eisenhower of its reality. General Montgomery was already driving for the Elbe. He reported to Eisenhower, "My Tac HQ moves to the northwest of Bonninghardt on 29 March. Thereafter my HQ will move to Wesel, Muenster, Widenbrueck, Herford, Hanover, and thence by autobahn to Berlin, I hope."

With that message, Eisenhower lost his temper. He sent a message to Montgomery, "There will be no drive on Berlin."

The Ninth U.S. Army was to revert to Bradley's command as soon as it had joined with the U.S. First Army to complete the encirclement of the Ruhr.

Bradley would then turn his armies southeast to link up with the Russians on the Danube. The mission of Montgomery's army would be to protect Bradley's northern flank. And that very day Eisenhower sent a message to Stalin, telling him of his intentions.

That is when the fiction of Allied unity exploded. For the next few days the British–American alliance was in danger. As for Stalin, he was so suspicious of the Western Allies that he did not believe Eisenhower's message, holding that it was part of a plot to get to Berlin before the Russians reached it.

Secretly, he made plans to step up the Russian effort and ordered Zhukov to Moscow to make the plans firm. The key to the drive on Berlin was the capture of Kuestrin, which had been reported but not accomplished.

Zhukov conferred with General Chuikov, who agreed to make an all-out effort to take Kuestrin if Zhukov would support him with adequate air forces. Zhukov agreed before he went to Moscow. Just after Zhukov's arrival in Moscow, Chuikov reported that the Russians had captured Kuestrin.

✳ ✳ ✳

Stalin called Zhukov into his office in the Kremlin late that night. He had just finished a conference with the State Defense Committee and was settling down to work all night, as usual. Puffing his pipe, he greeted Zhukov briefly and then got down to business.

"The German Front in the west has collapsed," he said. "Probably the Hitlerites don't want anything to halt the advance of the Allied force." He suggested that the Germans were doing a deal with the Western Allies that would give them Berlin.

It was important that the Russians get there first, Stalin said. How soon would Zhukov be ready to move?

"No later than two weeks," Zhukov replied. He thought Koniev would be ready then, too, but that Rokossovsky would only be in position on the lower Oder River by mid-April.

"Well then," Stalin observed, "we shall have to begin operations without him. And even if he's a few days late, that's no problem." He left Zhukov to work out the details on his maps, moved to another room and ordered Koniev to come to Moscow, too, to present his plans for the First Ukrainian Front. Then he replied to Eisenhower on April 1, giving him the disinformation that the Russians would launch their main thrust toward Leipzig and Dresden, there to link up with the Western Allies.

"Berlin has lost its strategic importance," he lied. "We will commit only secondary forces in that direction." He told Eisenhower also that he intended to launch his offensive in the second half of May, another flat lie.

Then Stalin got ready to move his troops to Berlin—as rapidly as possible.

—⟋W⟍—

21

Twin Juggernauts

O N EASTER SUNDAY, WHICH WAS APRIL 1 THAT YEAR, Marshals Zhukov and Koniev reported to Stalin in his study in the Kremlin, both of them carrying briefcases overflowing with maps and documents.

They were able to witness a procession that filed into the room, the most powerful men in the Soviet Union, the members of the State Defense Committee: Vyachyslav Molotov, foreign minister and the committee's deputy chairman; Lavrenti P. Beria, head of the NKVD; Georgi M. Malenkov, secretary of the Central Committee of the Communist Party; Anastas I. Mikoyan, minister of Trade and Industry; Marshal Nikolai Bulganin, representative of Stalin to the fronts; Lazar M. Kagonovich, minister of Transport, Nikolai A. Voznesensky, economic tsar of Russia; chief of staff of the army, General A. A. Antonov, and his chief of operations, General S. M. Shtemenko.

As was his habit, Stalin got immediately down to business with no foofaraws.

The Western Allies, he said, intended to get to Berlin before the Russians.

"Read the telegram," he told Shtemenko.

Shtemenko read a telegram from the Soviet mission to Eisenhower's headquarters that indicated the British were poised on the north of the Ruhr, ready to take the short road to Berlin.

Stalin turned to his two marshals, "Well, now, who is going to capture Berlin, the Western Allies or the Russians?"

Koniev was the first to speak, "It is we who will be taking Berlin," he said.

"So that's the sort of fellow you are," Stalin said with a smile. Once again he had succeeded in his tactic of playing off one rival against another. But he probed further.

"How will you be able to organize your strike against Berlin?" he demanded. "Your main forces are on your southern flank. Won't you have to do a lot of redeployment?"

"You needn't worry, Comrade Stalin," Koniev said. "The front will be able to carry out all its necessary measures, and we shall organize the forces for the Berlin offensive in good time."

Stalin turned to Zhukov.

"The men of the First Belorussian Front are in position," the marshal said. "We shall have to do no regrouping. They are ready now. We are closest to Berlin. We will take Berlin."

"Very well," said Stalin. "You both shall stay here in Moscow and prepare your plans within the next forty-eight hours. You will report and then you can go back to your fronts."

"I must tell you," he said, "that the Stavka will pay special attention to the starting dates of your operations."

On the morning of April 3, the two marshals reported again.

Stalin heard Zhukov first, then Koniev. All that remained to be done was for Stalin to demarcate the boundary line between the two fronts.

He picked up a colored crayon from the desk and went to the map table. He drew a line between the First Belorussian Front and the First Ukrainian Front. The line extended only as far as Luebben,

The Germans, 1944

The Germans were at last outnumbered in the field. Yet the tendency to resist the Russians at any price was strong. The German soldier seemed to be less arrogant, some of them whined, tried to look pathetic, and spoke of Hitler— *Kaput!* By this time, the Russian desire to kill or beat up German prisoners had largely disappeared. They would even give the captured Germans food, say, "Go stuff yourselves, you bastards!"

But there was another side to the problem. Nearly every liberated village in Belorussia or the Ukraine had a terrible story to tell. Hundreds of villages had been burned, and their inhabitants murdered or deported. The Germans had deported a high proportion of young people. The Gestapo had been active and people had been shot or hanged. The *Einsatzkommandos* also had been active, exterminating partisans or their alleged accomplices. As a result, whole villages had been destroyed. In hundreds of towns, Jews had been massacred. In Kiev, for example, tens of thousands of Jews had been massacred in a gully outside the city called Babi Yar. It seemed that every city had its own horror story.

As the Red Army advanced west it saw the destroyed cities and heard the tales of terror. There were mass graves of Russian war prisoners who had been starved to death, murdered, and the Russian soldiers told the real truth of the Nazis with its Hitler and Himmler and its Untermensch philosophy, making it all hideously tangible. All that had been written about the Germans was mild compared to what the Russian soldier was to hear and see—and to smell—for wherever the Germans had trod they left the stink of unburied corpses.

But all this was amateur stuff compared with a place the Russian forces captured in 1944. Majdanek, the extermination camp near Lublin, had seen 1.5 million people destroyed in two years. It was with the whiff of Majdanek in their nostrils that the Russians were to fight their way into East Prussia. There was the ordinary German of 1944; there was also the professional murderer. How was anyone to tell the difference between the two? This problem was to dog the Russian high command for the rest of the war.

a town on the Spree about thirty-five miles from the southeast boundary of Berlin.

"In the event of stiff resistance from the Germans on the eastern border," he said, "the First Belorussian Front may be delayed. If so, the First Ukrainian will deliver a strike against Berlin from the south."

Thus, he put the two juggernauts in motion.

Later, Stalin would tell intimates, "Whoever breaks in first, let him take Berlin."

Although Rokossovsky was not included in the Kremlin meetings, he was not forgotten by Stalin. Rokossovsky was ordered to regroup his forces and take over Zhukov's right flank on the Oder by mid-April, in order to reduce Zhukov's Front by 100 miles and let him concentrate his forces on Berlin. This meant a major redeployment of the Second Belorussian Front, a U-turn followed by a trek across 185 miles of devastated countryside. The tanks went by rail, but the rail network was broken up and they traveled at a snail's pace. The rest of Rokossovsky's men traveled by truck and horse or on Shank's mare, marching along the roads, festooned with weapons and supplies, every man a walking arsenal. For security reasons, the starting date of the push was not included in the written orders, but it was agreed that it would be April 16, one full month earlier than the lying Stalin had told Eisenhower.

Early on the foggy morning of April 4, Zhukov and Koniev left Moscow in their separate planes, headed for their separate commands.

The race for Berlin had begun.

The Race for Berlin

O N APRIL 5, 1945, MARSHAL ZHUKOV'S SENIOR COM-
manders met at his headquarters, a gray house on the outskirts
of Landsberg. They trouped into what had been the dining room
where they stood around a large table covered with a dust sheet.

Zhukov pulled back the sheet to reveal a three-dimensional map
of Berlin and its suburbs, featuring rivers, streets, squares, railroad
stations, airfields, and other topographical features. The public buildings that were the major objectives were marked with green flags. For
example, the Reichstag was No. 105, the Reichschancellery No. 106.

For two days Zhukov used this model to conduct war games,
and then the commanders went back to their units and conducted
their own briefings and war games, down to the battalion level.

✳ ✳ ✳

Down south, Marshal Koniev was doing the same with complica-
tions engendered by the fact that he had not yet crossed the Neisse
River and had established no bridgeheads. He would have to begin

his trip to Berlin with a river crossing under fire—and another over the Spree.

North of Zhukov, Rokossovsky's armies were still on the move to their start line, on the east bank of the Oder River. The first unit reached here on April 10. They faced a formidable obstacle: two branches of the river, swollen with rains, plus flooded land, three miles wide. On the other bank the land rose sharply, giving the Germans a very good defensive position. Intelligence reports said that Field Marshal Manteuffel's Third Panzer Army was well-prepared on the west bank with an elaborate system of trenches and blockhouses, stretching back for six miles from the river, with a second line twelve miles from the Oder, and a third defense line behind that—and Rokossovsky was scheduled to attack four days after Zhukov, to protect the

New Problems

The war against Germany was going very well, Berlin was nearly ready to fall, and now a whole new series of problems arose to plague Stalin. Who would have thought that exposure to a foreign department store would threaten the sinews of the state? But that was what was happening, in Bucharest and other Westernized cities. Soviet soldiers were encountering consumer goods they had not known existed. They were coming home laden with luxuries forbidden to the Russian people. This could not go on.

First Belorussian Front's right flank as it headed into Berlin.

While the Russian juggernauts began to move in the east, a new threat to the Germans was developing in the west, where the American First and Ninth Armies had met near Paderborn. Surrounded in the pocket was an entire army group, Army Group B, with two Panzer armies—some twenty-one divisions, numbering 325,000 men. This left only a few disorganized divisions standing between the Ruhr and Berlin. The road was now open for the Americans to strike against Berlin.

But General Bradley chose not to seize the opportunity. He was still bemused by the myth of the Grand Alpine Redoubt. Instead of giving the Ninth Army the orders to take Berlin he committed eighteen American divisions to the reduction of the Ruhr pocket, with the result that the drive never materialized.

Bradley thought the price of capture of Berlin would be too high, "especially when you have to stop and let the other fellow take over."

The Russian vise was now closing around Berlin. Foreign Minister von Ribbentrop recognized that, and on April 12 he warned the remaining diplomats that it was time to leave the beleaguered city.

But the czar of Berlin, Goebbels, kept up a show of confidence. And when the word came on that night that President Roosevelt had died he broke out the champagne and telephoned Hitler in the bunker to tell him the good news.

✳ ✳ ✳

On Saturday, April 14, Zhukov's artillery opened up all along the front. After ten minutes the Russian troops attacked, caught the Germans by surprise, and made inroads of up to three miles in the line.

The Germans knew that this was only a reconnaissance in force, the attack would come in a couple of days.

By April 15, the position of the Germans on the Elbe Front was serious. General Heinrici's forces were outnumbered ten to one, the three Soviet Fronts had 2.5 million men, 41,600 guns, 6,250 tanks and self-propelled guns, 1,000 multiple rocket launchers, and 7,500 aircraft. German Army Group Vistula had only 250,000 poorly armed men with 850 tanks, 500 antiaircraft batteries, and 300 aircraft.

Heinrici anticipated Zhukov's coming attack would begin on the morning of April 16 and he ordered his troops to leave the frontline trenches and fall back to await the inevitable preattack bombardment. So the troops moved back to the second line of defense.

General Chuikov's command post was on a sandy hill overlooking the village of Reitwein on the west bank of the Oder.

Georgi K. Zhukov

Georgi K. Zhukov was marshal of the Soviet Union. He was the son of a village shoemaker and as a boy was apprenticed to a furrier. In 1915, he was
drafted into the Czarist Army. When the war ended, Zhukov was a highly dec-
orated cavalry sergeant. In 1918, he joined the Red Army and in 1919 he
joined the Communist Party. During the civil war in 1920, he was a squadron
commander and then a regimental commander after 1923. He attended cavalry school in 1925 and training courses for senior officers in 1929. In 1930,
he was made cavalry brigade commander.

From 1931–33, Zhukov was assistant to the inspector of the Red Army.
From 1933 to 1937 he was commander of a cavalry division. In 1937, he was
appointed commander of a cavalry corps. In 1938, he was appointed deputy
commander of the Belorussian military district, a post he held until 1939
when he became commander of a group of forces in the Far East.

In 1939, Zhukov led a successful offensive against the Japanese at
Khalkhin-Gol in Mongolia. In June 1940, he was appointed chief of the Kiev
military district, a post held until January 1941, when he was appointed chief
of the General Staff. After a quarrel with Stalin, Zhukov was relieved of this
job in June 1941 and assigned to command a reserve army group in the
Battle of Smolensk in July 1941, where he played a leading role in holding
up the Germans. In September 1941, he organized the defense of Leningrad.
The shelling of the city began on September 4, followed by air raids, particularly on September 8, a raid that caused 178 fires.

Zhukov is given credit for organizing the defense in three days, immediately after Marshal Voroshilov fumbled the job. This was one of his proudest
moments. In October 1941, when the Germans were driving on Moscow,
Zhukov was called by Stalin to lead the defense, and he commanded the
defense until January 1942. Then Zhukov became commander of the
Western Army Group in the winter of 1942. In August he was appointed first
deputy supreme commander in chief of the Soviet armed forces, a post he
held until the end of the war.

Zhukov had the responsibility for the battles of Stalingrad and Kursk, and coordinated the First and Second Ukrainian Army Groups in the winter offensive of 1943–44. In the spring of 1944, he commanded the First Ukrainian Army Group and in the summer offensive of 1944 he coordinated the First and Second Belorussian Army Groups.

Zhukov commanded the first Belorussian Army Group in the final assault on Germany in 1945. In 1945 and 1946, he commanded the Soviet occupation forces in Germany. In 1946, he was appointed to command all Soviet ground forces. He was commander of the Odessa, then the Ural military district, from 1947–52. In 1953, he became first deputy minister of defense and in 1955 the minister of defense. In 1956, he was elected to the Communist Party ruling presidium as an alternate member.

In June 1957, Zhukov was elected to full membership. In October 1957, he was removed from all posts and publicly disgraced for questioning party leadership of the armed forces. At that, he lived out his life in retirement from service.

Marshal Zhukov and his staff arrived well beforehand and on April 16, Zhukov had decided to assure surprise of the Germans by starting his attack in the middle of the night, at 3:00 AM local time, 5:00 AM Moscow time.

With three minutes to go, Zhukov and his staff emerged from the dugout and took their places in a specially constructed observation post. At exactly 3:00 AM, three red flares shot into the sky, "Now, comrades, now!" Zhukov muttered.

The darkness was shattered by the flash and roar of guns and mortars, the screech of Katyusha multiple rocket launchers. Guns were lined up wheel to wheel, one every four yards, 400 guns for every mile of the front. They produced a stupefying concentration of firepower. The whole Oder valley seemed to rock, as the barrage crept over the first German line.

The bombardment continued for thirty minutes, pouring half a million shells on the German lines to a depth of five miles. There was no response from the German guns.

Then a searchlight beam pierced the blackness, shining vertically upwards. Thousands of multicolored flares followed, and this was a signal for 143 other searchlights operated by women soldiers who had arrived at the front a few days earlier. The lights were positioned at 200-yard intervals along the front.

They were intended to be Zhukov's secret weapon, turning night into day for the Soviet troops. The British had used this tactic successfully in the west, bouncing the beams from the clouds to create artificial moonlight, but Zhukov had opted to go one better— using the searchlights to blind the enemy and light up the battlefield for the Russians.

At the signal, Chuikov's men rushed from their trenches and began moving toward the Kuestrin bridgehead. Behind them to the north and south other Russian units hurled themselves into the river, cheering and shouting. Engineers were launching pontoons and pre-fabricated bridge sections, but men were already paddling assault boats and some were swimming across.

In the center, the Chuikov army was running into problems. The waterlogged ground made going very difficult. They also felt like easy targets, silhouetted against the searchlights behind them, and the bright light gave them night blindness. The lights did not pierce the clouds of dust and smoke. Troop commanders sent back orders that the lights be turned off, only to become completely blinded in the darkness and confused when orders were given to switch the lights on again. Many units simply stopped and took cover. When they reached the German lines, they were unnerved to find them empty. The Russian troops faltered, suddenly unsure of themselves.

In the command post Chuikov and Zhukov could not see what was going on. For the wind bore the dust and smoke toward them. Visibility was zero and they had to rely on radio telephones and messengers to direct the advance. As reports came in that communications were breaking down, Zhukov lost his temper. The bridges across the old Oder River had been blown, creating obstacles, and the engineers could not get through with their bridging equipment. The armored vehicles jammed up the roads. If they got off the roads the tanks risked being blown up by mines or bogged down in the mud.

The air force had troubles, too. The visibility was bad, as the smoke and dust rose to 3,000 feet and the pilots had great difficulty in penetrating the dust clouds.

✳ ✳ ✳

General Heinrici's plan had worked to perfection. He had kept his guns and his armor intact and now had drawn the enemy into a trap. The heights were held by the Fifty-Sixth Panzer Corps, whose commander, Lt. Gen. Helmuth Weidling, was a grim-faced man with a monocle, known for his aggressive tactics.

Dawn broke and the sun came up, promising a bright spring day. Through the settling dust Weidling's gunners on the heights could see the Russians crowding the roads below. They opened fire on the troop carriers, tanks, and guns. "Heinrici had designed the last mile of the road as the killing field and tanks and self-propelled guns lay in the gulleys, all well-camouflaged," General Chuikov wrote later.

But, finally, the Russians gained control of a bridge and the troops rushed forward again. Beyond the canal the land was green with winter wheat. They ran across the green ground until they were met by a wall of fire. They stopped and dug in. The hills around them were not only high but rather steep, and some of them crowned by church spires.

"The Germans could see us as clearly as if we were in the palm of their hand," one Soviet infantryman said. "They spared neither shells nor bullets, but we held our ground. We did not fire back because that would have been useless, the enemy was well out of range of their submachine guns."

General Chuikov's troops were taking heavy casualties as the Germans poured fire into them, killing thousands and turning tanks into blazing funeral pyres. Chuikov called for support and tried to redeploy his artillery for a fresh barrage. Zhukov was almost apoplectic with rage, "They're pinned down . . . our troops are pinned down!" Chuikov shouted.

"What the hell do you mean, pinned down?" Zhukov screamed.

Chuikov was not dismayed; he had been subject to Zhukov's rages before. "Comrade Marshal," he said, "whether or not we are pinned down, this offensive will most certainly succeed. But resistance has stiffened and for the moment we are being held up."

Zhukov was not appeased. He swore long and loud. Berlin belonged to him and as he stood there, unable to move his armies, Koniev threatened to steal his victory away from him.

✳ ✳ ✳

Fifty-five miles south of Seelow, Koniev's operation was going very well. Spread across a front of 260 miles, but with the main thrust along an eighteen-mile stretch of the Neisse, they were between the towns of Forst and Muskau. Three armies led the way.

The German defenses on this bank of the river were strong, but his troops had a run of fifteen miles before they had to cross the Spree. And just south of Forst was an autobahn, sweeping into southeastern Berlin. This was the shortest route to Luebben, where Stalin's demarcation line between Koniev's forces and Zhukov's ended. If Koniev could reach Luebben before Zhukov cleared Seelow Heights, he could swing north and go for Berlin. His plan for this assault demanded crossing the river at no fewer than 150 places between Forst and Muskau. Once bridgeheads were established he could throw his armored forces into the attack. Everything depended on his engineers getting the bridges across the Neisse in place quickly—not an easy task because the Neisse was a fast river and here it was 150 yards wide.

✳ ✳ ✳

By 10:00 AM the Red Air Force had knocked out most of the German guns on the Seelow Heights, and Chuikov's Eighth Guards

Army had overrun the first two defense lines at the foot of the Heights, but the third line on the slope was proving tough going. Chuikov could not get tanks or self-propelled guns up because the grade was too steep. The only way was along the road to Seelow and the neighboring villages of Friedrichsdorf and Dolgelin, but it was controlled by fortified German strong points that could only be reduced by artillery fire. Chuikov ordered his guns to redeploy, then hit the slopes with a twenty-minute barrage to make way for a new infantry assault.

Zhukov's slender patience ran out and he swept aside Chuikov's plan, over the protests of his infantry commanders, and ordered his two tank armies to attack. All this was categorically opposite to the plan that had been agreed on in Moscow. The tanks were to be held until the Seelow Heights were taken and then deployed on the plateau leading to Berlin.

But Zhukov was beyond reason and he stormed out of the bunker, turned on General Katukov, commander of the First Guards Tank Army, and shouted, "Well, Get moving!"

✳ ✳ ✳

It was a desperate attempt to achieve an immediate breakthrough, sending 1,400 tanks and self-propelled guns across totally unsuitable terrain. It succeeded only in snarling the advance, hampering the movement of the artillery, creating nightmares for the infantry, and forcing guns and troop carriers off the roads. Tank crews and truck drivers, gunners and foot soldiers, struggled through the soggy morass, screaming and cursing at each other in the increasing chaos.

At 1:00 PM, Zhukov reported to Stalin, telling him how he had sent the two tank armies in and expected to take the Seelow Heights by evening of the next day.

It was just as well that Stalin could not see Zhukov's face or hear his cursing.

The High Cost of the Seelow Heights

A S DARKNESS FELL, GENERAL HEINRICI SURVEYED HIS
accomplishments of the day. Weidling's Fifty-Sixth Corps had
knocked out 150 tanks and 130 aircraft, turning Chuikov's attack
into a confused and bloody mess. The Germans had retaken a few
positions on the southern edge of the Heights. Still, General Heinrici
was under no illusion about the future, "The men are so exhausted
their tongues are hanging out," he said. "Still, we are holding. That's
something Schoerner couldn't do—that great soldier hasn't been able
to hold Koniev even for one day."

It was late night before Zhukov reported again to Stalin. He had
delayed as long as possible in making this call, hoping he would have
good news. Indeed, he did.

He had ordered Chuikov and Katukov to go on fighting in the
night, and they had made some headway at last. They had taken fear-

ful losses. The troops were blasted by German fire at pointblank range from 88- and 155-mm guns, which knocked out tank after tank, leaving little fires to light the way of the foot soldiers as they toiled up the slope. Those soldiers had been driven on relentlessly and around midnight captured three houses on the edge of Seelow. It was a foothold, but it was also a breakthrough.

Stalin was not impressed, however, and he was most unsympathetic as Zhukov spoke of the woes of the day. He lashed Zhukov for departing from the approved plan.

"You should not have sent the First Tank Army on the Eighth Guards Army's sector," instead of where GHQ had ordered. "Are you sure you will take Seelow Heights tomorrow?"

Zhukov struggled to retain his calm. He reiterated his claim that he would take the Heights, and declared that the delay might not be bad. "I feel that the more troops the enemy uses to counter our forces here," he said, "the quicker we shall capture Berlin, as it will be easier to smash the enemy troops in the open fields than in that fortified city."

Stalin was still grumpy. He rubbed salt into Zhukov's wounds, "We have been thinking of ordering Koniev to swing his tank armies toward Berlin from the south, and ordering Rokossovsky to speed up, forcing the river and also to strike at Berlin from the north."

Zhukov agreed that the movement of Koniev made sense, but he doubted if Rokossovsky would be able to cross the Oder and be in position to attack Berlin for a week.

Stalin was in no mood to continue the conversation.

"*Do svidaniye,*" he said. "Goodbye." And hung up the phone.

During the night, Zhukov regrouped and reorganized his artillery and armor, which was scattered all over the battle map, while 800 bombers attacked German positions, denying the exhausted defenders any rest.

By 8:00 AM, Zhukov began the assault on the Heights, once again with a thirty-minute artillery bombardment while wave after wave of bombers pounded the German defenses.

At 8:15, the first tanks rumbled forward while the barrage was still blasting with hundreds of Russian riflemen clinging to their sides and thousands more loping along beside as the attackers headed for the smoke-shrouded ridge. Again, they were met by devastating close range fire from 88s and Panzerfaust rockets. Heavy machine guns devastated the advancing infantry. Tank after tank was stopped and set ablaze by the Panzerfausts. The Russians had learned a method of protection. They tied mattresses from German beds onto the tanks to deflect the Panzerfaust projectiles.

As the attack continued, the volume of Soviet shells began to have their effect. German resistance on the Heights began to slacken. There were no German reserves left to throw into the line. Yet, somehow the defenders hung on and exacted a terrible price for the attackers.

Chuikov threw more and more men into the assault, and the carnage was appalling. By the end of the day he was dredging up men from the rear to send into the line as infantry. Just before nightfall he captured the small town of Seelow, but the Heights were still held by the Germans. It was very little progress to show for a day of hard fighting.

✳ ✳ ✳

Koniev, on the other hand, found the going on April 17 relatively easy. He had begun the day by telling his two assault generals, Rybalko and Lelyushenko, that they should forge ahead, avoiding frontal assaults, "Outflank the enemy where possible; concentrate on speed and maneuverability. Conserve your equipment. And above all, try to conserve enough strength for that final charge on Berlin itself."

He had unleashed the main assault at 7:00 AM after a brief artillery bombardment. His tanks raced through the blazing woods toward the River Spree. Koniev followed close behind to see Rybalko's Third Guards Tank Army cross the river. But, fast as they traveled, the Germans were even faster. They outran the Russian armor and established a defense line on the Spree. When the first tanks arrived they ran into heavy fire from machine guns on the western bank.

Koniev had to get his tanks across the river so he could bring up heavier weapons. The Spree was fifty yards wide at this point. The question was, could they ford it? Could tanks get across under their own power, without the help of engineers and bridging? There was only one way to find out. Rybalko ordered a single tank with a hand-picked crew to try. With German bullets pinging off its sides, the chosen tank plunged into the water, discovering that it was only about three feet deep. Other tanks roared across. In no time the tanks were across and the German line was broken.

The Tank Armies

Col. Gen. S. M. Shtemenko of the Soviet General Staff stated, "The employment of tank armies was the subject of serious discussion. Bearing in mind the existence of a strong tactical defense position on the Seelow Heights, it was decided to commit both tank armies to the battle after the Heights had been secured. Naturally, we did not base our plans on the possibility that our tank armies would rush into wide operational expanses following the rupture of the tactical defenses, as was the case, for example, in the preceding Vistula–Oder and East Pomerania Operations. In the course of battle when the force of the blow by Army Group's first echelon proved to be inadequate for rapid reduction of the enemy's defenses the danger arose that the offensive might be slowed. In the second half of the day April 16, after taking counsel with the Army commanders, we decided to reinforce the attack of the combined arms Armies with a powerful blow by all air and tank armies. The enemy threw all that he could into the battle, but by sunset of April 17 and the morning of April 18, we nevertheless succeeded in shattering the defensive forces on Seelow Heights and began to move forward. Hitler's generals took large forces from the Berlin defenses, including antiaircraft artillery, and threw them against our troops. This somewhat slowed the tempo of the offensive. And this is altogether understandable. It was necessary to break the resistance of the fascist German units coming from inside Berlin."

Koniev set up his headquarters in an old castle above the river, just outside Cottbus, halfway between the Neisse and the end of the demarcation line between fronts at Luebben, now twenty miles ahead. From the castle he called Stalin to report that his tanks were rolling forward west of the Spree.

Stalin interrupted him. Things were going badly for Zhukov, he said. He was still held up by the German defenses. Then, abruptly, Stalin fell silent.

Koniev held his breath. Was he at last to be given his chance at Berlin? Stalin came back on the line.

"Was there any way," he asked, "that Zhukov's mobile forces could be funneled through the gap torn by Koniev?"

Koniev seized his opportunity.

"That would take too much time, Comrade Stalin," he said. "It would only add to the confusion. There is no need to send the First Belorussian armored troops into the gap we have made. The situation on our front is developing favorably. We have enough forces and we can turn our tank armies toward Berlin."

He suggested using the little town of Zossen, fifteen miles south of Berlin, as the hinge on which his armies would turn.

"What map are you using?" Stalin demanded.

"The I:200,000."

Stalin searched his own map.

"Very good," he said at last. "Do you know that the German General Staff Headquarters is at Zossen?"

"Yes, I do," Koniev replied.

"Very good." Another pause.

Then the words Koniev had been lusting to hear, "Turn your tank armies toward Berlin."

✳ ✳ ✳

At 12:47 AM on April 18, Koniev issued directive No. 00215 to his commanders. Rybalko was ordered to force the Spree and advance rapidly to Fetschau, Golsen, Barut, Telnow, and the southern out-skirts of Berlin. He was also given a timetable.

The Third Guards Army was to break into Berlin from the south on the night of April 20.

The orders to Lelyushenko were equally precise. The Fourth Guards Tank Army, which was upriver and south of Rybalko, was ordered to force the Spree near Spremberg and advance rapidly in the general direction of Drepkau, Kalau, Dane, and Luckenwalde. By the end of April 20 he was to capture Beelitz, Treuenbritzen, and Luckenwalde, to take Potsdam and the southwest sector of Berlin that night.

"The tanks will advance daringly and resolutely in the main direction," Koniev said. "They will bypass towns and large communities and will not engage in protracted frontal fighting. The success of the tank armies depends on boldness in maneuver and swiftness of operations."

Let there be no question in the minds of his commanders what Koniev wanted.

✳ ✳ ✳

Stalin took a good deal of pleasure in telling Zhukov that Koniev was now on course for Berlin. It always pleased him to twist the knife in an open wound.

Zhukov's reaction was predictable: he erupted full-blast on his senior commanders. As Lieutenant General N. K. Popiel, chief of staff of the First Guards Army put it, "We have a lion on our hands."

He was a lion with sharp claws and a reputation of eating senior commanders for breakfast.

"Now take Berlin," he growled at them.

✳ ✳ ✳

On the morning of April 18, Zhukov issued fresh orders to his commanders. They were to go up to the front lines themselves and assess the situation of their troops and the enemy and be prepared to resume the main advance by noon on April 19.

Everything was to move, nothing was to hold back. This battle was consuming the Russian reserves; it must be ended quickly. Commanders who showed any irresolution, or proved incapable of carrying out their orders, were to be removed immediately. This meant instant demotion to private and assignment to a penal battalion, where life expectancy was almost like facing a firing squad.

✳ ✳ ✳

At 5:00 AM after another artillery barrage, Chuikov's troops attacked again and the furious day of battle began. The Germans tried a counterattack, but gradually they gave way before the Russian mass. Weidling's Fifty-Sixth Panzer Corps was desperately in need of reinforcement. He had been promised two more panzer divisions but there was no sign of them. The commander of the SS Nordland Division appeared late in the day to report that his division had run out of fuel miles away. The Eighteenth Panzer grenadiers arrived late that night when it was too late. Chuikov had broken through to the Heights and the entire corps was withdrawing.

This new division joined the retreat that was led by the Ninth Parachute Division, which had finally collapsed. "The paratroopers were running away like madmen," said the corps artillery commander.

The bulk of the corps withdrew in good order, to the next line of defense, but the Heights were lost.

Weidling had to move his headquarters back twice that day. By night he was installed in a cellar at Waldsieversdorf, a village just outside Muencheberg, ten miles back from Seelow.

There they had visitors. Foreign Minister von Ribbentrop came first, seeking information about the situation. After they told him, he disappeared quietly.

Then up came the thirty-two-year-old, one-armed head of the Hitler Youth, Arthur Axmann.

To Weidling's disgust, Axmann offered the services of twelve- to fifteen-year-old boys of the Hitler Youth, who were ready to fight to the death. Weidling was first speechless with fury, then told Axmann that he would not sacrifice these children to a cause that was lost.

"I will not use them and I demand rescission of the order sending these children into battle."

Axmann listened and then left in confusion, hurrying back to Berlin to find an alternate way of sacrificing his boys.

* * *

Chuikov had achieved his first objective: to control the Seelow Heights. To do this he had broken the first German defense line. Now his troops were astride the main road leading straight as an arrow to Berlin, which was thirty-seven miles away. The price had been terrible. The battle for Seelow Heights had cost the First Belorussian Front the lives of 30,000 men.

—w—

24

The Bear's Embrace

ZHUKOV HAD HOPED TO CAPTURE BERLIN BY APRIL 19, but the end of that day found him still twenty miles from the city line, held up by German resistance. Soldier Vladimir Abyzov's platoon had pressed forward again after taking the Seelow Heights, pausing only for a quick snack and to resupply themselves with ammunition. They rode tanks, meeting no opposition at first.

"Then we came to a populated place, call it a big village or a small town, and already on its outskirts there was a terrific exchange of fire. The Germans put up such a frenzied resistance that we could not gain even a meter of ground in half a day's battle. But what can you do when you are faced with tanks dug into the ground, not one or two but at least fifteen? We decided to wait until nightfall and close in on them under cover of darkness."

While Zhukov was fuming over the delays, Koniev was having another problem: too much progress. His two tank armies had gotten out ahead of the infantry, and Rybalko was particularly worried about their flanks and the possibility of a surprise attack on their rear by the enemy.

He called Koniev, who soothed him.

"Don't worry, Pavel Semonovich. Just keep going. Everything will be all right."

Rybalko and Lelyushenko did keep going. At the end of the day Rybalko's Third Guards Tank Army had made twenty-five miles. Lelyushenko's Fourth Guards Tank Army had done even better: thirty miles.

* * *

That evening of April 19, Rokossovsky reported to Stalin by telephone that he was in position and ready to attack the next morning. As he spoke Russian bombers, by the squadron, were blasting the German defenses on the west bank of the Oder. At the same time, special troops were paddling their inflatable craft across the river to gain control of the floodlands between the two branches of the Oder.

* * *

Vladimir Abyzov's platoon was now safely at Muencheberg, halfway between the Oder and Berlin, astride the main road into the city. The platoon had suffered heavy casualties and hoped for a night's rest. They chose a two-story mansion in the western end of the town. They ate in the spacious dining room on the ground floor, emptying their mess tins onto real porcelain plates.

Relaxing for the first time in days the men chatted. Yurka, the musician, pulled his mouth organ from the top of his boot and began to play a tune. Suddenly, Sasha Dymshyts, the battalion clerk, appeared in the doorway, looking excited. "Comrades!" he called, "Come and see our artillery firing on Berlin."

Suddenly everyone was laughing. A gun had been positioned five houses away and an artillery officer and several enlisted men were crowded around it. Abyzov and his comrades joined the crowd, and soon it was increased by twenty more, forming a tight ring around the gun. A row of shells was laid out on the carriage, each with a chalked inscription: "This is from Stalingrad, Hitler. This one is for you."

More officers arrived, including the commander of the Seventy-Fourth Rifle Division, Major General D. E. Bakanov. The artillery officer asked permission to begin firing and Bakanov waved his hand. "Go ahead," he said.

The artillery officer then said, "On the den of the enemy, Berlin—fire!"

The gun roared; the troops cheered and spontaneous bursts of submachine gun fire split the sky. Shell after shell sped on its way to Berlin, and the whole crowd, including the generals, burst into delighted laughter.

✳ ✳ ✳

The next day was Hitler's birthday, and the Allied bombers from both east and west contributed to the festivities. Shortly before 10:00 AM, the Americans sent another thousand-plane raid, the silver bombers were clearly visible in the blue sky, flying straight and level in perfect formation. The raid lasted two hours, the planes too high for flak and no German fighters were present. The raid was followed by several raids of mosquito bombers by the British.

Meanwhile, the Soviet artillery was firing on the city. At 11:50 AM, the Seventy-Ninth Corps guns fired a salute in honor of Der Fuehrer's birthday. Now the heart of the city was within range of the guns.

✳ ✳ ✳

On April 20, things were at last going well for Zhukov. His troops had already blasted their way through three German defense lines and were closing on Berlin. Koniev's armies were also streaking for south Berlin, driven by Koniev's threats, while the First Ukrainan Front was coming behind to split Germany in half.

Koniev was impatient. He sent a message to his two tank commanders: "Personal to Comrades Rybalko and Lelyushenko. Order you categorically to break into Berlin tonight. Report execution."

Zhukov was well aware of Koniev's progress and decided that a touch of the knout would spur on the First Guards Tank Army. He sent a message to Generals Katukov and Popiel, "First Guards Tank Army has been assigned an historic mission: to be the first to break into Berlin and raise the victory banner. Personally charge you with organizing and execution. Send up one of the best brigades from each corps into Berlin and issue following orders: No later than 04:00 (02:00 Berlin time) 21 April at any cost to break into outskirts of

---

I. S. Koniev

Of peasant origin, I. S. Koniev was a lumberjack before becoming a non-commissioned officer in the Czarist Army during World War I. He entered the Red Army and the Communist Party in 1918. Koniev was political commissar of armored trains during the civil war and political commissar of Seventeenth Maritime Rifle Corps until 1927, when he graduated from training courses. He became regimental then divisional commander between 1927 and 1932. Koniev graduated from the Frunze Military Academy in 1934. He was division commander from 1934–37, corps commander from 1937–38, and commander of the Second Red Banner of the Far Eastern Army from 1938–40. He became commander of the Trans Baikal then of the Trans Caucasia Military Districts from 1940–41. Koniev was awarded commander of the Nineteenth Army and Western Army Group in the Battle for Moscow, 1941. Afterwards, he became commander of the Kalinin Army Group from 1941–43, and commander Steppe, Second Ukrainian, First Ukrainian Army Groups in Soviet offensives in Ukraine, Poland, and the Battle for Berlin, 1943-45. He was commander of Soviet occupation forces in Austria and Hungary from 1945–46, and commander in chief of Soviet ground forces and deputy minister of war from 1946–50. Koniev was chief inspector of the Soviet army from 1950–51 and commander of the Carpathian Military District from 1951–55. He became first deputy minister of defense and commander in chief of the Warsaw Pact Forces between 1955 and 1960, and commander in chief of the Soviet Occupation Forces in Germany, 1961–62. From 1962 on, Koniev served as inspector general of the ministry of defense.

Berlin and report at once, for transmission to Stalin and press announcement."

Zhukov wanted not only Stalin but the whole world to know when he broke into the capital of the Third Reich. The only thing missing from the signal were the words "or else . . ." but there is no doubt that Katukov and Popiole knew the consequences of failure.

✳ ✳ ✳

The last barricades were being erected to create Fortress Berlin, but it was a paper fortress. The Forty-Second Volkssturm Battalion was typical. There were 400 names on the roll, but they had no uniforms and no ammunition for their Danish rifles.

No uniforms!

Soldiers without uniforms were not soldiers!

They were sent home. But there were some dedicated Nazis who were willing to fight to the death for Hitler. Some 2,000 volunteers made their way as the Freikorps Adolf Hitler into the heart of the city. There were also several dedicated SS units, including the 1,200 men of Hitler's personal bodyguard.

And, finally, there were the brainwashed youngsters of the Hitler Youth. Axmann had been denied the opportunity of sacrificing these children on the battlefield, but he now organized them to play their role in the defense of the city.

"There is only victory or annihilation," he told them. "Know no bounds in your love of your people, equally know no bounds in your hatred of the enemy. It is your duty to watch when others tire, to stand, when others weaken. Your greatest honor is your unshakable fidelity to Adolf Hitler."

Axmann had issued rifles to the boys, as well as grenades and Panzerfausts, and gave them basic training in how to use them. Then he dispatched them to join the Volkssturm in the trenches and on the barricades. Many of them were assigned to the special Hitler Youth Regiment to guard bridges. Others became part of the Axmann Brigade. Mounted on bicycles and armed with Panzerfausts, they rode off to hunt and destroy Soviet tanks or die in the attempt. Thousands did both.

* * *

In the north, Rokossovsky had succeeded in establishing two firm bridge-heads and was advancing on Prenzlau. In the center of the front, Zhukov's forces were taking Strausberg, and it could only be a matter of hours before they captured suburbs within the boundary of the city itself.

Back on the Oder, the whole of the Ninth German Army, apart from Weidling's Sixty-Sixth Panzer Corps, was about to be encircled and destroyed. Koniev's men had smashed a great gap between this and the Fourth Panzer Army to the south. His right wing was strung north behind the Ninth Army; his tanks were approaching Zossen due south of the city.

Berlin was half encircled from the north, the east, and the south. Its only vague hope of survival was if the Ninth Army was pulled back from the Oder, but Hitler stubbornly refused to allow any retreat. Heinrici, when told for the third time that day that he could not pull back, knew that his army was doomed. It was all academic. He had been driving around the front all day and everywhere encountering men who were fleeing the battle as fast as their legs or their vehicles would carry them.

Heinrici ordered Obergruppenfuehrer Felix Steiner to move his headquarters to Ebenswald and organize the scattered remains of the forces that were milling around in the forest. He threw in the still-forming Fourth SS Police Grenadier Division and ordered the Third Naval Division hurried by rail from Swinemunde on the Baltic, scraping together a few odd units from Luftwaffe personnel, store-keepers, clerks, and local Volkssturm. But, as of the moment, Steiner was a general without troops.

* * *

Koniev's tanks had run out of fuel and stalled outside Baruth. They were waiting for supplies but the Volkssturm and Hitler Youth got there first. The tankers sat helplessly and waited while their tanks were destroyed one by one. The few operational German aircraft found and attacked a column, thinking it was Koniev's tanks—instead it was the main convoy of OKH Headquarters, which had left Zossen for Obersalzburg.

* * *

Koniev was furious about the delays aggravated by the terrain, which was not suitable for tank warfare. One brigade of the Third Guards Tank Army was fighting, but the rest of the army was standing still. Koniev signaled Rybalko, "I order you to cross the Baruth-Luckenwalde line through the swamp by several routes, deployed in battle order. Report fulfillment." Prompted by Koniev's curses, by afternoon they had caught up and the local Volkssturm had run out of Panzerfausts. The advance resumed, with the tanks pressing along through the swampy ground. Even advancing cautiously it was not long before they were moving through the gates of the Zossen complex.

This large, sprawling compound was a masterpiece of German camouflage.

No casual observer would have guessed that it was a military headquarters. To the eye, it looked just like another village. Groups of red brick cottages and a red brick church stood on the edge of a picturesque pine wood. Pigeons still nested in the eaves. But there was a curious absence of humanity. There were no bits and pieces of farm machinery outside the sheds and barns and everything was too neat and tidy.

Grouped in clearings in the wood were twenty-four concrete buildings, linked by sandy tracks. All were heavily camouflaged, with netting hung across the concrete footpaths, so they would not be visible from the air. These comprised two main centers, named Maybach I and II, which housed the OKH and OKW, respectively. The most important parts of both, including the operations rooms, were buried deep underground. Between them, buried even deeper, was Exchange 500, the communications center linking OKW, OKH, and Hitler, the hub of the vast communications network that had once existed from the Arctic to the Black Sea, from the Atlantic coast of France to the Caucasus mountains. It was completely self-contained, with its own power generators, water supplies, and air-conditioning filtered against poison gas.

The first Soviet troops to arrive were treated to a tour by Hans Beltow, the engineer, who had stayed behind. He took them on a rambling walk (the lifts were not working) through a maze of corridors and spiral staircases, storerooms, offices, officers' bedrooms—all the discarded paraphernalia of an abandoned military headquarters.

In exchange, 500 telephones and teleprinters were still operating, the teleprinters spewing out long messages from Berlin. Some German clerk had left large printed notices in Russian on the teleprinters, warning, "Do not damage this equipment. It will be valuable to the Red Army."

One of the telephones rang and a Soviet soldier picked up the receiver. The voice on the other end demanded to speak to a general. With great delight the soldier said, "Ivan is here! You can go. . . . "

✳ ✳ ✳

The sole defenders of Zossen were four fat soldiers, and they were drunk. Three of them surrendered immediately. The fourth was too drunk to do so and had to be carried on a litter. The nerve center of Hitler's empire had ended not with a bang but a burp.

✳ ✳ ✳

Koniev wasted no time here. Major Boris Polevi, political commissar, was inspecting the room of the commander of OKH, General Krebs, and was listening to wire recordings of his last few telephone conversations with Berlin. But Koniev hastened the army along toward Berlin.

Lelyushenko's Fourth Guards Tank Army, on Rybalko's left, was also closing in on Berlin without pausing. During the afternoon they swept around to the southwest of Berlin, taking Babelsburg. There, one brigade liberated a concentration camp full of foreigners, which included former French Premier Eduard Herriot and his wife. By evening both armies had crossed the outer Berlin Ring Road and were heading toward the center of the city.

✳ ✳ ✳

East of the city, Zhukov's armies were already in control of the Berlin Ring Road from Bernau to Wusterhausen and some units had broken into the outer suburbs. Meeting fierce resistance on the Lindenberg-Malchow road, the First Mechanized Corps swung around Malchow and pressed on toward Weissensee, about four miles from Hitler's bunker.

Chuikov's Eighth Guards Army was sent south to storm the city from the south and southeast.

✳ ✳ ✳

Berlin was nearly squeezed to death in the embrace of the Russian bear. There were now nine complete Soviet armies engaged in the encirclement, with Zhukov's forces moving from the north, east, south, and southeast, and Koniev's advancing from south and southwest.

During the day, Zhukov extended his grip on the northern outskirts of Berlin. The Forty-Seventh Army lunged from the north, tanks fought across the Havel River, near Henningsdorf, then prepared to strike south to link up with Lelyushenko, who was driving north from Potsdam. Only twenty miles now separated the two fronts. When they linked up the capital would be locked up tight.

The armies that were now tracking around the perimeter reorganized for a plunge into the heart of the city. With each corps holding out at least one full division, they divided into battle groups and assault units specially designed for street fighting. Most groups were made up of an infantry company with several field guns, a few self-propelled guns, a platoon or two of combat engineers, and a flame thrower platoon. The flame throwers were used against bunkers, turning the inmates into screaming torches. Alongside these units, they were supported by massed artillery and Katyusha rocket launchers and the air force flew continuously overhead.

When the firing stopped, Soviet soldiers began to enter cellars and shelters. Once they had confirmed that there were no soldiers there, they turned to looting, taking valuables, especially wristwatches. To

---

K. K. Rokossovsky

Son of a Polish father and Russian mother, K. K. Rokossovsky's father was a locomotive engineer. He was orphaned at the age of fourteen and began to work in construction. In 1914, he was drafted into the Czarist Army. He ended the war as a cavalry sergeant. In 1917, Rokossovsky entered the Red Guard and in 1918 the Red Army. He commanded a cavalry squadron in the civil war and later a regiment. He joined the Communist Party in 1919. During the 1920s he was a regimental commander and then a student in training for cavalry officers, until appointed commander of a cavalry brigade in 1929, division commander in 1930, and corps commander in 1936. He was arrested in August 1937 and jailed for three years, released in March 1940, and reinstated as cavalry corps commander. In June 1941, he was commander of the Ninth Mechanized Corps in the Ukraine. In July 1941, he commanded the operational group of forces near Smolensk. In 1941, he was commander of the Sixteenth Army in the Battle for Moscow. In July 1942, he commanded the Bryansk Army Group until September.

In the Battle of Stalingrad in 1942–43, Rokossovsky commanded the Don Army Group. In the Battle of Kursk in 1943, he commanded the Central Army Group. He commanded the First and then the Second Belorussian Army Groups from 1943–45. From 1945 to 1949 he was commander in chief of Soviet forces in Poland and minister of defense and deputy prime minister of the Polish Peoples Republic, as well as the marshal of Poland, from 1949–56. From 1956 to 1962 he was chief inspector and deputy minister of defense for the USSR, and from 1962 on the inspector general of the Soviet ministry of defense.

---

everyone's surprise they did not bother the women. There was none of the rape that the civilians had dreaded that the Hitler organization had advertised as coming from the savage Russians.

But these were well-disciplined combat troops. The brutalized second echelon men—members of penal battalions and Asian troops were still to come and they would bring to life the most dreadful fears of Berlin's women.

✳ ✳ ✳

In the Hitler bunker that day, the dictator argued with his trusted military associates. He ordered Keitel and Jodl to leave Berlin but they refused to go. Hitler said, "I will never leave Berlin. . . . I will defend the capital to my dying breath. Either I direct the battle for the Reich Capital, or I shall go down with my troops in Berlin. That is my final and irrevocable decision."

Keitel went off to find General Wenck and tell him to forget all previous orders and march on Berlin at once, to link up with the Ninth Army. Jodl stayed behind to finish the arrangements for the transfer of the remaining OKW and OKH staff to Berchtesgaden.

✳ ✳ ✳

The one who did not try to persuade Hitler to leave Berlin was Dr. Goebbels. He was resolved that Hitler should go out in a burst of glory, and he would go with him and take his wife and children.

Hitler now invited Goebbels to move into the bunker with him and Goebbels brought his family—in two cars.

The six children were each allowed to bring a favorite toy.

They were assigned a suite with their mother, and they were told that they would soon receive injections so that they would not get sick.

✳ ✳ ✳

Hitler now devoted himself to sorting out his papers, burning those that he no longer wanted. He had the rest packed in metal boxes and taken to airfields around Berlin. The forty members of Hitler's personal staff who opted to leave were flown out that night in ten aircraft, nine of which reached Munich safely. The plane carrying the documents crashed en route, killing all the crew but the rear gunner. The documents disappeared, to become one of the living legends of the Third Reich.

Zhukov was afraid he might lose the race for Berlin and he awaited word of Koniev's progress anxiously. On April 22, he gave Chuikov and Katukov orders to ford the Spree and move into the southern districts of Tempelhof, Steglitz, and Marienfeld no later than April 24. Bogdanov and his Second Guards Tank Army were to drive for Charlottenberg and the western districts.

As night fell, some of Chuikov's units made an unexpected breakthrough near Koepenicke. They overpowered a German defense company, crossed the river, and rushed to the Dahme River beyond, which they also crossed.

Other troops followed and by dawn they had taken the suburb of Falkenberg.

After a short fight, the Thirty-Ninth Rifle Division captured Koepenick's two bridges and crossed the rivers with their artillery and armor. The last major obstacle between Zhukov and the city center had been removed. Zhukov, by morning, was less than fifteen miles away from meeting the forward units of Koniev's Front.

Stalin issued new orders to the three fronts involved in Operation Berlin. Rokossovsky was no longer needed for the assault, so he was sent to destroy German forces around Stettin and drive Manteuffel's Third Panzer Army into the arms of the British.

Stalin now defined the new boundary between Zhukov and Koniev to keep them from fighting each other. Stavka Directive 11074 carried the line from Luebben into the city through Mariendorf, south to Tempelhof, right through Anhalt station. This left Koniev just 150 yards west of the Reichstag, the ultimate Soviet target.

The final prize was to go to Zhukov.

✳ ✳ ✳

Keitel came back from his mission outside Berlin and again tried to persuade Hitler to leave the city for Bavaria.

Once again, Hitler refused. He had obviously decided that Berlin was to be his funeral pyre.

All the rest was anticlimax.

✳ ✳ ✳

Col. Gen. Nikolai Berzarin took command of Berlin on April 28 and issued his first order as military governor of the city. On that day, Hitler married Eva Braun in a civil ceremony performed in the map room of the bunker. On the next day, April 29, Hitler sent his last will and testament to Field Marshal Schoerner, who had been chosen commander of the army. Copies were sent to Admiral Doenitz, Hitler's successor as chief of the German state, and one was to be preserved in the archives at Munich.

In the chancellery, Goebbels gave a party for the nurses and children in one of the cellars. He was saying his last farewell to Berlin.

One of Hitler's staff poisoned his dog Blondi that day. Hitler had his last conference that evening, darkened by the news that his old ally, Benito Mussolini, had been executed by Italian partisans.

At 1:00 AM on April 30, it became apparent that there was no hope for Berlin. Hitler then realized that the time had come for him to commit suicide.

That day he lunched with his secretaries, and afterward said his goodbyes to the staff. Eva was with him, looking her best. Hitler and Eva then went into their room.

A few minutes later, a shot rang out. They found Hitler on the sofa, his body crumpled over the arm his head hanging down, dripping blood from a gunshot wound. He had taken cyanide and then shot himself just to make sure. Eva was curled up at the other end of the sofa, her legs tucked beneath her.

✳ ✳ ✳

Stalin had left his office for the night, and was in bed in his dacha at Kuntsevo. Zhukov called and insisted that the duty officer awaken him, saying the matter was too urgent to wait for morning.

Stalin came to the telephone. Zhukov told him that Hitler was dead. "So that's the end of that bastard," Stalin replied. "Too bad we couldn't take him alive."

✳ ✳ ✳

That night, Magda Goebbels murdered her children. First she gave each of them a chocolate spiked with a powerful soporific. Then she poisoned them by crushing a cyanide capsule in the mouths of each. Then she went into Goebbels' study and began playing solitaire. At 8:15 PM Goebbels told an aide that he and Magda intended to commit suicide. They wanted to do it in the open air. They put on coats and he grandly offered his arm to his wife. Together, they mounted the stairs to the bunker entrance. Both had cyanide capsules and Goebbels had a Walther P-38 revolver. They stood together. Magda bit her capsule and swallowed, she slid to the ground. Her husband shot her in the back of the head. He then bit his own capsule, pressed the revolver to his head and fired.

A few hours later, Berlin fell.

CHAPTER

―̴̴

25

Chinks in the Alliance

COL. GEN. S. M. SHTEMENKO OF THE SOVIET GENERAL Staff stated, "At 1:50 PM on April 20, the long-range artillery of the Seventy-Ninth Rifle Corps of the Third Assault Army commanded by Col. Gen. V. I. Kuznetsov was the first to open fire on Berlin, thereby starting the historic storming of the German capital. On April 21, units of the Third Assault, Second Guards Tank and Forty-Seventh Armies entered the outskirts of Berlin and began the struggle in the city.

"In order to demoralize the enemy decisively, to destroy his will to fight, to give maximum help to our weakened combined arms units, and also to accelerate the reduction of defenses in Berlin itself, by all possible means it was decided to commit the First and Second Guards Tank Armies, together with the Third Guards, Fifth Assault, and Eighth Guards Armies against the city so as to defeat the enemy rapidly, with the fire and avalanche effect of tanks. It should be added that at the time there was no space for maneuver and no specific missions appropriate to the maneuvering capacity of tank units could be set.

"The struggle in Berlin approached its climax. We all wanted to finish off the enemy's groupings in Berlin by May 1 in order to make the holiday for the Soviet people even more joyous, but the enemy, although he was in the last agony, continued to cling to every house, to every cellar, and to every floor and roof. Nevertheless, Soviet troops took block after block, house after house. The troops of General V. I. Kuznetsov, N. E. Berzarin, and S. I. Bogdanov drew closer and closer to the center of Berlin. Then came the long awaited signal from Commander V. I. Kuznetsov. The Reichstag was taken and our red banner raised over it. How many thoughts went through our minds at this happy moment!"

✳ ✳ ✳

The European War ended, and with the United Nations established, the alliance of Stalin with the West seemed to persist. Stalin had agreed to enter the Pacific War once Germany was defeated and reiterated that promise at the Potsdam Conference of the Big Three. There were some new players on the team: Vice-President Harry S. Truman had succeeded Franklin Roosevelt as president of the United States, and the British Labour Party defeated the Conservatives in elections that summer, so Winston Churchill attended only the first half of the conference and was replaced by Clement Attlee, the new prime minister.

Stalin was at his most affable. Although secretly he was hoping to secure more territory, he accepted the Western rejection of his pitch for a Mediterranean seaport with aplomb. When told of the American possession of the atomic bomb he seemed unimpressed, though privately he urged Soviet scientists to speed up their atomic researches. It was obvious that he did not understand the implications of The Bomb, and would not until after Hiroshima and Nagasaki, for he urged Truman to use the new weapon against the Japanese.

The Soviet Union entered the Pacific War on August 9, 1945, and swept through Manchuria with ease. Stalin wanted a piece of the action in the Occupation of Japan, but was firmly denied any role by

Truman. He accepted that rebuff stoically and in September 1945, the alliance still seemed strong. But it began to unravel and by the end of the year the chinks had become gaping holes. Once again, the communist system was extolled in Russia, and once again, the mind-set of International Revolution was returned. It was almost as if the Comintern had never been abolished.

In Russia, Stalin soon perceived that the greatest threat to his imperial power was posed by Lavrenti Beria, the chief of internal security, and he moved to curtail that threat by appointing Alexis Kuznetsov as party watchdog. A lesser threat, Georgi Malenkov, was controlled by removing him as party secretary and his talents turned to state administration. Andrei Zhdanov took over Malenkov's party duties and remained close to Stalin until Zhdanov's death in 1948.

The marshals who had been most responsible for Russia's victory over Hitler were soon retired to obscurity. Zhukov remained as Soviet commander in chief and member of the Allied control commission for Germany until spring 1946. He then was brought back to Moscow, given a subordinate position in the ministry of war, and subsequently assigned to provincial garrisons. History was rewritten to make Stalin the all-glorious leader responsible for all the victories and none of the defeats of the Red Army.

As to international relations, Stalin biographer Adam B. Ulam put it this way: "If the Americans had been less neurotic, Soviet-American relations following the war could have been 'correct' if distant. Of course, they could not have been friendly. For the Soviet Union any friendship with a democratic country was dangerous; with America it would have been suicidal. To have Americans as friends was like having a meddlesome wife: they always wanted to change you."

Many people in the West believed that after the war the Soviet Union would moderate her foreign policy, if not for fear of the atomic bomb then in exchange for American assistance. Many people in Russia hoped for that. A large American loan was discussed in 1944 and 1945, but the Russians did not want to look like they needed the money. The subject was not discussed again. Isolation from the West was a deliberate policy of Stalin's, based on his concept of domestic needs. The whole Russian society was undergoing reschooling to undo the effect of untoward foreign influences and Stalin would not allow any foreign ideas to interfere. The opening salvo in the campaign was a Communist Party Central Committee resolution of August 14, 1946.

Switchback

The spirit of Yalta did not endure. Within a month it had evaporated. Soviet action contrasted so greatly with the promise that U.S. State Department officials said Stalin must have had difficulties with the Politburo for being too friendly and having made too many concessions to the capitalist nations. The Soviet government vetoed most of the suggestions of the Americans and British for the future Polish Government of National Unity. In Bucharest, Deputy Foreign Minister Vishinsky bullied King Michael into appointing a communist government. President Benes appointed Zdenek Fierlinger head of the government. Fierlinger was nominally a social democrat, but had become a thorough fellow traveler of the communists.

The tone of the president's messages to Stalin became sharp, and the amiable Stalin of a few weeks earlier disappeared. So did sixteen members of the Polish underground connected with the London Polish government who were invited to Moscow with a promise of immunity, only to disappear into the woodwork. The president's messages now reflected unmistakable anger. Russian behavior regarding Poland threatened the Yalta Agreement, he said. The tone of the interchanges grew more strident, and finally Stalin accused Roosevelt of double-dealing, which the president angrily denied.

Where this might have ended is unknown—the situation was headed for crisis, but President Roosevelt died suddenly on April 12, and Vice President Truman became the president of the United States. Soviet policy suddenly was suspended while the new president was assessed in Moscow. The honeymoon would be brief; forces were already at work to drive Russia and America apart.

This resolution was obviously written by Stalin himself; it had all the earmarks including bad Russian grammar, excessive use of the past tense, and the piling up of venomous invective. The resolution took the form of a diatribe against the writer Mikhail Zoshchenko and the poet Anna Akhmatova. They were accused of attempting to "disorient our youth and poison its consciousness."

There was both genuine fury and cold calculation behind the attack. Before the war both culprits had been in disgrace, but during the war they were allowed to publish. Stalin sensed the need to give the people hope that the postwar Russia would not return to the past. But in Stalin's postwar mood these people were showing dark ingratitude and subversive interests. There was an element of deliberation in Stalin's choice of the Leningrad journals as his point of attack. Leningrad was Zhdanov's bailiwick. Such transgressions could not have taken place without deplorable lack of vigilance on the part of local party officials. Here, then, was also a test of Zhdanov. Would he put on hurt airs and argue, or would he go to work to "correct his mistakes"?

Zhdanov passed the test with flying colors. He took Stalin's complaint and improved on it. Zoshchenko became "that unprincipled literary hooligan." Anna Akhmatova became "not exactly a nun, not exactly a whore, but half nun and half whore, whose whorish ways are combined with praying."

Stalin had found the right man for the job. As the Beria of intellectual life, Zhdanov now attacked others. Zhdanov began a cultural pogrom. Writer Alexander Fadayev shot himself. The composer Shostakovich tried to get back into grace with an "Ode to Stalin's Afforestation Plan."

✷ ✷ ✷

At Yalta, Stalin's primary aim was security for the Soviet Union and security for Stalinism. He proposed to do this by, first, extending the frontiers of the Soviet Union to include all the territory that had ever been under Russian rule; second, by creating beyond her extended borders a sphere of influence as large as possible, both in Europe and in Asia, by securing regimes that could be relied upon to respond to the Kremlin's policies and needs. This remained undefined but included those territories occupied by the Red Army at the end of the war. Stalin would also insist on major contributions from Germany and her satellites for reparations of the damage done to the USSR. There was some hard bargaining at Yalta over the future of Poland and reparations in particular, but Yalta was the high point of the alliance, and the conference communiqué indicated that the three powers agreed on the terms of unconditional surrender for Germany. The Germans learned quickly enough about this development. In the daily situation conference one day Hitler turned to Goering, his expert on British attitudes, and asked: "Do you think that deep down inside the English are enthusiastic about the Russian developments?"

Goering responded, "They certainly didn't plan that we hold them off while the Russians conquer all of Germany. If this goes on we will get a telegram in a few days."

But instead of a telegram, they received the communiqué at the end of the Yalta meetings, announcing tripartite agreement on the fate of Germany: Unconditional Surrender.

The three leaders were aware how precarious their unity would be once the war ended. There is no doubt that Churchill and Roosevelt were sincere in what they said about the alliance, and in their compliments to Russia for the role she had played. But what about Stalin? Was he sincere in his praise of "the indispensable contribution the alliance had made to the defeat of Hitler," or was this only pro forma?

Stalin, no less than Hitler, was sustained by a certain idea about himself—a conviction that he held a place in history comparable to that of the greatest of his czarist predecessors. Not only was the Red Army under his direction about to win the greatest victory in Russian history but the two most powerful figures in world politics had accepted his insistence that they come to him. The symbolism of this was not lost on Stalin's imagination. To be accepted as an equal by the president of the United States and the prime minister of Great Britain was tribute that satisfied even Stalin's vanity.

Also, to the surprise of practically everyone, Stalin proved to be a skillful negotiator. There was none of the authoritarian behavior that marked his relations with the Politburo or the Stavka, where Stalin was "the boss." He bore well the cut and thrust of democratic debate in an international conference where he could not control the proceedings. He proved extremely skillful and impressed everyone who heard him speak. He had a remarkable memory, he never consulted notes, and had skill in debate and quickness to move from roughness to charm.

Yalta, therefore, was the high point of Stalin's career. The toast he gave at the closing banquet must be regarded as sincere—in his admiration for the alliance—but the emotion of an historic moment and future policy were separate in Stalin's mind. The test of the future viability of the alliance would not be in sentiment or mutual trust, but the extent to which the other members were prepared to accept Stalin's claims for the USSR in the postwar settlement.

✳ ✳ ✳

Soviet xenophobia hit new highs in 1946–1952.

It was followed by total rejection of the West. Politically, this began with the Truman Doctrine. In 1946, the Greek communists emerged in full-fledged rebellion, took to the mountains and began a civil war. The British, into whose sphere Greece had been committed, found themselves unable to meet their political and military commitments, and in 1947 the United States took these over. Turkey was under unremitting pressure to provide a Mediterranean naval base for Russia. Truman stepped in with military and economic aid for both countries.

Then, on the heels of this, came the Marshall Plan, which Winston Churchill characterized as "one of the most unsordid acts of history." The United States proposed a self-help program for European nations, Russia and Eastern Europe as well as the West, which would guarantee the restoration of the economies of the participants. Stalin was invited and one part of him wanted to accept. But another part of him was deeply suspicious. This part won out. Stalin rejected the Marshall Plan, and pressed his Eastern European satellites to reject it also.

✳ ✳ ✳

But, before this, there was trouble in the matter of cooperation with the West beginning in Korea in 1945.

At the Yalta Conference, Korea had been arbitrarily split at the Thirty-Eighth Parallel into two zones of occupation, one Russian, and one American, with the announced intention that the country should soon be unified by holding free elections. The Russians came to occupy the north and brought in Kim Il Sung, a popular anti-Japanese hero, as the leader of the People's Republic of Korea. The Americans were not so imaginative—they brought in a full-fledged military government and installed it in power. Later Dr. Syngman Rhee arrived. He was a celebrated leader of the anti-Japanese resistance. Elections were held in the south in 1946 and Dr. Rhee was elected president of the Republic of Korea

A joint Soviet-American commission had been set up at Yalta to guide the Koreans to independence and democracy. The first meetings of Russian and American soldiers along the Thirty-Eighth Parallel were very friendly. But then Stalin's xenophobia intervened. General I. M. Chistyakov, one of the heroes of Stalingrad, led the Russian delegation. They came down to Seoul in the winter of 1946, but already the atmosphere had been poisoned. There was virtually no exchange of personnel across the border of the two occupation zones, The Kim government and the Rhee government lined up on opposite sides of the Thirty-Eighth Parallel gazed across the line like angry dogs. The meetings of the Joint Commission failed to achieve any progress and were finally abandoned.

The icy atmosphere of Korea was soon duplicated in Vienna and Berlin. Cooperation gave way quickly to confrontation, and soon an iron curtain was pulled down, blocking Eastern Europe off from the west.

The stage was set for the Cold War.

—⟋⟍—

26

The Iron Curtain

WHEN THE WAR AGAINST THE NAZIS ENDED IN 1945 the Soviet Union was left in a perilous state. Thousands of population centers lay in ruins and the famine of 1946 was imminent in the failure of Soviet farmers to produce food. The western part of the country was ravaged by partisan warfare, which threatened to spread. In the Baltic region and the western Ukraine, armed gangs carried on the fight against the Soviet regime.

In March alone, 8,300 partisans had been killed or captured by government troops in the western Ukraine, along with eight mortars, twenty machine guns, 700 submachine guns, 2,000 rifles, 600 pistols, and 1,700 grenades. Also captured were a number of leaders of the Ukrainian rebellion. In this, 200 troops of the security administrations, as well as Red Army troops, had been killed. Armed clashes had occurred in Belorussia, Latvia, Estonia, and Lithuania, where 145 partisans had been killed and 1,500 captured.

Stalin ordered Beria again and again, "to finish off these outlaws," but the warfare continued, and would for half a decade.

On March 6, 1946, just as Stalin was preparing to leave the Kremlin for his dacha, Secretary Poskrebyshev handed him a coded telegram from the Russian Embassy in Washington, reporting on a speech made in Fulton, Missouri, by Winston Churchill. Stalin was surprised at Churchill's harsh tones. While expressing his respect for the accomplishments of the Russian people and Stalin during the war, Churchill warned of the communist threat hanging over the Western democracies, "From Stettin in the Baltic to Trieste in the Adriatic, an Iron Curtain has descended across the continent."

It was, of course, true. In 1946, Stalin had lowered the curtain to prevent the contamination of the Russian people by foreign ideology. The one way he knew to do this was to prevent any normal contact with the West—for Stalin knew better than anyone that once the Russian people had a taste of freedom, the socialist myth he had so long propagated would soon disappear. The realities of the Russian dictatorship could not withstand comparison with Western standards, either pragmatically (consumer goods) or intellectually (the free play of ideas). The only way to keep the Russian people under control was to isolate them from the rest of the world. And so, for the rest of Stalin's life the Russian people were to be kept behind an Iron Curtain.

What concerned the West was the growing realization that despite all the honeyed words—and on reflection there weren't so many of these—the Bolsheviks had never abandoned their dream of world revolution and an international socialist society, led by the Soviet Union. Just recently, George Kennan, the U.S. Charge' d'Affaires in Moscow, had sent a long report to Washington reporting on a speech Stalin had made in February, in which he spoke of the inevitability of a third world war, one with the communist world pitted against the Western democracies. This was the nightmare of the West, particularly the United States, as Stalin turned his country and his satellite states into an armed fortress.

Another aspect of the Cold War was Russian espionage. Washington, in the late 1940s, was a virtual beehive of Russian espionage, much of it successful. Such bright lights as Alger Hiss of the State Department were suborned. Hiss was convicted of perjury for lying about his espionage, served a prison term, and would go to his death uttering fervent denials, but he was a Russian spy—one among many.

Much of the espionage was directed at getting information about the American atomic program. This was fairly productive, although to say that the Russians got the secrets of the atom through espionage is an oversimplification. They would have divined those secrets in time, anyhow—the Americans had no monopoly on brains—but what the espionage program did do was shorten the interval. In December 1946, the Russians achieved their first chain reaction. The first Soviet atomic bomb was tested in the summer of 1949.

The successful employment of slave labor in the Russian atomic program is greatly underestimated in the West. For example, in 1946 a camp was built in Siberia to house 1,000 prisoners engaged in scientific research. The next year 5,000 prisoners were relocated and supplies allocated to build a tent city to house more scientific prisoners. It is remarkable what effect a few crusts of bread or prospects of a hot bath will have on those long deprived of the modalities of civilization.

But Stalin knew. He would and did use any device to assure his continued power, and the success of his efforts.

By 1949, Stalin had all of Eastern Europe in his pocket. Communist leaders were ruthlessly purged either for sympathy with Tito or for standing up for their country's economic interests against Soviet imperialism. It was Stalin's position that the communist parties of these countries be protected against Tito heresy. Therefore, they had to have some of the lessons that he had taught Russians.

Let them do it their own way, said some protesters. No, Stalin said. It was his express wish that the educational experience gained in the USSR be shared by the people's democracies. Soviet advisors would teach them how such things were done. So what Adam Ulam

J. V. Stalin, Cold Warrior

Faced with multiple problems at home, Russia was also totally isolated in the United Nations, though at least there she had the veto power in the Security Council. Stalin felt that a difficult and unequal confrontation had begun but he had no thought of yielding. He decided to turn his country into a fortress. In his view the anticommunist policy indicated in the Truman Doctrine had made it impossible to accept the Marshall Plan. The USSR was desperate and could have used Marshall Plan aid but to accept it would be to sacrifice some degree of control of the Soviet economy. Through Molotov, at the Paris Conference at the end of June 1947, Stalin said no.

The long Cold War had begun. The only way out, Stalin believed, was to break the American monopoly on the atomic bomb. So the USSR set out to do so with her own scientific efforts, aided by successful espionage. Stalin also devoted most of Russia's resources to the buildup of heavy industry.

In 1946, Soviet scientists achieved their first chain reaction and commissioned the first nuclear reactor the following year. In November 1947, Molotov announced that the secret of the atomic bomb was secret no more. The first Soviet hydrogen bomb was tested in 1953. Apart from the economy, Stalin now devoted his major effort to defense matters and a substantial section of the Soviet prison camp system (Gulag) was devoted to that purpose. Beria was put in charge of the program. As one official put it, "We were building socialism with the help of a vast army of prisoners." The system served two of Stalin's purposes: cheap labor and a way of "reeducating hundreds of thousands of enemies and traitors."

In the fall of 1947, Stalin also reestablished the International Revolution with the creation of the Cominform, the successor to the Comintern that had been abandoned in 1943. But the Cominform fell by the wayside in the breach with Yugoslavia, and it never achieved the status of the old Communist International.

has called the "obscene drama" of the Moscow Trials of 1939–1940 was repeated in 1949–1952 in Sofia, Prague, and Budapest.

I happened to be in Prague in February 1948, when the communists seized power. The reason: they knew that they would lose the free elections scheduled for that spring.

The communists controlled the Interior Ministry and had strong representation in the army. Therefore, the revolution could be—and was—carried out overnight. The plight of the most independent newspaper in Prague is an illustration of what happened. That paper had been famous for its political column, which ran in column one on the front page.

On the morning after the revolution, readers discovered that the political column had been replaced by a chess column.

By May the communists imposed a new Soviet-style constitution, and thereafter a Stalinist regime imposed harsh Stalinism on the Czechs. It lasted all the rest of Stalin's life and was met by a popular uprising in 1968, which was put down with Stalinist terror. The communist regime finally collapsed in 1988.

✳ ✳ ✳

One of the many communist institutions, established in 1947, was destined to awaken the unbelievers in the West to the dangers of Stalinism. This was the creation of the Cominform, successor to the Comintern, in the rigors of the Cold War. The Cominform was established at a meeting of Russians and their satellites in Szklarska Poreba, Poland, in September 1947. The Yugoslavs were anointed to carry the headquarters, but something went wrong. Tito was Stalin's favorite boy and had been cordially welcomed to Moscow by Stalin in the spring of 1945. Yugoslav military personnel by the thousands were being trained in Russia; a large contingent of Soviet military experts was in Yugoslavia.

But then Tito outdid himself. Without consulting Stalin first, he made a treaty friendship with the Bulgarians, sent an air mission to Albania, and said it was possible to organize a federation of European socialist states.

Stalin was outraged. Tito had broken the basic rule: thou shalt do nothing without first consulting J. V. Stalin. At a meeting with the Yugoslavs in Moscow on February 10, 1949, Stalin so expressed himself. His first thought was to insist on federation of Bulgaria and Yugoslavia. The Yugoslav delegation resisted his demands. He became more enraged. The Titoites had broken rule number two: Stalin's word is law. The Yugoslav delegation was packed off back to Belgrade without ceremony.

Sanctions followed. The Soviet advisors were recalled from Yugoslavia.

But to that Tito answered with a letter, "Much as we all respect the USSR as the land of socialism, none of us can love any less our own countries, which are also building socialism."

✳ ✳ ✳

Stalin lost his temper completely and sent a twenty-five-page letter filled with threats and invective to Tito. He tried to enlist the Cominform in the battle, but failed to persuade the Yugoslavs that Cominform interference was desirable. The split was a fait accompli.

Stalin had suffered his first great defeat since the war, by wagging his fingers when Tito refused to respond like a puppy dog. The breach became formal and irretrievable in November 1949. In Budapest the Cominform passed a resolution castigating Yugoslavia as "the power of murderers and spies." The Yugoslav leaders were compared to the Nazis.

But the expulsion of Yugoslavia was the end of the Cominform. Stalin, seeing that his attempt to impose authoritarianism on the indigenous communist movements of Europe, lost interest in the Cominform, and it quietly disappeared in 1949.

Stalin's efforts to bully his Western Allies were no more successful. In 1948, he attempted to force them out of Berlin, by imposing a land blockade that prevented vehicles and trains from reaching the city. But President Truman organized a massive airlift, which kept

Berlin supplied with food and other necessities for more than a year. In 1949, the blockade was lifted without fanfare.

The brightest element in Stalin's international efforts was the success of the Chinese Revolution, wherein after thirty years the Chinese communists triumphed over the nationalists in 1949. But even here the success was illusory. Mao Zedong proved singularly independent and resistant to Russian efforts to guide the Chinese Revolution, which, he held, was based on the peasantry. When the United States withdrew its military forces from South Korea, the North Korean government, with a nod from Stalin, attacked the south to unify the country by force. America was on record as declaring Korea outside the American zone of influence, Secretary of State Dean Acheson having so stated. Therefore, the North Koreans expected an easy victory and soon had cornered the remaining American forces around Pusan. President Truman again surprised Stalin by ordering South Korea defended and, because the Russians were boycotting the meetings of the UN Security Council and it was therefore immune from a Soviet veto, managed to make the defense of South Korea a UN effort. The expected North Korean victory did not materialize. The war went on for three more years, China intervened, and the war became stalemated.

Stalin's one satisfaction on the international front was the success of the Chinese.

After the enormous promise of the war's end, where it was not too much for Stalin to hope to dominate all of Europe, the performance of the last few years of Stalin's life was disappointing.

Stalin's Death and the Death of Stalinism

STALIN DID NOT BELIEVE IN DOCTORS, AND SO HIS HIGH blood pressure was scantly treated. On the night of March 1, 1953, he suffered a massive brain hemorrhage. A few hours later, he was dead. The supreme ruler of Russia, the God of millions, the devil of millions, was seventy-three years old and dead. Immediately, the bargaining began around his deathbed for shares of that vast communist and Soviet Empire.

At 10:05 AM on March 10, the eight senior members of the Presidium of the Central Committee of the Communist Party lifted the coffin of their leader and placed it upon an artillery carriage. They had just completed their provisional allocation of power. They had hurriedly ejected the claims of newcomers for parts of the succession, and reestablished their own supremacy. Georgi Malenkov held the first place, shakily. Next came Lavrenti Beria, head of the security forces. Molotov was next, but he seemed fated to be discarded. Then came

Stalin's Place in History

Ilya Ehrenburg concluded that Stalin missed a great chance of immortality by not dying at the end of World War II. Had he done so he would have been recalled as a great war hero, and all the horrors of his past would have been attributed to others. By living into the next decade he forced recollection of his crimes against the Russian people, including his many purges and terrors.

In the later years, Stalin would often talk about growing old, but this was mainly to register his companions' reactions to such statements. In a 1948 play, which won the Stalin prize, the Stalin character says he will live to be a hundred. He was sure those around him were asking themselves, "When will the old bastard die?" Actually his anguish at aging showed through in his turning on old servants whose aging appearance reminded him of his own. People like Voroshilov, Molotov, his secretary Poskrebyshev, all found themselves thrust into disgrace.

He was determined to live as long as possible and not to relinquish control. He knew that to rebuild after the war's destruction, people were going to have to work harder than ever. Who else was there to make them keep their shoulders to the wheel? Certainly he would not entrust the affairs of the nation to Beria, who itched to take over. Malenkov, Khrushchev, and all the rest lacked something—that drive for power that had guided Stalin all his life. Besides rebuilding, his people had along way to go to catch up with America, that single superpower that had emerged from the war almost unscathed. Someday the Americans were going to realize how powerful they were, and might move to use that power. What if Russia was not ready to oppose them?

Then there were millions who had failed the mark during the war, men who had allowed themselves to be captured by the enemy, the people of the Baltic states, those Ukrainians who even now were forcibly opposing the state's authority. There was the constant danger of ideas from the West creeping in and destroying all that he had built.

And there was the revolution, too. The suspension of revolutionary activity would have to be lifted. Socialism must go forward; Soviet power must expand. There was no quitting this game. He must go on and if necessary drag Russia and the satellites after him.

Klementi Voroshilov, Lazar Kaganovich, Anastas Mikoyan, Nikita Khrushchev, and Nikolai Bulganin.

Stalin was entombed and the others could turn their attention to what concerned them most: the struggle for power. As biographer Ulam put it: "To the tragedy of a great and obsessed man who had stamped his resolution and his criminal obsession upon a whole society, there would now succeed the drama of oligarchs struggling for his inheritance and for the credit of removing the blight of his ways from Russia and Communism."

Beria was the first to fall. All the members of the Presidium were aware that Beria had compiled extensive dossiers on them. They were also aware of his ambition to succeed Stalin and very much afraid that he was preparing a coup to seize power.

On June 17, 1953, he went to Berlin to investigate the spontaneous revolt there by workers. He took with him two Soviet divisions. Twenty-one demonstrators were killed in the disturbance.

Beria in Berlin was keeping a wary eye on his rivals. When he learned that a meeting of the Presidium had been set for an unusual hour, he called the Presidium secretary to demand a reason. He was told there was nothing on the agenda to necessitate his return. Nonetheless, he flew back to Moscow immediately. When he got there he gave a cynically accurate assessment of the German Democratic Republic, "The GDR? What does it amount to, this GDR?" he asked with a sneer. "It's not even a real state. It's only kept in being by Soviet troops, even if we do call it the German Democratic Republic."

The other members of the Presidium reacted badly to Beria's arrogance.

Nemesis was waiting. The plot to bring Beria down was led by Nikita Khrushchev, along with Nikolai Bulganin and Marshal Zhukov.

In May they won out over Georgi Malenkov.

A special meeting of the Presidium was set for June 26. Khrushchev arrived with a pistol in his pocket.

Beria came in, sat down, and asked, "Well, what's on the agenda today? Why have we met so unexpectedly?" Khrushchev prodded

Malenkov with his foot and whispered, "Open the session. Give me the floor."

"Malenkov went white," Khrushchev later wrote. "I saw he was incapable of opening his mouth, so I jumped up and said, "There is one item on the agenda: the antiparty, divisive activity of Imperialist agent Beria. There is a proposal to drop him from the Presidium and from the Central Committee, expel him from the party, and hand him over to the court martial. Who is in favor?"

Molotov, Bulganin, and others denounced Beria, in turn. Before a formal vote on Khrushchev's motion was taken, Malenkov pressed a button. Zhukov entered with an armed group of army officers, arrested Beria, and took him away. Fearing an attempted coup by Beria, Zhukov moved a tank division and a motor rifle division into Moscow.

It was several days before Beria's NKVD officials knew that he had been arrested. For most people the evidence of Beria's downfall was the disappearance of his pictures.

Beria's arrest was announced on July 10. Khrushchev, the leader of the coup, now emerged as the dominant figure. In September he replaced Malenkov as party first secretary.

Beria disappeared into the cells of the NKVD and was never heard of again. His crimes against the Russian people were so heinous they could not be mentioned. On December 24, it was announced that Beria and six other conspirators had been found guilty of "a plot to revive capitalism and restore the bourgeoisie." Beria's most serious crimes, obeying Stalin to carry out mass murder, could not be mentioned without endangering the remaining oligarchs of the old regime. But the announcement of his execution referred to "crimes that testify to his moral degradation."

In the years that followed, the men of the Kremlin played musical chairs. Khrushchev was in charge in 1956 when he made his historic secret speech to the Twentieth Communist Party Congress, denouncing Stalin and all his works. One result was the removal of Stalin's body from the Lenin-Stalin mausoleum, and the anti-Stalin campaign that followed.

Stalin Lives in History

Dmitri Volkogonov's biography of Stalin paints him as a "dark and deadly personality," to quote Sovietologist Robert Conquest. Indeed it does. Volkogonov and his family were among Stalin's victims; he was exiled to Siberia along with his mother, brother, and sister after his father was executed. Two of his uncles also seem to have been executed; they simply disappeared. Volkogonov himself as a youth was a marked man. On his graduation from tank officer school with honors one of his friends confessed that for three years he had been spying on Volkogonov, forced to do so by higher authority, "Been looking after you, reporting what you said you know, keeping an eye on you in general."

"It may be said that this book is my way of avenging the wrongs done to my family, but I would deny it," Volkogonov wrote. "When Stalin died I was a young tank commander and I thought the sky would fall in. I understood nothing when my family was taken away, and even later did not link that tragedy with Stalin. They told me that my father had died. My mother wept in secret. Not until July 1952, did I discover that I was myself a marked man. . . . This digression into my personal background serves as a reminder that it is senseless to try to take revenge on history."

Volkogonov had joined the army in 1945 and rose rapidly in rank, becoming deputy chief of the main political section of the Soviet army and navy. He was shaken by Khrushchev's denunciation of Stalin in 1956. He led a kind of dual life for many years, outwardly a hard-line political instructor of the armed forces, inwardly planning, researching, and writing his biography of Stalin, which *glasnost* allowed him to publish.

His last word on Stalin, "If his physical death came to Stalin sooner than expected his political demise was long delayed. His historical death is unlikely, since the people will never forget what was done in his name."

Khrushchev oversaw the Red Army suppression of the Hungarian and Polish uprisings. He continued arming the USSR with atomic weapons, but advocated peaceful coexistence with the capitalist world. He assisted Fidel Castro in the Cuban Revolution and made the error of bringing atomic weapons to Cuba, which provoked a crisis with the United States. Soviet missiles were withdrawn from Cuba after the confrontation in October 1962.

Khrushchev was suddenly deposed in the fall of 1964 and replaced as first secretary of the party by Leonid Brezhnev. Four years later, the Red Army invaded Czechoslovakia to put down a government rebellion against Russian interference with Czech affairs. Brezhnev called for support from Polish, East German, Hungarian, and Bulgarian allies, and dutifully these satellites sent their soldiers to do Moscow's bidding.

In these days, Russian foreign policy was aggressive, often verging on confrontation with the West. In the late 1960s and 1970s the USSR gave open support to the North Vietnamese in the Vietnam War, but they did not seem to learn anything from the disastrous American experience of interfering with such native revolutions. In 1979 the Soviets invaded Afghanistan to support a left-wing regime against rebels. They remained bogged down there until 1988, when they withdrew their forces, cogently admitting a defeat that paralleled America's in Vietnam.

In all these postwar years, the USSR stuck with Stalin's policy of guns before butter, keeping the average Russian citizen in want, which became desperate in times of famines, unfortunately common due to the failure of Soviet agriculture.

In 1985, a new era opened in Russia with the coming of Mikhail Gorbachev to power as first secretary of the Communist Party. This was a peaceful revolution, signaling a change from the old policies of Stalin's day. Gorbachev began a program of reform that included personal freedom and *glasnost* (openness of government). These policies were opposed by the old hard-line Stalinists, which resulted in several confrontations.

The 1990s were years of change. Boris Yeltsin was elected president of Russia. He closed *Pravda* and disbanded the Communist Party. Even Gorbachev was put under house arrest, but released in 1991. Latvia declared her independence from the old Soviet Union; the Ukrainians voted for independence by 90 percent; and the Soviet Union was formally abolished. Freedom to import and export was established in Russia. Everywhere the movement was toward a market economy. In 1992, prices were freed and immediately skyrocketed. The various segments of the old Soviet Union sought American aid.

President Yeltsin became the center of controversy, and efforts were made to impeach him. But they came to no more than the American efforts to impeach President Bill Clinton. Yeltsin served until ill health forced his resignation early in 2000. His chosen successor, Vladimir Putin, was elected to succeed him, once more proving the point that only in a free society can a man choose his own successor.

Most important, Stalinism and all it stood for—authoritarian government, cruelty, murder, lawlessness, and injustice—had been replaced by rule of law. The cult of personality was as dead as Stalin, and virtually no one in Russia wanted to revive it. Looking back from the vantage point of the twenty-first century, it was hard to believe that such a monster as Stalin had existed and ruled Russia with an iron hand for thirty years.

In the destruction of Stalinism, Russia came of age.

Malenkov was the front runner.

Notes

Chapter 1

This chapter depended on Adam Ulam's and Dmitri Volkogonov's biographies of Stalin. The story of the Japanese trial balloon sent up on the Mongolian-Manchurian border is from research I did for my *Japan's War*. The story of the Nazi-Soviet Pact is from Anthony Read and David Fisher's *The Deadly Embrace*. The story of the Soviet war games of 1941 is from Ulam's biography and M. I. Kazakov's essay in *Stalin and His Generals,* edited by Seweryn Bialer. Stalin's stubborn rejection of the many reports of German military buildup along the border is from *Stalin and His Generals*, essays by N. N. Voronov and I. T. Staranov.

Chapter 2

The story of the German Balkan campaign is from my *Hitler's War.* The account of the Russian military buildup is from Alexander Werth's *Russia at War.* The story of General Kazakov's assignment is from his essay. The story of Admiral Kuznetsov's vigil is from his essay in *Stalin and His Generals*. The story of General Tiulenev is from his essay in *Stalin and His Generals*.

Chapter 3

The Starinov tale is from his essay in *Stalin and His Generals*. General Boldin's story of the first hours of the German attack is from his essay in *Stalin and His Generals*.

Chapters 4 and 5

General Guderian's account of his first hours in battle is from his book *Panzer Leader*.

The story of Yakov, Stalin's first son, is from Volkogonov.

Chapter 6

The account of the beginning of the war depended on *Zhukov's Greatest Battles*, the Ulam biography, and *Stalin and His Generals*. The minute by minute account of the proceedings is from *Zhukov's Greatest Battles*. Stalin's reaction is described in Volkogonov. The visit of Zhukov and the others to Stalin's dacha is from the Volkogonov book. The story of General Eremenko's adventure is from his essay in *Stalin and His Generals*.

Chapter 7

The Starinov story is from his essay in *Stalin and His Generals*. Zhukov's account of his relief as chief of staff is from *Zhukov's Greatest Battles* as was his account of his employment in the defense of Moscow. The material about Stalin's bumbling in the first few weeks is from Volkogonov, as is the account of his first lesson in strategy. The story of the defense of Kiev is from Alexander Werth's *Russia at War*.

Chapter 8

The account of General Guderian's activities is from Heinz Guderain's *Panzer Leader*, that of Hitler's strategic considerations from my *Hitler's War*. The accounts of Zhukov's and Rokossovsky's activities are from the Zhukov book and Volkogonov as is the story of Stalin during the panic of October in Moscow. The story of von Rundstedt's relief of command is from *Hitler's War*. The story of Stalin's argument with Zhukov is from the Zhukov book, as is the story of Zhukov's confrontation with Rokossovsky, supplemented by Volkogonov.

Chapter 9

The source for this analysis of Stalin's military skills is Volkogonov. The Stalin-Zhukov telephone conversation is from Zhukov. The marshal learned in this first winter offensive that it was useless to argue with Stalin because the dictator was impervious to reason and insisted on having his own way. The story about Stalin's second son, Vasilyi, was pieced together from materials found in Zhukov, Volkogonov, Thaddeus Wittlin's biography of Beria, Ulam, and Werth's *Russia at War*.

Chapter 10

The story of the German assault on Sevastopol is told by Werth. Hitler's ruminations are described in *Hitler's War*. The German dictator changed his mind at least twice that winter and spring about his next objective, since Operation Barbarossa had failed. Stalin's concept of "active defense" was left over from his association with Kulik, who had put many wrong ideas into his mind. One of the odd anomalies of the war was Stalin's preoccupation with Moscow, even after the Germans had abandoned their efforts to capture it, in favor of taking the Caucasus. This played directly into the Germans' hands by strengthening the Russian Bryansk and Western Fronts.

The Germans had a marvelous deceptive ploy working, "Operation Kreml," which concealed the real Operation Blau, which was aimed at the Don River Basin.

Chapter 11

I depended on my own *199 Days—The Story of the Battle for Stalingrad* and *Hitler's War*. The famous Order No. 227 is described in Volkogonov's chapter on Stalingrad.]

Stalin's appointment of Zhukov to be his special assistant was carried out with the dictator's usual secrecy, as described by Volkogonov. "Tell them precisely what you have to and no more," was Stalin's fashion. The promotion of General Rokossovsky to Marshal is described by Volkogonov. The plight of the Germans at the end and the surrender of General Paulus are from my *199 Days*.

Chapter 12

By the time Stalingrad loomed, Zhukov had won Stalin's confidence more than any other general had. That it was not misplaced is indicated by this chapter. The essential source here was *Marshal Zhukov's Greatest Battles*.

Chapter 13

Kursk was the greatest tank battle of World War II. I used Werth for the Russian side, and Ziemke's *Stalingrad to Berlin* for the German.

Chapter 14

Rokossovsky was emerging as one of Russia's best generals. I tell of his progress, using Seaton's *Stalin as Military Commander*. For the Moscow and Tehran conferences I used Ulam, Volkogonov, and Perlmutter's *FDR & Stalin*.

Chapter 15

By far the best source on Russia in Eastern Europe is Shtemenko's *The Last Six Months*, and for the German side *Hitler's War*.

Chapter 16

Again I turned to Shtemenko for this chapter. Ziemke was also useful.

Chapter 17

Central to this chapter was Shtemenko's chapter "Along the Trail of the Heroes of Shipka Pass," which describes the events in Bulgaria in the summer and fall of 1944.

Chapter 18

For this chapter on Tito and Yugoslavia's relations with Stalin, I turned to Ulam, Volkogonov, and Werth.

Chapter 19

One of the anomalies of the war is why the Red Army chose to sacrifice hundreds of thousands of men in the last days of the war, to take Berlin, but more odd, also to take Budapest for which the Germans fought as desperately as they did for Berlin. The only conceivable answer is that long before the Cold War, Stalin was determined to create his own fortress state within a *cordon sanitaire*. The details are given in Shtemenko's *The Last Six Months*.

Chapters 20, 21, 22, 23, 24

These chapters describe the fighting and capture of Berlin, and Hitler's last days in the Bunker of the *Reichskanzlerei*. I used Read and Fisher's *The Fall of Berlin* and O'Donnell's *The Bunker*.

Chapters 25 , 26, 27

Given Stalin's insistence on maintaining absolute control of the government of the USSR it was inevitable that the alliance should break up. No dictatorship can stand the competition of a free society. Stalin had no recourse but to make of Russia a prison state if he was to keep control. How he did this is detailed in the Ulam, Volkogonov, and Radzinsky biographies.

Bibliography

Barnett, Corelli, ed. *Hitler's Generals*. New York: Grove Weidenfeld, 1989.

Bialer, Seweryn, ed. *Stalin and His Generals*. London: Souvenir Press, 1970 .

Andrew, Christopher, and Oleg Gordievsky. *KGB: The Inside Story*. New York: Harper Collins, 1990.

Axell, Albert. *Stalin's War, Through the Eyes of His Commanders*. London: Arms and Armour, 1997.

Bullock, Alan. *Hitler and Stalin, Parallel Lives*. New York: Vintage Books, 1993.

Guderian, Heinz. *Panzer Leader*. Washington, D.C.: Zenger, 1952.

Hoyt, Edwin P. *199 Days—The Battle for Stalingrad*. New York: Tor Books, 1993.

———. *Hitler's War*. New York: McGraw Hill, 1988.

———. *Japan's War*. New York: McGraw Hill, 1988.

Medvedev, Roy. *All Stalin's Men*. New York: Anchor Press, Doubleday, 1984.

O'Donnell, James P. *The Bunker*. Boston: Houghton Mifflin, 1978.

Perlmutter, Amos. *FDR & Stalin, A Not So Grand Alliance*. Columbia: University of Missouri Press, 1993.

Radzinsky, Edvard. *Stalin*. New York: Anchor Books, 1997.

Read, Anthony, and David Fisher. *The Deadly Embrace: Hitler, Stalin and the Nazi Soviet Pact, 1939–41*. London: Michael Joseph, 1988.

———. *The Fall of Berlin*. New York: W. W. Norton, 1992.

Richardson, Stewart, ed. *The Secret History of World War II*. New York: Richardson and Steirman, 1986.

Salisbury, Harrison E., ed. *Zhukov, Georgi K.: Marshal Zhukov's Greatest Battles*. New York: Harper & Row, 1969.

Seaton, Albert. *Stalin as Military Commander*. New York: Praeger, 1976.

Shtemenko, S. M. *The Last Six Months*. New York: Doubleday, 1977.

Spahr, William J. *Stalin's Lieutenants*. California: Presidio Books, 1997.

Topitsch, Ernst. *Stalin's War*. London: Fourth Estate, 1987.

Ulam, Adam B. *Stalin: The Man and His Era*. New York: Viking, 1973.

Volkogonov, Dmitri. *Stalin, Triumph and Tragedy*. New York: Grove Weidenfeld, 1988.

Werth, Alexander. *Russia at War*. New York: Carroll & Graf, 1964.

Wittlin, Thaddeus. *Commissar: The Life and Death of Lavrenty Pavlovich Beria*. New York: Macmillan, 1972.

Ziemke, Earl F., and Magna E. Bauer. *Moscow to Stalingrad: Decision in the East*. New York: Military Heritage Press, 1985.

Ziemke, Earl F. *Stalingrad to Berlin, Defeat in The East*. New York: Military Heritage Press, 1966.

Index

OTHER COOPER SQUARE PRESS TITLES OF INTEREST

THE GI'S WAR
**American Soldiers in Europe during
World War II**
Edwin P. Hoyt
with a new preface
664 pp., 29 b/w photos, 6 maps
0-8154-1031-X
$19.95

HITLER'S WAR
Edwin P. Hoyt
with a new preface
440 pp., 60 b/w photos, 4 maps
0-8154-1117-0
$18.95

JAPAN'S WAR
The Great Pacific Conflict
Edwin P. Hoyt
with a new preface
568 pp., 57 b/w photos, 6 maps
0-8154-1118-9
$19.95

THE U-BOAT WARS
Edwin P. Hoyt
with a new preface
272 pp., 32 b/w photos
0-8154-1192-8
$17.95

WARLORD
Tojo against the World
Edwin P. Hoyt
with a new preface
280 pp., 10 b/w photos
0-8154-1171-5
$17.95

GUADALCANAL
Edwin P. Hoyt
314 pp., 43 b/w photos, 10 maps, 1
diagram
0-8128-8563-5
$18.95

INFERNO
**The Fire Bombing of Japan, March
9–August 15, 1945**
Edwin P. Hoyt
188 pp., 10 b/w photos, 2 maps
1-56833-149-5
$24.95 cl.

THE INVASION
BEFORE NORMANDY
The Secret Battle of Slapton Sands
Edwin P. Hoyt
212 pp., 22 b/w photos, 4 maps
0-8128-8562-7
$18.95

'44
**In Combat from Normandy to
the Ardennes**
Charles Whiting
240 pp., 29 b/w illustrations, 4 maps
0-8154-1214-2
$17.95

ANZIO
The Battle that Failed
Martin Blumenson
224 pp., 4 maps
0-8154-1129-4
$17.95

CANARIS
Hitler's Master Spy
Heinz Hohne
736 pp., 29 b/w photos, 3 maps
0-8154-1007-7
$19.95

CORREGIDOR
The American Alamo of World War II
Eric Morris
560 pp., 23 b/w photos, 4 maps
0-8154-1085-9
$19.95

DEFEAT INTO VICTORY
Battling Japan in Burma and India,
  1942–1945
Field-Marshal Viscount William Slim
New introduction by David W. Hogan, Jr.
576 pp., 21 b/w maps
0-8154-1022-0
$22.95

THE DESERT FOX IN NORMANDY
Rommel's Defense of Fortress Europe
Samuel W. Mitcham, Jr.
248 pp., 20 b/w photos, 8 b/w maps,
9 tables
0-8154-1159-6
$17.95

GENERAL OF THE ARMY
George C. Marshall, Soldier
  and Statesman
Ed Cray
876 pp., 24 b/w photos
0-8154-1042-5
$29.95

GOODBYE, LIBERTY BELLE
A Son's Search for His Father's War
J. I. Merritt
Foreword by Samuel Hynes
240 pp., 26 b/w photos, and 1 b/w map
0-8154-1231-2
$24.95 cl.

HANGED AT AUSCHWITZ
An Extraordinary Memoir of Survival
Sim Kessel
New introduction by Walter Lacqueur
192 pp., 26 b/w photos
0-8154-1162-6
$16.95

HEROES NEVER DIE
Warriors and Warfare in World War II
Martin Blumenson
648 pp.
0-8154-1152-9
$32.00 cl.

HITLER
The Survival Myth
Updated Edition
Donald M. McKale
304 pp., 12 b/w photos
0-8154-1128-6
$17.95

HITLER IN VIENNA, 1907–1913
Clues to the Future
J. Sydney Jones
344 pp., 54 b/w illustrations, 16 maps
0-8154-1191-X
$24.95 cl.

THE HITLER YOUTH
Origins and Development, 1922–1945
H. W. Koch
382 pp., 40 b/w photos, 2 maps
0-8154-1084-0
$18.95

HITLER'S COMMANDERS
Officers of the Wehrmacht, the
  Luftwaffe, the KriegsMarine, and
  the Waffen-SS
Samuel W. Mitcham, Jr. and
Gene Mueller
384 pp., 52 b/w photos, 8 maps
0-8154-1131-6
$18.95

HITLER'S FIELD MARSHALS
and Their Battles
Samuel W. Mitcham, Jr.
456 pp., 26 b/w photos, 9 tables,
22 maps
0-8154-1130-8
$18.95

HITLER'S SHADOW WAR
The Holocaust and World War II
Donald W. McKale
504 pp., 39 b/w illustrations
0-8154-1211-8
$29.95 cl.

THE HOUSE OF KRUPP
The Steel Dynasty that Armed
the Nazis
Updated Edition
Peter Batty
360 pp., 17 b/w photos
0-8154-1155-3
$18.95

HUNTERS FROM THE SKY
The German Parachute Corps,
1940–1945
Charles Whiting
with a new preface
240 pp., 12 b/w photos, 8 maps
0-8154-1145-6
$17.95

THE JEHOVAH'S WITNESSES AND
THE NAZIS
Persecution, Deportation, and Murder,
1933–1945
Michel Reynaud & Sylvie Graffard
Introduction by Michael Berenbaum
304 pp., 40 b/w photos
0-8154-1076-X
$27.95 cl.

JULIUS STREICHER
Nazi Editor of the Notorious Anti-
Semitic Newspaper Der Sturmer
Randall L. Bytwerk
with a new afterward
264 pp., 31 b/w illustrations
0-8154-1156-1
$17.95

KASSERINE PASS
Rommel's Bloody, Climactic Battle
for Tunisia
Martin Blumenson
358 pp., 18 b/w photos, 5 maps
0-8154-1099-9
$19.95

MARSHAL ZHUKOV'S
GREATEST BATTLES
Georgi K. Zhukov
Edited by Harrison E. Salisbury
New introduction by David M. Glantz
328 pp., 1 b/w photo, 5 maps
0-8154-1098-0
$18.95

THE MEDICAL CASEBOOK
OF ADOLF HITLER
Leonard L. Heston, M.D., and Renate
Heston, R.N.
Introduction by Albert Speer
192 pp., 3 b/w photos, 4 graphs
0-8154-1066-2
$17.95

THE MEMOIRS OF FIELD-
MARSHAL WILHELM KEITEL
Chief of the German High Command,
1938–1945
Edited by Walter Gorlitz
New introduction by Earl Ziemke
296 pp., 4 b/w maps
0-8154-1072-7
$18.95

MENGELE
The Complete Story
Gerald L. Posner and John Ware
New introduction by Michael
Berenbaum
400 pp., 41 b/w photos
0-8154-1006-9
$18.95

MUSSOLINI
A Biography
Jasper Ridley
464 pp., 24 b/w photos, 3 maps
0-8154-1081-6
$19.95

OCCUPATION
The Ordeal of France, 1940–1944
Ian Ousby
384 pp., 16 b/w photos
0-8154-1043-3
$18.95

OPERATION VALKYRIE
The German Generals' Plot
   against Hitler
Pierre Galante
328 pp., 23 b/w photos, 3 maps
0-8154-1179-0
$17.95

SIEGFRIED
The Nazis' Last Stand
Charles Whiting
312 pp., 24 b/w photos, 6 b/w maps
0-8154-1166-9
$17.95

SWING UNDER THE NAZIS
Jazz as a Metaphor for Freedom
Mike Zwerin
with a new preface
232 pp., 45 b/w photos
0-8154-1075-1
$17.95

THE TRAGIC FATE OF THE
U.S.S. INDIANAPOLIS
The U.S. Navy's Worst Disaster at Sea
Raymond B. Lech
336 pp., 52 b/w photos, 2 maps
0-8154-1120-0
$18.95

TRIUMPHANT FOX
Erwin Rommel and the Rise of the
   Afrika Korps
Samuel W. Mitcham, Jr.
376 pp., 26 b/w photos, 8 maps
0-8154-1055-7
$17.95

THE WEEK FRANCE FELL
June 10–June 16, 1940
Noel Barber
336 pp., 18 b/w photos
0-8154-1091-3
$18.95

Available at bookstores; or call 1-800-462-6420

COOPER SQUARE PRESS
200 Park Avenue South
Suite 1109
New York, NY 10003